NAVIES, DETERRENCE, AND AMERICAN INDEPENDENCE

This book focuses on British defence policy in the period between the Seven Years' War and French intervention in the American Revolution. It is a study of coercive diplomacy and of the influence of defence considerations in foreign policy, particularly as applied to the naval relationship between Britain and France at the outbreak of the American Revolution—a subject of considerable significance in understanding how American independence was made possible.

Nicholas Tracy has worked in Canada, England, and Singapore. He now lives in Fredericton, New Brunswick, and has written about eighteenth-century British history, twentieth-century Canadian defence policy, and naval strategy.

Navies, Deterrence, and American Independence

BRITAIN AND SEAPOWER
IN THE 1760s AND 1770s

Nicholas Tracy

UNIVERSITY OF BRITISH COLUMBIA PRESS
VANCOUVER 1988

© The University of British Columbia Press 1988
Printed in Canada
ISBN 0-7748-0298-7

This book has been published with the help of a grant from the Social Science Federation of Canada, using funds provided by the Social Sciences and Humanities Research Council of Canada.

Canadian Cataloguing in Publication Data

Tracy, Nicholas, 1944-
Navies, deterrence, and American independence

Bibliography: p.
Includes index.
ISBN 0-7748-0298-7

1. Seapower—Great Britain—History—18th century. 2. Great Britain—History, Naval—18th century. 3. Great Britain—Foreign relations—1760-1789. 4. United States—History—Revolution, 1775-1783. 5. Great Britain—Colonies—America—History. I. Title.
DA87.T73 1988   327.41   C88-091277-4

In Memory of Antoinette

Contents

Illustrations

Preface

Analysis of Britain's strategic system in its successes and failures between 1763 and 1778 has depended on a wide range of documentation, primarily from Admiralty records and State Papers, but also including the private papers of statesmen. The constant focus of attention has been on the questions of what the British government thought they could do with Britain's naval force, what they felt obliged to do because of Britain's dependence on naval force, and on what information they based their decisions. Other aspects of naval institutional history, and of British diplomatic history, have had to be given no more than slight attention. The study of British policy does not depend on foreign documentation, and I have made only limited use of foreign published material. It is possible that some insights into British policy-making have thus been missed, but the most important implication of this one-sided approach to diplomatic history is that I have been able only to give second-hand answers to the question of why foreign governments reacted as they did to British *démarche*. There have been a number of studies made of French foreign policy in the period, however, J. R. Dull has added his study of French naval policy in the years leading to the French intervention in the American Revolution, and James Pritchard his study of the French navy in the period 1748-62.

I am indebted to the Canada Council and the Social Science and Humanities Research Council of Canada for financial support over the years that I have worked on this project. Without a subvention in aid of publication by the Social Sciences Federation of Canada it is problematical whether this book would ever have been published. The privilege of attending Ian Christie's seminars at the University of London has contributed fundamentally to my understanding of the historian's craft, and I am indeed grateful to Professor Christie for his advice. The technical support of the University of New Brunswick, and the National University of Singapore, have been gratefully received. Especially, however, I thank my wife Antoinette for her support during my years of study. This book is dedicated to her memory.

NICHOLAS TRACY
FREDERICTON, NB

1

Introduction:
The Direction of Britain's
Security Policy in the 1760s

The French decision in 1777-78 to render active military support for the revolutionaries in British North America marks the failure of the British policy of employing the naval superiority secured during the Seven Years' War to deter French efforts to reverse their defeat. During the first twelve of the fifteen years between the Peace of Paris of 1763 and the French declaration of support for the American Congress, British statesmen had responded with such consistency to a series of attempts on the part of Bourbon France and Spain to recover their power and influence that it may be said that a system of behaviour had been established. For the British it was a system of deterrence by which a graduated escalation of naval response was employed to coerce the Bourbon powers into more acceptable behaviour. The antagonism of rival powers and the need to coerce with threatened armed force were taken for granted. Ultimately the system failed when the preoccupation of London with the revolution in North America persuaded the French government that there existed a fleeting opportunity to destroy the mercantile basis of the British fleet.

For the British government the navy, which had become the premier force in the world's oceans, was the essential instrument of coercion. In consequence the crises which particularly called for vigorous British action following the Peace of Paris were those which appeared to put at risk the power of the British fleet, and the respect given to it. Dependence upon naval strength not only defined Britain's ability to satisfy foreign policy objectives, but also to a considerable extent determined what such objectives should be.

Denied for political and economic reasons a substantial peacetime army, the British recognized a need to form an alliance with a continental military power in order to give Britain greater influence in European affairs and, especially, to ensure that the French could not concentrate on building naval forces. The classic expression of this concern, "France will outdo us at sea, when they have nothing to fear by land," had been made by the Duke of Newcastle in 1749, and there was little reason to doubt in 1763 that if the French should ever be able to dispense with their army the British would find it difficult to maintain their naval supremacy.[1] Britain had allied with Prussia in the Seven Years' War, but the successful reduction of French power had ended the need for her continental neighbours to seek alliances against France, and the precipitate haste with which the Earl of Bute had concluded peace between Britain and France estranged Frederick of Prussia.[2]

The need to build up Britain's influence in Europe, to attract an ally, but also to protect their interests in the absence of an ally, obliged the British to take an active part in continental politics. The only available means of giving British diplomats weight in Europe being the power of the British navy, the British government especially had to concern itself with developments that might diminish the respect given to British naval power. Naval dominance of the Mediterranean was necessary if Britain was to have influence in central and southern Europe. Naval control of the Baltic was even more important because of the continuing need for naval building materials from the north despite the supplies now available from North America. The area of conflict extended to the trading and colonial empire, which Britain in any case valued, but control of which was also regarded in the days of restrictive navigation acts as the necessary foundation of the merchant marine, which in turn was the foundation of naval strength.

The central tenet of British foreign policy in the 1760s and 1770s was that France was the irreconcilable enemy. Until the Seven Years' War, Britain's gallophobia could be justified by concern that the Bourbons would acquire control of a disproportionate amount of Europe, and by so upsetting the balance of power acquire a position then known as "universal monarchy." The war had eclipsed French power, but British gallophobia remained and encouraged a belief that the French were determined to reacquire a position of military domination of Europe and maritime competition with Britain. William Pitt, who had been driven from his leadership of the government in 1761 because he wished to precipitate war with Spain following the latter's signature of the Family Compact, had wide public support for his belief that France could only be kept honest by ensuring her inability to risk war. He was thus a great critic of the concessions to France in the peace treaty, which had been made in the hope that a measured generosity would reduce French determination to plan révanche. Canada was permanently ceded to Britain, but Martinique and Guadeloupe were returned to France. Pitt, like many Englishmen, was convinced that possession of a maritime trading empire was a no less powerful support for the military greatness of European states than was control within Europe itself. Canada, it was known, had been a continual disappointment and expense to France. The French sugar islands, on the other hand, were increasing their prosperity and trade, and the French trade to India sustained a substantial marine.[3]

Pitt's assessment may have been simplistic, but the policy of succeeding British administrations was not greatly different. Following a standard formula, the "separate and private" instructions given to the Duke of Richmond when he was dispatched as ambassador to France in 1765 noted: "it is not easy to imagine, that, after so great Disgraces both by Sea and Land, and after the Cession of so vast a Territory to Our Crown in Consequence of their late unsuccessful War, the Court of France, as well as That of Spain, should not have Thoughts of putting Themselves in a Condition to recover in Time their lost Possessions, and retrieve the Reputation of their Arms."[4] It is ironic that it was recognition of the need to maintain strong imperial defences, occasioning as it did the attempt to tax the American colonists to pay for their own defence, that disrupted the empire and gave France her chance for révanche.

The British belief that France was determined to overthrow the peace settlement was not unfounded. Louis XV had no desire to repeat the experience of war, but his chief minister, the Duc de Choiseul, had other views. Choiseul had negotiated the Family Compact with Spain during the Seven Years' War with the private intention of diverting British military effort away from French interests at the expense of Spain. In order to retain the Spanish connection when the Peace of Paris was concluded Choiseul had felt constrained to offset some of Spain's consequential losses, and Louisiana had been ceded to Spain to compensate for the loss of Florida. But these losses were looked upon as temporary and tactical. Choiseul was determined to rebuild French naval power for a war of révanche, and for this purpose he took the office of Minister of Marine and Colonies. To achieve his objective he needed to have a period of peace and to establish secure relationships with France's continental neighbours. In the Seven Years' War the French had attempted to obviate the necessity of defeating the British navy at sea by, instead, winning such resounding victories on land that the British would have to abandon their maritime conquests in a deal to restore a balance of power on the continent. This strategy had failed and Choiseul was determined to reverse it, securing the land frontiers of France by treaty so that France could fight Britain at sea. His policy was facilitated by the weakness of France, which made her no longer a threat to her neighbours. The temporary peace with Britain, however, was to be no more than superficial. Not only was the French navy to be prepared for war, but every effort was to be made to undermine Britain's position by subterfuge and encroachment, using all means short of war.[5]

Spain's attitude was just as inimical to British interests. The Marchese de Grimaldi, Foreign Minister to Bourbon Charles III, had negotiated the Family Compact out of concern that the triumph of British naval forces was giving Britain indisputable power over maritime affairs. Such a situation was regarded as dangerous to the continued integrity of the Spanish empire, and certainly the arguments put forward by the Earl of Egmont in 1765 for the establishment of the British post on the Falkland Islands justified Spanish fears. The Falkland station, he wrote to the Duke of Grafton, "is undoubtedly *the Key to the whole Pacific Ocean.* This Island must command the Ports & Trade of Chile, Peru, Panama, Acapulce, & in one word all the Spanish territory upon that Sea.''[6] Since Spanish imperial territory was closed to foreign traders, Egmont was clearly urging breaking into the Spanish trade illicitly. The war had brought only disaster to Spain, defeat at Havana and Manila, and the loss of Florida. However, the Spanish navy had survived relatively intact, and the Spanish government was convinced that it was necessary to plan for a renewal of the conflict with Britain. The attitude of Charles III and his countrymen was well summed up by an "old Spaniard," de Munian, who told the British chargé d'affaires in Madrid in 1766, Mr. Devisme, that the British "as Masters of the Sea, [were] too powerful not to be oppressive, and [that he] is firmly of opinion that no Peace with them can be secure.''[7] In 1767 the Comte d'Ossun, French ambassador in Madrid, warned Choiseul that there was "une différence essentielle dans les vues des cours de Paris et de Madrid, la première ne voulant avoir la guerre avec l'Angleterre ni maintenant, ni plus tard, la seconde désirant seulement l'éloigner jusqu'à ce que les deux nations fussent en état de la faire, c'est-à-dire dans deux ans.''[8] In reality Choiseul's own position was little different, although there never was complete harmony between French and Spanish objectives, nor complete co-operation in preparing for them.

British isolation was the more complete because of the separation between the policies of Britain and Hanover which had taken place with the accession in 1760 of George III to the British throne. The military alliance between his kingdom and his electorate did not continue after the end of the Seven Years' War. In Britain there was no enthusiasm for the link with Hanover which, without a Prussian or Austrian alliance, could be regarded as more of a liability than an asset. It might have been possible to make greater use of the Hanoverian connection to foster a north European anti-French alliance. It is evident, however, that British statesmen did not feel that Hanover was a factor they needed to consider either as an asset or as a vulnerable point to be guarded.

The 1760s was a period of instability in British political life. In 1763 Bute was driven from power because of jealousy for his relationship with King George III, whose tutor he had been. Between that date and January 1770, when Lord North was made First Lord of the Treasury and Prime Minister, the leadership of the government changed hands four times. George Grenville succeeded the Earl of Bute, one of whose chief critics he had been despite having held high office in the government under Bute. Grenville had disagreed with Bute's determination to make a conciliatory peace treaty, and he was asked to resign his secretaryship. Nevertheless he was given the Admiralty in its place, and when Bute fled from office in April 1763 he put Grenville at the head of the administration to save the King from the Whigs. George III found Grenville intolerable, especially because of the latter's criticism of Bute. In 1765 Grenville was dismissed, and when the King found he could not form a ministry centred on William Pitt, he made the Marquis of Rockingham his prime minister. Rockingham in his turn was brought down by an inability to replace one of his ministers, the Duke of Grafton, who resigned owing to his loyalty to Pitt. George III was then forced to allow Pitt to form a government on his own terms, which included a seat in the Lords for himself with the title of Earl of Chatham. The nominal leadership of the administration was left in the incapable hands of Grafton. When within a year Chatham became incapacitated by what must have been a depressive illness, Grafton became prime minister in fact. Unable to stand the burden of that position, he soon resigned.

Nonetheless, the conduct of Britain's foreign relations during these years and on into the 1770s was remarkably consistent. In 1769 von Nolcken, the Swedish ambassador in London, observed:

> However much the views of the various parties have differed among themselves, yet all new members of the Administration have been forced when it comes to foreign policy to lay aside their private opinions and follow in their predecessors' footsteps, and have seen the necessity of pursuing uniform and common measures. Lord Chatham, contrary to his own expectation and that of the whole nation, was not able to break out of George Grenville's limited political system, and his weariness, discontent, and resignation may well have been caused not so much by his illness as by his conviction, acquired during the course of his last ministry, that it was no longer possible to lead the country in the old style.[9]

Continuity in foreign policy was facilitated by the limited size of the British political system at the time, and by the informality of opposition, which provided an underlying stability despite the short tenure of prime ministers. Individuals moved from office to office and in and out of office, and it was rare for a cabinet not to contain at least one member of the previous cabinets and others who had been in high office within a few years. The Earl of Sandwich, for example, having been First Lord of the Admiralty before the Seven Years' War, and briefly so again in 1763 before the fall of the Bute administration, became Secretary of State for the Northern Department under Grenville, returned to that office in 1770 during the Falkland Islands crisis, and shortly thereafter moved back to the office by which he is chiefly remembered, the Admiralty.

In theory the conduct of Britain's foreign relations was the independent duty of the Secretaries of State, who were responsible only to the King and whose duties were divided between the northern and southern states of Europe. The reality was that the administration of the King's government was more or less a collective cabinet affair. Not all members of the cabinet had much influence outside their own departments, but each cabinet had its dominant members who owed their influence less to their offices than to their personal or political importance. Grenville's cabinet had a clear inner group consisting of Grenville, the two Secretaries of State—the Earls of Halifax and Sandwich—and the Duke of Bedford, who was Lord President of the Council. Bedford was an elder statesman who had negotiated the peace treaty that Grenville had criticized for its generosity. They were paired in office by George III in order to control Grenville. Sandwich and Halifax were political dependents of Bedford, although in reality their views were similar to those of Grenville. Sandwich and Grenville had both been junior lords of the Admiralty under Bedford in 1744. The First Lord of the Admiralty under Grenville, the Earl of Egmont, had little direct influence on foreign policy. It was not his office, however, which limited his importance, for when Sandwich was at the Admiralty in Lord North's administration he had an important voice in cabinet control of foreign policy. Both Egmont and Sandwich at times took departmental decisions with major international implications without authorization from a secretary of state. The cleanest sweep of offices occurred when Rockingham formed his government in 1765, only Egmont keeping his place. Rockingham brought in General Seymour Conway and the Duke of Grafton to be Secretaries of State. When Grafton brought down Rockingham it was he who nominally led the next administration under Chatham. However, when he was in political difficulty during Chatham's illness, Grafton brought back into office members of Bedford's group, Viscount Weymouth, and Earl Gower, who had been a minor member of Grenville's administration. Grafton also brought into the government as a Secretary of State, at the King's suggestion, the Earl of Rochford, who as a career diplomat at

Madrid and Paris had been closely associated with Grenville's policies. Grafton's cabinet, in contrast to Grenville's, was disastrously divided. When Grafton resigned, and Lord North, who had been his Chancellor of the Exchequer, accepted the Treasury, he changed none of the cabinet posts. When vacancies occurred he brought back first Sandwich and then Halifax.

It has often been remarked that there was little brilliance among the men who so continually occupied the great offices of state. Certainly this observation is correct, but there was considerable mediocre talent, and, as Nolcken has remarked, the international situation was not one where there was much room for brilliant initiatives. Mediocrity helped to ensure continuity, and the limited political interest there was in foreign relations further reduced efforts at innovation. It was not until the Corsican crisis of 1768 that George III became significantly involved in the direction of foreign policy, although by 1770 he was taking a considerable interest in this aspect of government, which historically was a king's prerogative.

The only direction popular opinion gave to foreign policy was confined to a consistent policy of confrontation with the French, a concern for economy, and reliance upon naval supremacy for security. Within the administration there was little interest in departure from this broad policy, only a statesman of the rank and stature of the Duke of Bedford being able openly to advocate rapprochement. North and Rochford secretly considered such a possibility in 1772, but this did not imply much departure from the traditional attitude that France could only be kept honest by British superior strength. Ministerial acknowledgment of the value of placating the French served more to modify the British policy of confrontation, with a view to making British power more acceptable to France, than it did to suggest an ability to dispense with confrontation altogether.

2

The British Navy
after the Seven Years' War

The conflict with France and Spain revolved equally around maritime empire, which was the source of naval and commercial power, and European diplomatic influence, which determined the extent to which the French could concentrate their resources on naval forces. The keystone of British strategy, upon which depended London's ability to defend colonial possessions and to achieve influence in Europe, was the maintenance of naval power capable of overawing France and Spain and an economy strong enough to support a war.

In 1768 Charles Jenkinson, later 1st Earl of Liverpool but at the time a commissioner of the Treasury, epitomized the conflicting influences on post-war naval planning. When preparing "Heads of Defence of the Extra Estimates of the Navy" he wrote: "The two great ends of security & oeconomy may seem at first view to combat each other but it is our duty to reconcile them. Security must have the first place."[1] The cost of naval armament was high. Following Sandwich's brief tenure at the Admiralty from April to August 1763, an account was made of the value of the fleet. With five first rate line-of-battle ships, fourteen second rates, fifty-seven third rates and fifty-two fourth rates, the value of the capital ships was estimated at £5,117,941.7.11¼, the entire fleet rising to £6,624,311.16.3¾. If the life of the fleet averaged sixteen years, the annual cost would be £414,819.8.6. Such figures probably related little to reality. The accountant gave figures for a life cycle of anything from twelve to sixteen years, and those epochs can only have been more or less well-informed guesses.[2] Nonetheless, the cost of maintaining hulls and equipment was unquestionably high, and so was the cost of commissioning.

In 1764 the Navy Board, the administrator of naval matériel, made an estimate of the cost of maintaining ships on Channel or foreign service or of fitting them as "guardships, ready at short notice to proceed to sea." A first rate of 100 guns fitted for service in the English Channel cost £40,750; a third rate of 74 guns cost £30,688 for the same service, but only $6,198 when fitted as a guardship with a complement reduced from 650 men to 150. A thirty-two-gun frigate cost £12,418 to keep in sea pay. Eighteenth-century standards of accounting were notably inaccurate, but these figures are nonetheless valuable because they indicate what the decision-makers at the time thought were the costs involved (see Table 1).[3]

TABLE 1: Costs of maintaining or fitting ships

Rate	Guns	Men	Channel (£)	Foreign (£)	Guardship (£)
1st	100	850	40,750	41,073	
2nd	90	750	35,664	35,949	
3rd	80	650	31,246	31,403	
3rd	74	650	30,688	30,935	6,198 (150 men)
3rd	70	520	26,008	26,228	6,198 (150 men)
3rd	64	500	24,396	24,586	6,198 (150 men)
4th	60	420	21,186	21,346	5,433 (130 men)
4th	50	350	18,123	18,256	
5th	44	280	14,353	14,459	
5th	36	240	13,313	13,404	
5th	32	220	12,418	12,502	
6th	28	200	10,906	10,982	
6th	20-24	160	8,480	8,541	

The peacetime deterrent function of the British navy did not require the maintenance of major units on active service. In 1763, during his brief period at the Admiralty in Bute's administration, George Grenville drew up a peace establishment for the navy, planning a reduction of manpower from the 85,650 men then in service to 16,000.[4] To effect this, and yet to be able to maintain a small squadron on each of the principal stations, it was necessary to lay up "in ordinary" all the ships of the line save for twenty guardships. It took some time for the peace establishment to be implemented. In January 1764 there were still 26,168 men in the navy and it was not until September 1765 that the size dropped nearly to 16,000. The fleet was by then much as it had been envisaged. Only the Jamaica station had any major units, and they had been sent out as a result of Spanish and French attacks on British interests there. Grenville's plan had not stipulated forces for the East Indies, nor had it foreseen the need for cruisers, but in the end provision was made for both those services (see Table 2).[5]

TABLE 2: Fleet disposition, September 1765

Station	Rate:	3rd	4th	5th	6th	Frig.	Slps	Other
East Indies					2	1		
Jamaica		2	1	2	2	1	2	
Leeward Islands			1	1	3		2	
Mediterranean			1	2	2		1	
North America			1	1	6	2	10	6
Newfoundland			1	3			2	1
Convoys and cruisers			1	1		1		
Home waters			1	4	2	11	36	

NOTE: These figures can be used only to show trends, as the source is somewhat imprecise.

These ships were not expected actually to "defend" British interests. Grenville had decided that the navy should be used to enforce the customs laws, resistance to which was stiffened by the Sugar Act of 1764. Accordingly small warships were in great demand for purely domestic purposes.[6] With respect to the great powers the job of the ships on active service was to observe events, report developments, and symbolize a British "presence." A sample of twenty-two ships whose period of commissioning fell between 1763 and 1765 shows that they spent a total of 6,462 days in harbour and only 2,079 days at sea.[7] Britain's defence depended on the ability to reinforce when necessary the active squadrons with ships of the line from the ordinary reserve or the guardship squadron.

The cost of guardships had risen considerably from the early 1750s when a squadron of twenty had cost an estimated £33,814, but they still provided a comparatively inexpensive alternative.[8] The guardships were cleaned annually in the spring, carried part of their stores and armament on board, and were given a complement of 150 men. Guardships were principally intended as a security against a sudden mobilization of the Bourbon fleets, and were theoretically moored at Plymouth, Portsmouth, Chatham, and Sheerness. However, they also served as a ready reserve of ships to reinforce other squadrons or to transport troops. Twenty guardships were kept on the books from July 1765, but anything up to four of them were often away performing various services, generally on foreign stations. Furthermore, from July 1766 until 1771 there were never fewer than two of them paid off or being repaired. This was not a matter of routine maintenance because during most of the period the same two ships were paid off without any crew other than the watchmen. By keeping on the books more ships than the international situation required it was possible to expand the squadron quietly at a time of crisis without endangering the peace by announcing the mobilization of ships in ordinary. Similarly it was possible to increase the number of men in

TABLE 3: State of the guardships, 1764-70

Date		Total guardships	In commission	Paid off	On service
31 Dec.	1764	18	18		
29 July.	1765	19	17		2
12 Aug.	1765	20	18		2
23 Sept.	1765	20	20		
14 Apr.	1766	20	19	1	
21 July	1766	20	18	2	
22 Feb.	1768	20	14	3	3
9 May	1768	20	16	3	1
23 May	1768	20	17	2	1
13 June	1768	20	18	2	
29 Aug.	1768	20	17	2	1
5 Dec.	1768	20	16	2	2
13 Feb.	1769	20	15	2	3
27 Mar.	1769	20	16	2	2
8 May	1769	20	15	2	3
15 May	1769	20	14	2	4
5 June	1769	20	15	2	3
10 June	1769	20	16	2	2
19 July	1769	20	17	2	1
11 Sept.	1769	20	18	2	
27 Aug.	1770	20	17	2	1
3 Sept.	1770	20	16	2	2

the guardships, thus shortening the notice required before the squadron could go to sea (see Table 3).[9]

It was the "ordinary" reserve of battleships which ultimately provided the British navy with the ability to defeat Bourbon révanche, and it was the maintenance of the ordinary which presented naval administration with the greatest difficulties in balancing security with economy. In September 1764 it was estimated that out of 149 ships of the line existing at the end of the war, including those building, nine had already been scrapped, and forty-one had been completed or put into good condition. Ninety-nine remained to be completed or repaired, of which nineteen were more fit to be scrapped and replaced, at a total cost for the ninety-nine ships of £2,003,785.[10] In Sandwich's papers is another estimate for building and repair which, exclusive of eleven ships that had not yet been surveyed, amounted to £1,889,381.2.7¾, or an estimated five and a half years' work for 3,000 shipwrights.[11] The dockyards, the efficiency of which was vital to the operation of the fleet, also required considerable expenditure. They had been neglected during the war, partly because the increased size of ships made reconstruction of the yards necessary in any case.

Some attempt had also to be made towards paying off the large navy debt which had accumulated during the war. It was the practice during the eighteenth century for the navy to meet its financial requirements by issuing bills in excess of the parliamentary vote, and by the 1760s there was little incentive to pay off the debt entirely. The navy debt was a profitable investment for businessmen, but only so long as there remained confidence that the government could pay. It was appreciated that the high costs of naval warfare could only be sustained in a future conflict if British naval credit were sound. Accordingly it was necessary to sustain the pattern of debt repayment in peacetime, and it had to be accepted that it was impossible to finance the maintenance in good condition of more than a part of the ships in ordinary.[12]

THE FRENCH AND SPANISH FLEETS IN THE 1760S

The first requisite for the maintenance of Britain's naval supremacy without squandering limited financial resources was reliable intelligence.[13] When Charles Jenkinson reminded the Commons that security must have priority over economy, he remarked that "We shall begin the next war with two Enemies at a time." This was the general belief in Britain, notwithstanding the efforts which were made to detach Spain from the French alliance. A simple two-power standard could be adopted because only France and Spain had navies that could be a danger to Britain and were likely to be so. The Swedish navy was insignificant outside the Baltic, although in 1764, when it appeared possible that Sweden might barter the wartime commitment of ten ships of the line for resumption of the French subsidy, London was alarmed. The British ambassador-designate to Sweden, Sir John Goodricke, reported that the Swedish navy possessed twenty-six ships and six frigates. However, he estimated that only five of the ships, or at most twelve, were fit for service.[14] The Danish navy was more respectable. The British resident in Denmark, Dudley Cosby, reported thirty-one ships and fourteen frigates. The Dutch navy, despite British pressure for reform, was but a remnant of its former self, and the Russian navy, which with British assistance had acquired considerable size, was not highly regarded, even after its destruction of the obsolete Turkish navy in 1770. No other navy reached even those strengths, and none but those of the Bourbon powers were a major concern to the British. Consequently British naval intelligence was primarily concerned with France and Spain.

An insight into Bourbon intentions sometimes could be acquired through the interception and decipherment of diplomatic correspondence in the British and Hanoverian post offices.[15] Tactical information about the state of readiness of the Bourbon fleets for war could be obtained by sending a frigate to "look into" the Bourbon harbours to count ships at moorings and observe the state of their rigging. For information on the size and condition of the Bourbon fleets, on new construction, and on the repair of ships, the Admiralty had to have reports from the continental dockyards and from Paris and Madrid. Travellers and merchant officers sent regular reports, but no reliance could be placed on their accuracy. The principal channels of information were Britain's diplomatic and consular representatives. They provided considerable information themselves and also controlled a number of paid agents. The consul at Turin was the best continuous source of information about the Toulon dockyard, and the Cologne consulate controlled a well-placed agent in Versailles.

Of far greater importance than either of these was the secret service of Robert Wolters, who held the post of consul at Rotterdam. He had agents in Paris, Madrid, Brest, Toulon, and elsewhere who corresponded with him regularly, and he forwarded the reports and abstracts of the French and Spanish fleets to the Secretary of State's office. Part of the expense of acquiring this information, the most valuable part of which was the naval reports, was paid for by the Admiralty, where duplicates of the naval papers were kept.[16] Wolters' agency was expensive. In the last quarter of 1769 his office expenses and the payment of the Paris, Brussels, Furnes (?), and Geneva agents came to £2,756, and in 1767 for a similar period the Madrid bill alone came to £1,574.[17] Little is known about Wolters' agents, but it is evident that his reports were considered the best available. When he was Secretary of State for the Northern Department, Sandwich is known to have read Wolters' reports, and when Sir Edward Hawke as First Lord of the Admiralty wanted information about the French dockyards in the winter of 1768-69, it was to Wolters that he applied. Wolters' answer reflects the difficulties: "Sending a person on purpose to a French Port I have long since been obliged to give up, as I have not been able to find one that would have courage to see clearly and to make a true report."[18] Ambassador Lord Harcourt reported the same thing in November; the fate of a Mr. Gordon, who was hanged by the French for spying in the dockyards, made it impossible to recruit agents for that purpose.[19] Often Wolters' agents supplied the only information available, and their reliability was borne out by Hawke's own opinion when he visited France in 1770.[20] The reports were detailed, although they were based on a slow accumulation of information, so that out-of-date reports on individual ships were often repeated year after year. News of works undertaken in the yards was regularly received, however, and accordingly abstracts of the condition of fleets were unlikely to underrate the state of readiness. Unfortunately Wolters died in 1770. His wife and Hake, his clerk, continued the service, but the information received from that source gradually became less useful.[21]

In the 1770s Sandwich built up his own intelligence system in France, which in some respects more than replaced Wolters' agency. The ambassadors and consuls continued to provide what intelligence they could both of a political and a naval nature in order to supply strategic warning. These reports were supplemented by a voluminous and frequent correspondence from agents in Normandy and Brittany, especially one at Morlaix, who reported the details of naval preparations at Brest and Rochefort and warned when ships sailed.

Defeat at sea, blockade of naval stores, and the failure of finances had all contributed to the ruin of the French navy during the Seven Years' War, but the British realized that Choiseul intended to give first priority to its restoration. As early as January 1763, the British agent in Versailles reported that Choiseul was inclined "to reduce the Army to Nothing, in order to increase the Fleet, to introduce the same Oeconomy into every Office, and to pursue it, so far as to enable Him to discharge the Debt contracted this War . . . to put the Finances in about Twelve Years . . . on a better Footing, than they were on in 1755."[22] While the Versailles agent also reported that there was doubt about what success Choiseul would have, since it cost France more to prepare a navy than to maintain an army, Wolters forwarded reports from Paris and Geneva confirming that Choiseul's plans were to prepare for a naval war of révanche.[23] Choiseul took the post of Minister of the Marine in order to oversee the reconstruction of the navy. He instituted a series of reforms designed to improve naval morale, and he embarked on a program of ship construction.[24] Later, in 1765, he wrote a "Mémoire Justificatif présenté au Roi" in which he described his success. In 1763 there were forty-five ships and ten frigates in various states of repair; he claimed that two years later he had built up the fleet to sixty-three ships and thirty-one frigates "tous en état d'aller à la mer et en état de tous points."[25]

British intelligence agreed with Choiseul's account of the French fleet in 1763. On 29 November Wolters had been able to forward to Sandwich a report which revealed a war-shattered fleet which contained only forty-six ships of the line which were not known to require major repair. Of those only eighteen were reasonably certain to be in good repair (see Table 4).[26] There were eight ships and nine frigates under construction, and British intelligence did report improvements in the French fleet during the following years, but not such as to justify Choiseul's boast. There were constant reports that lack of timber was holding up repairs. New construction and repair was apparently not even adequate to hold the decay in check. On 30 May 1765 an unknown Admiralty intelligence source drew up an "Abstract of the French Navy" which reported no more than a total of thirty-six capital ships fit for service (see Table 5).[27] These were divided into a

TABLE 4: Abstract of Walters' intelligence of the French fleet, 1 November 1763

---

1 × 116 guns: *Le Royal Louis*, which reportedly had been condemned after survey to be reduced to 80 or 90 guns;

1 × 90 guns: *La Ville de Paris*, which had been commenced in 1757, but was rotting on the ways, work being held up by timber shortages;

4 × 80 guns: of which only the *Duc de Bourgogne* was in good condition. *Tonnant* needed repair, *Orient* needed major repair having suffered an accident in 1761, and *Languedoc* was still under contruction and little advanced;

24 × 74 guns: of which 7 were known to be in good repair, 3 others were new ships, 6 had not yet been surveyed, 2 were unfit for service (including the *Dauphin Royal* 70), and 3 were under construction;

24 × 64 guns: of which 4 were known to be in good repair, and 3 others were new ships; *Rencontre* and *Hazard* were listed as "médiocrement bon," *Actif* was in the Indies, 4 needed survey, 2 were being repaired, 5 were in bad condition, and 3 were under construction;

3 × 48-50 guns;

27 × 18-36 guns: of which 9 of 30 guns were under construction, and *L'Hebe* 30 was believed to be condemned.

TABLE 5: Estimate of French fleet, 1765, classified by their number of guns

Guns:	116	90	80	74	70	64	60	Total
Fit for service	1	1	1	11	1	21		36
Being repaired			2	2				4
In bad condition				11		5	2	18
Building	1		2	2				5

NOTE: From Abstract of the French navy, 30 May 1765.

squadron of eighteen at Brest, thirteen at Toulon, and four at Rochefort, and there were also reported to be a further three 64s in the East Indies. Another nine ships of the line were thought to be under construction in the provinces.

It appeared that the French were still optimistic. The report continued: "it is represented that it is in the power of France to complete the 5 ships which are building, the 4 which are repairing, and the 5 which are ordered to Brest to be repaired, in the course of twelve months, so that France may at that Period have 50 Capital Ships fit for Service, including the 36 which appear by the foregoing Abstract to be so ready." However those fifty were slow in making their appearance. In January 1766 further information was received dated 30 November 1765 from Wolters about the building and repair undertaken in French yards since 13 November 1763.[28] It was reported that one ship of 90 guns (*Ville de Paris*), one 74, and two 56s had been launched in 1764, and in 1765 one 64 (*Artesian*) and two more 56s had joined them.

One 90 (*Bretagne*, which had been intended to have 110 guns), two 80s (*St. Esprit*, which was nearly finished, and *Languedoc*) and three 74s (*Lyonnais, Marseillais,* and *Bourgogne*) were being built. One 80 (*Orient*), three 74s, and one 64 were being rebuilt. The same agent remarked, however, that none of the ships under construction were being built at the expense of the Crown. They were all ships laid down late in the war as patriotic gifts from various cities at a time of national crisis. Furthermore, fifteen ships at Brest were in need of extensive repair, amounting to rebuilding. There was no ship timber available for the purpose.

It was apparent that the French did not have the resources to build the fleet they wanted in the 1760s. In 1767 the Versailles correspondent expressed his opinion that the French court "sincerely wish to avoid war" because "the Finances are so ruined." Three months later he added that "the Duc de Choiseul & every other Minister must avoid War for, at least, Ten years."[29] By the mid-1760s Choiseul's program had ground to a halt. Abstracts of the French fleet dated 10 September and 26 November 1766 in the Chatham and Liverpool papers list only thirty-nine and forty-two ships of the line which were thought to be in good condition.[30] On 1 January 1768 Wolters provided a "Liste de la Marine de France" which showed a maximum of only forty-one capital ships which could be in good condition, out of a total of fifty-nine. There was good evidence of sound condition for only twenty-three (see Table 6).[31] Below the line the French fleet was expanding more rapidly, it appeared. Five ships of 56 guns had been built since 1764, making a total of eight of that rate. In the 20 to 36 gun range, there were eleven new ships, with ten others under construction, and fourteen old ships, of which it was known that one had been condemned. Discouraged by his lack of success, Choiseul returned to the Foreign Ministry. His cousin, the Duc de Praslin, who had been acting as Foreign Minister, took over the Marine.[32]

It was only towards the end of the next two-year period that intelligence sources began to report an increase in the number of French ships of the line believed to be in good condition, although even so the number remained small. In March 1769 Harcourt in Paris calculated a total French fleet of sixty ships.[33] In December 1769 he forwarded a report that the French had a total of seventy-four ships which he could "no otherwise Account for, than by supposing that the enclosed list comprehends the whole Navy, Old and New Ships, unserviceable as well as serviceable."[34] The number included 50-gun ships, which reduced the total ships of the line to sixty-three. It was not until 1 January 1770 that Wolters drew up a list of the French fleet, which included thirty-three ships of the line for which there was evidence that they were in good repair, out of a total of fifty-eight, of which six were definitely not fit for service (see Table 7).[35]

Rotterdam the 2.d February 1768.

Sir

Recd. 8 Feby

I have the Honour to send you inclosed a new List of the french Navy. I have directed my Correspondent to endeavour to gett me a still more minute Account of such Ships as are judged to be totally unfit for Service.

It is with great Satisfaction that in comparing this List with the former, I see that not one new Ship of the Line has been built for the french King's Account since the Peace, all the new Ships being those that were built from the particular Gifts: The Cesar just begun at Toulon, is the only Ship that can be excepted out of this Class.

I have the Honour to be

Sir.

your most humble and most Obedient Servant,
RWolters,

P. Stephens Esqr.

14

Letter from Robert Wolters, Consul at Rotterdam, to Philip Stephens, Admiralty Secretary, 2 February 1768, forwarding an intelligence report containing an abstract of the French Navy, 1 January 1768.
Courtesy of the Public Record Office, ref. no. ADM 1/3972

Toumant	00.	Juin An 1743 Refuse de se reparer. le bon état	
Languedoc	00 . 76 .	1766. Donné par les Etats du Languedoc	
2.e Rang.			
Sophie	74. 96.	Brest. 1766. Vieng Vaisseau refondu. le bon état.	
Conquerant	74. 96.	1766. D.°	
Diadème	74. 96.	1766. D.°	
Palmier	74. 96.	1766. D.°	
Defenseur	74. 96.	1754. En bon état.	
Robuste	74. 96.	1754. En Radoub. en Nov. 1767.	

Liste de la Marine de France
rectifiée et continuée jusqu'au 1.er Janvier 1760.

N.B. Ceux marqués d'un trait sont de l'échange pays, cinq marqués de deux traits sont des Vaisseaux refaits.

Vaisseaux.	Lieu où construit. Age.	Particularités.
1.er Rang.		
Royal Louis.........	116. Brest. 1759.	Marqué dans trois ans, parties, &c.
Ville de Paris.......	90. Brest. 1764.	Lorsqu'on a voulu le Vaisseau Louis à Brest en 90 Canons
Duc de Bourgogne..	80. 94. 1751.	Ce Vaisseau part le Roi. à la Ville de Paris pour ses Dons. On le vit en charge...
L'Esprit...........	80. 94. 1766.	Donné par la Couronne...

TABLE 6: Abstract of Walters' intelligence of the French fleet, 1 January 1768

Royal Louis in bad condition (belying the 1765 abstract), but *Ville de Paris* 90, *Bretagne* 90, *Duc de Bourgogne* 80, *St. Esprit* 80, and *Orient* 80 (but mounting 74) were all listed as good. *Tonnant*, 80, ordered repaired. 25 ships of 74 guns listed, but two were under construction, two under repair, one other was noted as being in bad condition; 5 had been rebuilt in 1766, 6 completed since the war; it was known that one of the old ships was in good condition. 17 probably serviceable 64s. The ships of the first four rates were divided among the major ports as follows: Toulon 2 × 1st, 8 × 2nd, 6 × 3rd, 2 × 4th; Brest 6 × 1st, 15 × 2nd, 19 × 3rd, 6 × 4th; Rochefort 2 × 2nd, 1 × 3rd.

TABLE 7: Abstract of Walters' intelligence of the French fleet, 1 January 1770

7 × 80 to 90 guns (including *Couronne*, a built-up 74, and *Tonnant*, but not *Orient*, reduced to a 74); 27 × 70 to 74 (only the *Dauphine Royal*, 70 known to be in bad condition, 2 under repair, 6 new since the war, and 11 rebuilt); 23 × 64 guns (2 in bad condition, one of which (*Rencontre*) had been condemned, 3 new ships, and 6 rebuilt); 8 × 50-56 guns; and a total of 44 small ships.

The French deficiency in numbers was somewhat made up by the alliance with Spain. It was known that Charles III was eager to rebuild his forces, and Choiseul was encouraging him. Partly at the expense of the Admiralty, Wolters had hired an agent at Madrid. Because he proved unreliable, the information available was never as precise as that on the French fleet. On 15 November 1763, for instance, Wolters admitted that "the Intelligences which we have hitherto had from thence are no ways equal to the Price given," although he remarked that "if we dismiss him, it will I fear be difficult to find an other." Nevertheless, the correspondent reported that a target had been set of forty ships of the line in European waters. During the 1760s the Admiralty was forced to pay considerable attention to the Spanish naval building program.[36]

On 9 April 1764 the Spanish navy was reported to be in a bad way with thirty-six ships of the line, for the most part in poor condition, of which only twenty-seven carried 68 guns or more. The average age of the thirty ships for which completion dates were available was thirteen years, and the remaining ships were marked as "old."[37] Throughout 1765 the news of the Spanish navy was no more impressive, with reports of inadequate finances and ineffectual workmen. Its strength in Europe and the West Indies was calculated by the Admiralty on 30 May to be a total of thirty-seven ships of the line, of which ten were in the West Indies.[38] On 14 October a calculation showed only twenty-four available for service in Europe.[39] The list of the Spanish capital ships in the Chatham Papers, dated 10 September 1766, still only gave a total of thirty-nine ships of the line.[40] The Spanish fleet was then reported to have two 80s, three 70s, and twenty-two of 68 guns. Nine of the total, including two of new construction at Havana, were in American waters. An abstract dated 1 November 1766 in the Liverpool papers repeated this figure, with the addition of one 80-gun ship in European waters which had apparently been one of the two ships built at Havana.[41]

It was the reports of new construction that obliged London to take the Spanish navy seriously. On 1 October 1767 Wolters reported that the thirty-eight-ship fleet included nine ships built since 1763.[42] On 11 March 1768 he reported that the fleet numbered forty-two ships, with one 80, three 70s, and two 60s under construction.[43] In another Admiralty intelligence file is a list of the Spanish navy which was drawn up on 1 October 1767, apparently using Wolters' information and then brought up to date on 11 March 1768 and at some time one or two years later. Of the forty-eight ships of the line, which it noted had generally been rationalized by increasing the armament of the 68s to 70 guns and reducing those of 64 guns to 62, it showed that eleven were ships built since 1764. Furthermore, although six were considered to be unfit for service, it was noted that they would soon be replaced by new construction. On the other hand, although listed as "new ships," two of the 80s were thought to be still under construction.[44] On 27 April 1769 Wolters reported that three 70s were building at Ferrol, six 70s at Havana, and one 80 and one 70 at Cartagena where an 80 and a 14 had recently been launched.[45]

The concern felt for Spanish ship construction is indicated by the presence in the Admiralty papers of an abstract dated 1 May 1769 listing the hulls known to be laid down and noting the discrepancies between the intelligences.[46] The abstract showed that two 74s were begun in May 1768 at Ferrol, and at Carthagena were an 80 nearing completion and a 70 lately begun which would be the last of six built under contract by Genoese workmen. Three 70s, two 60s, and three frigates were under construction at Guarnizo, near Santander, by M. Gautier, a Frenchman who had already launched three 70s at that place. At Havana an 104 and an 80 were nearly finished. The two 60s at Guarnizo were suspected actually to be 74s completed at Ferrol, but later intelligence reported three more 70s building at Ferrol, six ships of unknown force building at Havana, one at Guajaquit (Guayaquil?), and two chebecs at Yodca (?). A list of the Spanish fleet drawn up on 15 May 1769 by Commodore Spry, commander-in-chief of the British squadron in the Mediterranean, gave a total of fifty-two ships and nineteen frigates.[47] Wolters reported on 31 December 1769 that the Spanish fleet numbered forty-nine ships, including five new 80s, with one 80 and three 68s building, and that the average age of the fleet had fallen to nine years.[48] Against this intelligence, however, were more vague reports like one in

December 1766 which remarked: "nous pourrons avoir dans peu d'Années beaucoup de Vaisseaux; mais alors il faudra aussi fabriquer des Matelots et des Gens capables à les commander."[49] The reports agreed that the Spanish fleet was unlikely to be as dangerous as it was large, and the Admiralty does not appear to have considered it as of the same class as that of France.[50]

Despite its limitations, Bourbon naval rearmament in the 1760s made it difficult for the British government to reconcile the dichotomy of economy and security. During the Grenville administration between April 1763 and July 1765, the champions of the competing objectives of strength and economy were, respectively, the Earl of Egmont at the Admiralty and Grenville at the Treasury. Egmont is best known for his interest in colonial development of an idiosyncratic nature. One of his more far-reaching adventures of this kind was his order to establish a British post on the Falkland Islands as an Admiralty departmental measure, seeking cabinet approval only after the deed was done. By the 1760s he was a much less dynamic politician than Grenville, whose prestige in the Commons was to remain high until his death in 1770. Grenville's experience at the Admiralty, and, in 1744 as a junior Lord under the Duke of Bedford, and again briefly after the Seven Years' War, strengthened his hand when seeking economies.

There were separate naval parliamentary votes, for the maintenance of ships laid up "in ordinary," the ordinary estimate; for running expenses calculated at a flat rate of £4 per man per lunar month of twenty-eight days; and the extra estimate to make good the deficits on the other votes and to pay for construction.[51] A dispute began in 1763 when Grenville would only agree to £100,000 for the extra estimate although the Admiralty asked for £197,877. The next year he objected to any increase when the Admiralty demanded £259,739. This touched off a strong reaction from Egmont, who claimed that the French marine was in a better condition than the British guardships and that he had an intercepted a letter from "a principal minister of France" saying that they would be ready for war in 1764. He insisted that £150,000, which it was rumoured might be made available, was insufficient even to meet pledges, let alone undertake rebuilding. The sum was eventually increased to £200,000, but in April 1764 when Grenville was circulating the draft of the King's speech for approval, Egmont renewed his demand. He objected to the statement that ample provision had been made for the navy: "Let who will inform you otherwise, I maintain and prove that you have not now (guardships included) in Great Britain seventeen ships of the line complete." Grenville disagreed on many counts. A total of £1,450,000 was allowed for the fleet, "nearly double the sum which used to

John Perceval, 2nd Earl
of Egmont, 1711-70.
Engraving by J. Faber
after a painting by F.
Hayman.
Courtesy of the British
Museum (Class II period 4;
1870.10.8.2680) Negative
191646

be allowed in times of peace,'' and Grenville thought that ought to be
sufficient. In part he was right. Egmont's alarm at the French fleet was quite
unfounded. At great expense the secret service was providing the opposite
information, that the danger from the French was not immediate. Sandwich,
at any rate, read the reports, and passed them on to Grenville with his
comments.[52]

Egmont did have difficulty in keeping his program of construction and
repair within Grenville's budget, if indeed any effort was made to do so. In
April 1764 the Navy Board waited upon the Admiralty Board and reported
on the slow progress in the repair of the fleet, the result in part of labour
shortages. It was therefore decided to allow the men in the yards to work
overtime ''one tyde extra'' during the summer months when daylight
allowed. A tide equalled one and a half hours per day overtime, for which
one-third of a day's wages was paid. The Victualling Office and Navy Office
were both instructed to prepare estimates of the stores which should be
maintained so that the fleet could be quickly expanded by 10,000 men and to

Rt. Hon. George Grenville, 1712-70. Engraving by James Watson, after a painting by William Hoare. Courtesy of the British Museum (Class III period 4; 1868.8.8.1631) Negative W/P 22440

thirty ships stored for eight months' service. The state of the guardships was improved by increasing their complements to 180 men for a third rate and 160 for a fourth rate so that the total complement of the guardship squadron would be sufficient to man some of their number fully for services such as transporting troops to the West Indies without stripping the remaining ships unduly. This extra expense, furthermore, had only been made possible by improving the victuals issued to seamen in the guardships to attract recruits.[53] In this same optimistic mood the Admiralty ordered the Navy Board to prepare a long-range plan for rebuilding the dockyards.[54] Their capacity was set as the only limitation on ship repair, and priority was given to repair over new construction. The Navy Board was informed that the Admiralty thought "it proper to recommend that for the future, no Ships shall be built but on Slips, so that the Docks may be always free for the reception of Ships wanting repair."[55] Priority was to be given to the repair of those ships of the line which required least attention.

In December 1764 when the Navy Board sent up to the Admiralty their estimate for the naval ordinary which incorporated these forward-looking plans and called for an increase of £87,374 over the preceding year's £388,568, they had a rude shock. The Admiralty sent it back accompanied by a "suggestion," which presumably had originated in the Treasury, that there could be no increase in the ordinary that year. A reduced estimate was accepted and Parliament granted £407,734 for the ordinary.[56]

As frequently happened in British naval finance, the economy on paper was ignored in practice.[57] In March 1765 the Secretary of the Navy Board reported that their expenditure was likely, despite all efforts at economy, to exceed their grant by £83,961.[58] A week later the Navy Board minutes noted that consideration was being given to retrenchment.[59] The Admiralty sent them a "secret and private" letter in April asking them whether economy could be effected by reducing the amount of overtime they allowed the yards to work. The Navy Board, however, replied that reducing the number of shipwrights to the number which could be paid for out of the grant would cripple the rebuilding program because those retained would not keep ahead of wear and tear, and certainly could never take in hand out-of-condition vessels. To stop overtime work would save £24,000, but many shipwrights would leave the King's service, and the rate of rebuilding would be reduced. There were twenty-two ships in commission and only twenty-five ships in ordinary that were in good condition. By working the shipwrights one tide extra for seven months the Navy Board hoped to raise that number to sixty-three by the end of 1767, but if overtime were stopped, their time and motion analysis cut out the repair of five ships in the two-and-a-half-year period.[60] The Admiralty, in consequence, applied to the King on 30 May for an increased grant to reduce the deficit (see Table 8).[61] No direct reply is preserved, perhaps because of the political confusion that came with the fall of the Grenville administration in July 1765 and its replacement by that of the Marquis of Rockingham. On 2 July, however, the Treasury Board directed the Admiralty to prepare an estimate of the probable expense of the navy for the present year. The Admiralty, still under Egmont, passed the directive to the Navy Board. When the estimate was presented on 11 September it noted an excess of £78,763 expenditure over grant, and Rockingham appears to have accepted it.[62]

Despite his inability to persuade Pitt to return on mutually acceptable terms to office, George III had in the end been unable to bear the continuation of the Grenville-Bedford ministry. Dismissing them, he turned to Rockingham, who was a firm Whig supporter of the Hanoverians but who had had no administrative experience. He did not consider it necessary to pursue as rigorous an economy as Grenville had, and perhaps his retention of Egmont at the Admiralty is an indication that his support for the navy was at least initially the result of inattention. However, he did give a

TABLE 8: Estimated discrepancy between parliamentary grants and expenditures, 30 May 1765

	Estimate expenditure (£)	*Granted by Parliament (£)*
Ordinary	245,419	385,842
Extra estimate		200,000
Wear and tear for 16,000 men	658,828	280,000
Wages to seamen and marines	358,356	312,000
	1,262,604 (sic)	1,178,642 (sic)
Estimates exceed grants by	1,178,642 (sic) 83,961 (sic)	

seat on the Admiralty Board to his kinsman Admiral Keppel, and as was shown when in 1778-79 Keppel was tried by court-martial for his conduct at the battle of Ushant, Rockingham was prepared to go a long way to support him. At any rate there was no immediate recession. On 6 September the King had agreed to the long-range plan for improving the dockyards at a cost of £352,240 for Portsmouth and £379,170 for Plymouth, and in October the Navy Board was advised to insert in future estimates sufficient sums to carry on each year's instalment of the program.[63]

Grenville's economies, despite the evasion of them, made possible parliamentary grants of £650,000 in 1764 and £1,500,000 in 1765, which helped to reduce the navy debt from £5,065,152 where it had stood at the end of 1762 to £2,449,058 by December 1765. By December 1769 it was down to £1,076,960, which effectively meant that British naval finances would not suffer the fate of those of the French navy.[64] On the other hand, the immediate financing of the British navy had been adequate to set in motion the repair of a fleet large enough to contain Bourbon naval rebuilding. The program was continued and extended under Rockingham.

On 18 November 1765 the Navy Board and Admiralty had a joint meeting at which they discussed the state of the fleet and the means of putting it into good order. The Navy Board, it is recorded in the Admiralty minutes, unanimously agreed that it would be possible to increase the establishment of ships of 60 guns and above to ninety ships by 1768 with the existing number of shipwrights, 3,150 men, and other artificers in proportion, providing they were employed one tide overtime in the summer months. If it were desired to increase the line of battle beyond nineteen ships, then it would be necessary to hire at least twenty-six additional shipwrights for every additional ship of the line. Fourteen shipwrights were needed for routine maintenance of every 1,000 tons of shipping. If it were required to keep in good condition the total list of the navy, which was given as about 300,000 tons of shipping, of which about 140 were ships of the line, the shipwright force would have to be increased by a third to 4,200. The Navy Board also took the opportunity to remind the Admiralty that the dockyards were in a state which would be dangerous should a war occur. In return they were enjoined to prepare estimates to carry out the long-range plan already approved.[65]

The Admiralty decided to keep the establishment of shipwrights up to strength, but not to increase the force. It thus appears that the goal of ninety ships of the line by 1768 may have been adopted temporarily; and certainly that was the recommendation made to Rockingham in December by Admiral Keppel. He envisaged the need for 33,000 more seamen to man them in an emergency and foreshadowed the expedient adopted in 1771 of laying up the cutters on coastal revenue patrol in order to release men for the ships of the line. He wanted to reduce the guardships by four or five so that the rest could be manned to within 100 men of full complement, and he wished to reduce the manpower tied up in foreign squadrons.[66] Keppel's extreme reshaping of the fleet was not adopted, but when the Navy Board asked for £277,300 for the 1766 extra estimate for building and repair, Rockingham did not refuse it.[67] No questions were asked when the expenditure for 1765 exceeded the grant by £398,024.[68] Instead, another £1,200,000 was voted towards the reduction of the navy debt.

Admiral Hawke later remarked that "from the commencement of 1764 to the close of 1766 . . . the building and repairs of the navy had been carried out with great diligence."[69] There was no further mention of the ninety-ship goal, but on 10 September 1766 the Navy Board reported that besides the twenty ships in commission there were thirty-eight laying up in ordinary in good condition, and four more were expected to be ready by the end of the year. Eight more ships, including the *Royal George* of 100 guns, and two of 90 guns, were scheduled to be ready at the end of 1767, and a further six ships were scheduled to be put in condition at the ends of 1768 and 1769. That would make a fleet of eighty-two ships of the line in good condition by the beginning of 1770, but as it was expected that three of the ships could not be preserved more than three years, the number fell to seventy-nine ships.[70] The figure was virtually repeated in January 1767 when eighty-one ships were predicted for 1770, one of the doubtful ones presumably having already been taken from the list.

When the Rockingham administration collapsed in the summer of 1766 and William Pitt was asked to form the administration on his own terms, Egmont was quickly driven from the Admiralty. It appears that Chatham hoped to increase the strength of the navy. On 10 September Admiral Sir Charles Saunders was promoted in the Admiralty Board to First Lord, but his term of office was short. He quarrelled with Chatham and resigned in December. After making an attempt to split the Bedford group by offering the Admiralty to Earl Gower, Chatham gave it to Admiral Sir Edward Hawke.[71] Hawke was the hero of the battle of Quiberon Bay in 1759, in which he had destroyed the French Brest fleet while embayed in a full gale on the Brittany coast. A star from Pitt's past glories, he has not acquired much reputation for his abilities at the administration of the Admiralty. However, it is only in comparison with his more articulate successor Sandwich that Hawke shows up poorly, and perhaps unfairly so. He certainly did not ruin the navy, as was later to be claimed, and he might well have done better than Sandwich did at the strategic direction of naval war and the handling of politicized admirals. Be that as it may, Hawke was not to be able to count for long on the support of Chatham. When in 1767 the Duke of Grafton was left holding the government in his weak hands, there were renewed efforts to reduce naval expenditure.

On 29 January 1767 the Navy Board sent to the Secretary of the Admiralty their extra estimate for 1767, but had it returned to them because of the substantial increase shown over the last year. On 2 February they submitted a revised estimate, reduced "to nearly the same sum allowed for the last year," but in fact up from £277,300 for 1766 to £328,144. When £30,000 of that had been made a special grant supposedly for the purchase of hemp, the estimate was allowed.[72] On 19 February, however, the Admiralty directed the Navy Board to prepare a general plan for expenditure which was to conform as nearly as possible to the distribution authorized in the grant and definitely not to exceed the total grant.[73] Charles Jenkinson may have instigated this directive. He had been Joint Secretary of the Treasury when it first asked for a plan of expenditure in July 1765, and although he was in opposition during the Rockingham ministry, Chatham gave him a seat at the Admiralty when Hawke formed his board. He became particularly well known for his abilities in finance and in the late 1770s Lord North considered him for Chancellor of the Exchequer.

The Navy Board's plan was ready on 24 March, and it predicted an expenditure of £57,232 more than the grant.[74] This the Admiralty would not allow. Jenkinson prepared a draft speech to Parliament in which he explained that the administration would not permit the application to general repair of funds voted for specific purposes such as repair of the docks and the purchase of hemp.[75] The Navy Board was summoned to wait upon the Admiralty, and when they did so on 3 April, they were invited to propose ways to effect economies.[76] They were only able to suggest reducing the purchase of reserves of stores and dismissing 297 of the least productive tradesmen from the yards.[77]

The 1768 estimate provided £33,000 for the docks and £246,000 for the repair of ships, and the extra estimate was £7,225 over that of 1767. It may be significant that in October 1767 Lord North had been made Chancellor of the Exchequer. Jenkinson, who had returned to the Treasury, drafted a speech defending the increase, which he said was necessary to ensure that the navy and dockyards were on a war footing in four years' time. "The only question," he wrote "is over how many years that Expence shall be distributed, that is how many years the Peace is likely to last, the present plan has assumed four years thinking that a reasonable period."[78]

Nevertheless funds continued to be short. In 1769 and 1770 the extra and ordinary naval grants remained about the same as they had been in 1767 and 1768. In February 1770 Hawke failed to get Commons approval for an additional 2,000 seamen, which would have increased the ordinary estimate by £8,000 per lunar month. He warned the Commons "that whosoever sh[oul]d be first L[or]d of the Admiralty next year would be obliged to h[ave] 5 or 6000 additional Seamen."[79] Hawke admitted that it was impossible during these years to keep the guardships fully manned; they were later described as sinecures, little ready for sea.[80]

The limitations imposed by budgetary expediency upon the reconstruction of naval matériel may have been of little importance. The determinant of the size of fleet which a state could mobilize was its resource of naval manpower. Britain's was comparatively large, but there were undeniable limitations. Among Chatham's papers is a memorandum dated 10 March 1767, soon after Hawke was made First Lord of the Admiralty, which noted that in the first year of the Seven Years' War it had only been possible to raise 25,824 men, enough to man 39 ships of the line. After seven years of war the navy had been able to muster 84,770.[81] Presumably that would have provided full complement for about 129 ships of the line. That, then, was the real top limit of British naval strength. It is interesting to note that a memorandum in the Chatham Papers dated 22 August 1756 considered 125 ships of the line as "requisite for the total stagnation and extirpation of the french trade, upon the seas, and general protection of that of Great Britain upon the seas."[82] The 80-odd ships which it had been planned would be fully fit for service in 1770 were more than double the number that was expected could be manned within a year. With a total fleet strength on paper of 153 ships of the line it was reasonable to expect that ships could be made ready as rapidly as they could be manned.[83]

Intelligence sources ensured that the British government could count on a degree of strategic warning before naval war would be forced upon them. The instructions given on 30 December 1768 to Lord Harcourt when he was sent as ambassador to Paris required him to observe the state of the French navy, "on which both their inclination to engage in any hostile measures, and their ability to prosecute them with effect, will principally depend."[84] In 1768 the British had little reason to fear the French fleet, which it will be remembered was reported by Wolters to have only forty-one ships of the line which could be in good condition, out of a total of fifty-nine, and of which there was good evidence of sound condition for only twenty-three.[85] Wolters also reported on 31 December 1769 that the Spanish fleet numbered forty-nine ships, including five new 80s.[86] An abstract of the Spanish fleet preserved in an intelligence file kept by Lord Grantham, who was to be ambassador to Madrid from 1771, gave the Spanish fleet in Europe in 1770 as "3 of the line & 2 frigates at Cartagena, 5 of the line & 4 frigates at Cadiz, 24 of the line & 8 frigates at Ferrol, in all 32 of the Line & 14 Frigates."[87] Nevertheless it is apparent that there was no apprehension in Britain that the British navy was not competent to defeat the fleets of the Family Compact.

The British navy had not fallen behind in technical development. The ships designed during the Seven Years' War by Sir Thomas Slade, who was Surveyor of the Navy from 1755 until his death in 1771, met with general approval. In the years following the war the objective of Admiralty Boards was to standardize the fleet upon the dimensions of the successful *Dragon* 74 and *Essex* 64. The 74s were regarded as the most useful ships of the fleet because they could carry 32-pounder cannon and were as swift as a frigate.[88] The experimental introduction during this period of copper-plating to reduce the fouling of ships' bottoms and protect them from marine worm gave the British a decided tactical advantage in the American war. The superiority of British cannon was acknowledged by Choiseul himself when he sent agents to investigate British founding techniques and to entice British founders to France. All navies suffered during peacetime from the inexperience of their officers on half-pay, but this was particularly disadvantageous to the Family Compact because the need for the two national navies to act together presented problems of language, different traditions, and national antipathy. During 1767 the Admiralty and the Navy Boards were worried about the ability of the dockyards to support a war effort.[89] On the other hand, the Navy Board's report of their 1767 visitation of the dockyards clearly satisfied the Admiralty: "It is with pleasure that the Lords observe in the said Report, that the Ships lying up in the several Ordinaries were found in excellent order, and that the Regulations on that head have been well and punctually observed."[90] In the 1769 budget debate North disputed Grenville's contention that economies had ruined the navy.[91]

After his resignation from the Treasury in 1770, Grafton put out feelers to Lord North to take Hawke's place at the Admiralty. As First Lord of the Treasury he should have been able to ensure that the navy was not short; nevertheless, his secretary Thomas Bradshaw reported: "I have talked seriously to him [i.e., North] upon the wretched & dangerous state of the navy." Urging that a good man be appointed to replace Cockburne as Comptroller when the latter died, Bradshaw "apprised Lord North of the importance of filling up this office properly, especially at this time, when, from the weakness of the Admiralty it was doubly necessary that the Comptroller of the Navy should be a man of ability & diligence."[92] According to Bradshaw and Grafton, North agreed that the navy needed greater attention and that a vote to reduce the debt would serve to meet current expenditure while it would not raise alarms.[93] A good man, Palliser, was appointed Comptroller, but the 1770 vote to reduce the debt was only £100,000, and every rival's efforts to unseat Hawke failed. Even Sandwich was put off with the assurance that North was "firmly desirous of seeing that department under your management" but that no vacancy was foreseen.[94] The evidence of government concern for the success of their efforts to match Bourbon naval rebuilding is in fact slight, while the events of 1770 make it clear that the North cabinet were ready to trust the fleet in war.

REORGANIZATION OF THE ROYAL NAVY, 1770-75

The outcome of the Falkland Islands crisis of 1770 gave the British every reason to believe that their navy remained adequate to defend their maritime interests and to perpetuate the settlement of the Peace of Paris. Choiseul's policies were discredited and he was disgraced. The Duc d'Aiguillon, who was eventually appointed to take Choiseul's place, told Colonel John Blanquière, the new Secretary of the British embassy in Paris, that the Spaniards "have been constantly reproaching me ever since with having suffered the critical moment to escape, when Your navy was in a rotten condition, and that You would have been an easy prey—that we are now suffering you to prepare and arm and that in a couple of years, it would be too late."[95] From the evidence, however, the pseudonymous letter-writer Junius seems correct in his view that it was Britain which had missed the opportune moment to crush the Bourbon revival by defeating an isolated Spain before the American revolt reduced Britain's strength.[96]

The events of 1770 did break the momentum of French preparations for révanche, but in London the return of Choiseul to power was not expected to be long delayed, and d'Aiguillon's pursuit of French foreign policy was aggressive enough. The credibility of British seapower had been re-established, but the British triumph had been a holding operation, and the respite it gave was small. British naval preparations had to be continued at a redoubled rate because of the evident hostility of the Bourbons and the weakness in the system revealed by the mobilization. In 1772 Edmund Burke described the situation as "an armed peace. We have peace and no peace, war and no war. We are in a state to which the ingenuity of our ministry has yet found no apt name."[97]

In later years, when defending his administration of the navy, Sandwich was to describe the fleet he had inherited as rotten. It had not appeared that way to him in the spring of 1771. When he made the first of his visitations of the dockyards which he undertook every year until 1778, he discovered that the program outlined in 1767 had been carried out. He recorded in his journal that "there are now at least 80 Ships of the Line fit for immediate Service, & 43 others that will come in course & be made serviceable, so that the whole Fleet consists at present of 123 effective Line of Battle Ships."[98] This estimate of the number of ships fit for service, slightly below the 86 the Navy Board had estimated in October, was later confirmed when in 1781 a paper was prepared for Rockingham making a case for an investigation of Sandwich's administration. It observed: "It will appear that when Lord Hawke resigned he left *Eighty one sail of the line* fit for service and building" (see Table 9).[99] The 123 which could readily be made serviceable came very close to the 129 which an extrapolation from Chatham's 1767 memorandum suggested was the maximum for which Britain could find men. Sandwich had continued with the observation "that considering the very sever Services on which our Fleets were employed during the last war . . . it seems to me rather to be wondered that we have so many good ships still in our Ports, than that . . . we should have met with some of them who have not lasted so long as we *wished* they should."

In the course of 1771, progressive decay, and the discovery of decay where it had not been suspected, caused a considerable reduction in the estimate of ships in good condition. On 18 January 1772 the Navy Office provided a list of the fleet showing a total of thirty-one ships in commission, thirty others in good condition, and fourteen in dockyard hands.[100] North assured the Commons that Britain could put to sea "tomorrow" sixty ships, or seventy-five to eighty by the end of the year. He put a good face on it. "I do believe th[at] when Great Britain is in the situation she will soon be she may laugh at the junction of France, and Spain, put numbers against numbers, an hundred, and thirty, double theirs."[101]

That was the lowest estimation which was made. Sandwich's building and repair program steadily increased the number of ships he considered to be in good condition. In his 1773 visitation of the dockyards he reported, besides the thirty-two ships of the line in commission, thirty-six out of commission in good condition, a total of sixty-eight. To this he added fifty-four ships either building, repairing, or needing small to middling repair, making a total of 122 ships which he considered could be quickly put into condition, but as yet with a larger proportion needing some work than there had been thought to be in 1771 (see Table 10).[102] In June 1774 these figures had risen to thirty-five ships in commission, forty-one others in good condition, and fifty-two which could be quickly brought into service, a grand total of 128 effective (see Table 11).[103]

Sandwich was an exceptionally dedicated and inventive First Lord.[104]

TABLE 9: Sandwich's estimation of the condition of the British fleet, 1771

Rate	Guns	In commission	In good condition	Building & repairing	Total
1	100		3		3
2	90	2	6	1	9
	84		1		1
3	80	1	1		2
	74	12	15	6	33
	70	4		1	5
	64	10	3	5	18
4	60	2	1	1	4
TOTALS		31	30	14	75

TABLE 10: Abstract of Sandwich's estimation in 1773
of the number of ships requiring work at British naval yards

	Portsmouth	Plymouth	Chatham	Sheerness	Woolwich	Deptford
Good condition	12	12	7	5		
Wanting:						
small repair	2	5	4			
small to mid.	2		3			
middling	5	6	2		1	
mid. to great	2		2			
great repair	2					
Building	4	4	4		2	6

TABLE 11: Abstract of Sandwich's estimation in 1775

	Portsmouth	Plymouth	Chatham	Sheerness	Woolwich	Deptford
Good condition	15	12	6	4	1	3
Wanting:						
small repair	3	5	2			
small to mid.	3		2			
middling	3	4	2		1	
great repair	1	1				
Repairing	2	3	3		1	
Building	4	4	4	1	2	3

Unfortunately his ideas did not always prove to be practicable in the circumstances of the 1770s. His attempt in 1775 to substitute piece-work for day labour in the dockyards in order to effect economies and speed up building and repair was thwarted by the shipwrights, who went on strike.[105] Another good but unrealistic idea, evidently Sandwich's own, was for the development of a permanent naval force which would replace the guardship system with a three-tier fleet structure according to "some settled plan." The size of the permanent force was to be deduced by abstract reasoning from the extent of British territory, the size of the Bourbon fleets, and the maximum naval force which could be supported by Britain's maritime resources, especially of manpower. Consideration was also to be given to the need "for an Expeditious Armament at the Beginning of a War" and to the ability to follow-up the first armament with "a proper & ready Succession of Ships."[106]

Sandwich's review of Britain's resources of naval manpower was more pragmatic and differed little from that produced for Chatham in 1767. The optimum time for commencing a naval mobilization was in October when the ocean trades began to return home. They remained home until March, but once there the seamen would hide themselves until they could find work in a protected trade. Accordingly, protection should not be granted early. In 1770, during the Falkland Islands crisis, North said he was guided by this consideration, but he handled the 1777 mobilization much less effectively.

The royal dockyards were in no condition to sustain Sandwich's idealistic organization, which would have required the permanent occupation of twenty-four slips for capital ships in reserve and the simultaneous repair of ships of the line at eight others, over and above the maintenance work needed on the seventy-five ships of the first fleet. Sandwich's actual achievement between 1770 and February 1778 was less spectacular, but it was nonetheless very good. Decay was a constant factor. According to his reckoning only seventeen of the eighty-six ships on the serviceable list in December 1770 would need no repair before February 1778. Another twenty-six had been given repairs to keep them fit for service, and five more were still undergoing repair. Seventeen ships could not be made fit and were reduced to harbour service or storeships, fifteen others were unfit in February 1778 and awaited major repair, and six were condemned and sold, broken up, and made into breakwaters.[107] A vigorous program of new construction was needed to keep up the size of the line of battle.

The numerical strength of the fleet is only a rough guide to its effectiveness in war. Much depends on what standard is used in the subjective judgment Sandwich made of ships "fit for service." The defeats of the Revolutionary War led contemporary politicians and subsequent historians to look for the roots of defeat in Sandwich's failures to maintain adequate naval matériel. On the basis of the evidence, however, it appears that Sandwich's failings were more those of political leadership and possibly strategic judgment. He more than held his own in the repair and expansion

John Montagu, 4th Earl
of Sandwich, 1718-92.
Engraving by V. Green
after a painting by J.
Zoffani.
Courtesy of the British
Museum (Class II period 4;
1864.8.13.263) Negative 1/2
pl. 36875

of ships, and largely through his own efforts the supply of shipbuilding
timber was built up between 1770 and 1778 to nearly the three-years' reserve
he thought necessary. Eighteenth-century accounting techniques kept him
from knowing how far he had fallen short of that goal, but he had built up a
stockpile, broken a "combination" of timber merchants by importing Baltic
oak, and had arranged proper storage for the timber under cover. A paper
prepared in the Navy Office in April 1779 to support Sandwich in the
defence of his administration gave an abstract contrasting the supplies
available in 1770 and 1778 not only of timber, but also of masts, hemp,
pitch, tar, and iron. There were improvements in every category, but
especially in timber and tar supplies, of which the stocks had doubled (see
Table 12).[108]

The introduction of copper-plating was greatly accelerated during
Sandwich's administration. The technique of protecting hull fastenings from
the corrosive effects of bimetal electrolysis had not been perfected.
Consequently only small ships were coppered until February 1779, when

wartime pressures led to the order being given to copper the first ship of the line. Sandwich's administration also saw the large-scale introduction of carronades, which were short cannon capable of firing a heavier ball at short range for a similar deck-weight as the long guns. At first the carronades were greeted with great suspicion in the fleet, especially after some of them burst on firing, but by 1778 they had been accepted and were to prove valuable in the war.[109]

The experience of 1770 suggested the need for strategic and administrative changes in Britain's fleet organization. In November 1771 Sir Guy Carleton, later the governor of Canada, drew up a memorandum in which he expressed the conviction that any future conflict with France would be fought at home. He believed that the French strategy of colonial attacks had been frustrated and that, in future, the most likely attack should be considered to be an invasion of the British Isles.[110] North's policy of avoiding foreign deployments in peacetime was in agreement with Carleton's ideas, and the Franco-Spanish invasion attempt of 1779 proved them to have been at least partly correct. It was only the failure of North's and Sandwich's strategic control which gave the French an opportunity of fighting the war outside European waters. Carleton reasoned that the only effective defence against invasion was an increase in the regular army, but the administration preferred to strengthen the home naval forces.

The first requirement was an increase of the vote for seamen. When the Admiralty presented to Rochford its plan for a peace establishment on 1 March 1771, they asked for 25,000 men.[111] The increased vote, arrangements made for the workmen to guard the dockyards so that the marines would be free for sea duty, and reduction of the number of ships employed on routine duties, such as the cutters aiding the revenue service, allowed for an improvement in the readiness of the fleet to fight for command of the sea. In January 1774 there were only 107 ships in sea pay, whereas there had been from January 1767 to July 1770 between 132 and 144 ships. In the earlier period there had been an average of only 99 to 104 men per ship. The mobilization of large ships during the crisis increased the average number of men per ship to 218.6, in the April 1770 returns. After the resolution of the crisis there was no equivalent reduction. During 1772, 1773, and 1774, there was never less than an average of 169 men per ship. This represented an increase in ship size of slightly less than 70 per cent over the pre-crisis days (see Table 13).[112]

All the squadrons had been given larger ships, but the implications were most dramatic in home waters. In April 1767 there had been in the Mediterranean squadron, in British ports, guardships, and cruising on the coasts of Great Britain, fourteen third rates, six fourth rates, seven fifth rates, ten sixth rates, one frigate, fourteen sloops, thirty-four cutters, and

TABLE 12: Navy Board comparison of stocks in 1770 and 1778

	31 Dec. 1770	*31 Dec. 1778*
Masts (New England		
and Riga)	1,759	3,263
(Norway)	3,308	6,084
		Plus 3,470 Riga and
		Norway masts on order.
Timber	31,366 loads	72,317 loads
Hemp	6,135 tons	7,150 tons
Pitch	4,674 barrels	6,812 barrels
Tar	12,072 barrels	30,780 barrels
Iron	3,588 tons	4,255 tons

TABLE 13: Numbers of ships in sea pay, and average number of men per ship, 1763-78

Date	*(1)*	*(2)*	*(1) Number of ships*					
1763	154	267	*(2) Average number of men per ship*					
1764	179	146						
1765	159	122						
1766	148	107	*Date*	*(1)*	*(2)*	*Date*	*(1)*	*(2)*
1767	136	99	1771	180	209	1775	102	169
1768	135	99	1772	153	177	1776	146	163
1769	136	101	1773	130	169	1777	210	220
1770	142	103	1774	107	171	1778	274	228

eight other small craft: a total of 9,440 men in ninety-five ships, or 99.3 men per ship. The increase in manpower and reorganization meant that in April 1772, in the same services, there could be two second rates, nineteen third rates, two fourth rates, twelve fifth rates, nine sixth rates, one frigate, nineteen sloops, ten cutters, and eight others: a total of 14,092 men in eighty-two ships or an average of 171.8 men per ship.

The size of the ships in the seagoing squadrons had been increased, but the most important alteration was the reorganization of the guardship squadron. The Admiralty did not agree with a proposal made by Lord Howe to the King that a small standing force was preferable to a larger guardship squadron.[113] The experience of the guardships sent to Ireland to receive troops for Gibraltar, however, indicated that reforms were necessary.

Several alterations were made in the organization of the guardships to improve their readiness for battle, most of which had only been made possible by the increases of the naval vote, which provided both more men and greater funds. The first step was to change the practice of cleaning the guardships annually each spring to a biannual cleaning in rotation, so that the entire squadron would have been cleaned within six months and many more recently whenever an emergency should arise. This degree of excellence was, in fact, more than the dockyards could produce without detriment to their other duties. In Sandwich's papers is a memorandum dated 30 January 1773 suggesting that the guardships be returned to an annual cleaning, but that one-third of the force should be cleaned every four months. Since the number of guardships did not drop below twenty, that would have ensured at least thirteen ships cleaned within eight months.[114] In the end it was decided to retain the rotational system of cleaning but to extend the period to nine months.[115]

Perhaps the most important change in the guardship squadron was the simultaneous increase in its size and in each ship's peace complement. After 1770 the guardship squadron was maintained at its full strength of twenty ships, the size of the individual ships was increased so that the two largest were second rates, and the ships' complements were increased from 180 to 350 men for a third rate.[116] This allowed a greater degree of self-maintenance and allowed another reform—the institution of training cruises. It was ordered that the Portsmouth and Plymouth guardships should meet during the summer for joint manoeuvres to improve seamanship and to test the ships' condition. North used this important reform to justify the increased naval vote to the Commons in January 1772, remarking: "it is thought right to h[ave] a squadron out in summer, by way of exercising the men, now th[at] could not be done upon the old complement."[117] Sandwich found that the training cruises met an enthusiastic reception from the fleet's officers.[118]

The increased complement reduced the mobilization time needed for the guardships. The third rates only needed another 250 men to proceed to sea, 80 of whom were held ready on shore. North expected they could be ready in three or four weeks. The 350-man complement of the guardships permitted them to be anchored ready for service in Plymouth Sound and at Spithead, where it was ordered that they should carry their full complement of guns. The revised complements of men were maintained in practice. In July 1772, sixteen third rate guardships bore an average of 337 men each.[119]

The result of these reforms was, as the Honourable Augustus Hervey told the Commons in 1772,

> you have twenty ships [of the] line now ready for sea, I repeat it ready for sea, wh[ich] is clearly ready. The H[onourable] G[entlemen] may shake his hat. In ten days they shall be at sea, w[ith] the assistance of some marines wh[o] are now on shore. Th[e] proof of it is, a few Guardships now O[rdered] for the East Indies, if it is his Majesty's pleasure they shall sail in ten days every necessary thing to fit them out will be ready in twenty-four hours warrant.[120]

In 1773 fifteen guardships were in fact to be mobilized in about ten days, justifying Hervey's boast.

Owing to the size of the navy vote, it had not been necessary to sacrifice the foreign service squadrons to strengthen the home battle fleet. The proportion of men serving in home waters or in the Mediterranean to those serving in foreign stations was not changed appreciably. This proportion was in April 1767 68 per cent, and in April 1771, 73 per cent. In April 1768, 1769, and 1770 there had been over 62 per cent, and in 1773 deployment of forces to India reduced the proportion of manpower at home to 53 per cent.[121] However, when it became necessary to reduce the size of the navy vote, it was the foreign squadrons which were reduced.

Sandwich had to struggle continually with North's quite proper concern to protect British credit, which might be damaged by large expenditure on the navy. Calculations of the state of navy debt vary considerably, but one official abstract shows it on 31 December 1771, after all deductions had been made for cash in hand and disbursements made on the transport service which were paid for by the Ordnance Department, as standing at £1,179,375. It continued to rise thereafter. Sandwich's insistence upon building up a stock of sound timber and stores necessarily involved expense, and so did the foreign establishments. At the end of 1775 the debt was up to £2,453,617 and by the end of 1777 it was at £3,410,602.[122] In order to prevent the debt going even higher consideration was given in 1772 to reducing the complements of ships on foreign service, but in fact no economies were possible that year until an end had been put to the danger of a French attack on India.[123]

According to secret service reports, as North told Parliament in 1772, throughout the first half of the 1770s the British fleet remained adequate to match the combined Bourbon fleets. The number of French ships discovered in 1770 to be defective had reduced the effective French fleet strengths. The *Royal Louis* of 112 guns had been "judged totally unfit for service and laid up to serve in the port to lodge troops," and the *Duc de Bourgogne* of 80 guns was reported "upon the stocks to refit, but in so miserable a condition that it was doubtful if they would be able to make anything of her." Four 64s had been broken up or condemned, and two 74s and a 64 were "upon the stocks to refit, but [their] head timbers being found rotten, work [is] provisionally suspended." At Brest were "good, doubtful, and bad, 35 ships besides the 5 at L'Orient; of which 8 were already condemned, and it is feared that more would undergo the same Fate upon close Examination. Of this Number 17 ships of the line had December the 31st their masts in, and were ready to be fitted out at the first notice." The report ended with the information that all the rest of the ships in Toulon and Brest were to be inspected.[124]

The disgrace of Choiseul had brought to a standstill his efforts to build up the naval strength of France. Louis XV turned his attention to domestic concerns, and his appointee to the naval ministry, Bourgeois de Boynes, produced calamitous disorganization by an ill-advised attempt to reorganize the officer corps. In the beginning of 1772 the Rotterdam net reported there to be sixty-one ships in the French fleet, of which two were under construction and twelve were known to be in bad condition, leaving forty-seven ships presumed in good condition.[125] Another "Etat de la Marine de France" in the Sandwich Papers, dated 1 April 1772, listed fifty-three ships of the line, only four of which were known to be in poor condition.[126] Between 1771 and 1774 only six ships were built to replace eight which were struck from the list.[127]

London was aware of the quiescence in French dockyards but may not have realized quite how much French fleet strength had fallen. In Sandwich's 1773 memorandum on a permanent establishment for the British fleet he said that the French line of battle consisted of sixty-six ships plus eight of 50 to 56 guns.[128] According to French reckonings, in August 1774 they had only thirty-four ships ready for sea, including ships of 50 guns.[129] Admiralty intelligence reckoning of 1 January 1775 estimated the French to have forty-four ships in good repair and ten out of condition. It is hardly surprising that the Admiralty erred on the side of safety, however, and rightly so, for in 1775 French naval reconstruction revived under the stimulation of the American Revolution. Even as early as January 1775 it was known that France had ten hulls under construction.[130]

Despite the efforts of Charles III, the Spanish fleet continued to be regarded in London as second-rate. In particular, the quality of the newly constructed ships, built by the French contractor Gautier, was believed to be poor. Lord Grantham, sent in 1771 as ambassador to Madrid, kept a file of intelligence reports on the Spanish navy which contain several notes in 1773 on their poor performance. They were built with so little freeboard that the lower gun decks could not be used "with the least fresh breeze of wind which the others do with facility."[131] On the other hand, because of its size the Spanish fleet could not be discounted entirely. A Spanish fleet list for 1 April 1772 in the Sandwich Papers shows only fifty-two ships of 58 guns or more, but in a duodecimo booklet Grantham drew up giving a state of the Spanish navy each year, he noted, for 1773, that Spain had twenty-nine ships of the line "ready careen'd" at Cartagena or Ferrol, with another 6 at Cadiz, and with no less than twenty-nine ships on the stocks.[131] The next year's abstract gave a total of fifty-four of the line, which closely resembles a list supplied by the Rotterdam agency that gave fifty-three Spanish ships not known to be out of condition, of which twenty-eight had been built or rebuilt since the war.[132] Nevertheless, the availability of the Spanish fleet could never be entirely relied upon by the French, and the allied fleet could never work together as efficiently as the homogeneous British fleet. The

120-odd ships of the Bourbon paper strength challenged Britain's naval supremacy, but had not supplanted it.

The revolt of the American colonists brought a return to the policy of Choiseul. Once again naval preparation for war with Britain became a dominant focus of state activity, although that policy was not the official one of the young King Louis XVI, who had no desire for war. By 1778 the French ministers considered they had stolen a sufficient march on the British that there was a reasonable prospect of winning a naval war. There is no reason to suppose that that judgment was correct, but the statecraft of the British government had supported the illusion. Not too much should be made of the fact that French naval intervention did make possible the success of the Revolution. That was primarily the result of political weakness in Britain, and bad strategic planning. British wartime errors gave substance to the French illusion of British naval weakness.

3

The Utilization
of Naval Supremacy, 1763-68

Dependence upon naval power significantly constrained and channelled Britain's foreign policy. The scale of the triumph in 1763 which established Britain's general naval predominance emphasizes the limits there were to the utility of naval power. In the years following the Seven Years' War, successive British administrations found themselves grappling with those limitations. The ability to employ naval forces to protect British interests was dependent upon circumstances. When it was possible to take direct naval action, there was always a price to pay for humiliating her former enemies. Coercion of those governments by naval action unconnected with the direct subject of dispute incurred an even higher price because the humiliation was all the more apparent. Yet failure to protect national interests undermined the credibility of British seapower, and failure to protect the economic and politico-geographic foundations of naval strength could lead to irrecoverable loss.

THE HONDURAS AND TURKS ISLAND INCIDENTS

In 1764-65, when British interests were threatened consecutively in Honduras, Turks Island, and the Gambia, the Grenville administration managed to employ Britain's naval strength with considerable success as an instrument of foreign policy.[1] The troubles with Spain and France respectively in Honduras and at Turks Island were apparently unconnected in their origins, but their juxtaposition in time and location meant that it was possible to take concerted action against both dangers, and the sudden appearance of two threats at the same time may have enhanced governmental awareness of danger.

The first news of trouble came from Honduras. The long history of Anglo-Spanish disputes over British claims to rights to cut logwood and mahogany in the Spanish territories of Honduras and the Mosquito Coast ensured that any development in those places would be closely watched. The dispute had been one of the principal reasons for the Spanish entry into the Seven Years' War, and any violation of Article 17 of the Peace of Paris, which had secured British rights, could be regarded as the first step in an attempt to rob Britain of her victory.[2] The attention of the Grenville cabinet was immediately held when on 12 June 1764 a letter was received from Governor Lyttleton of Jamaica reporting that Philip Remirez de Esterios, the governor of Yucatan, had decided that the arrival of Englishmen to cut logwood on the Rio Nuevo and Rio Hondo in Honduras could not be justified by the treaty. Acting on instructions from the anti-British minister of the Marine and Indies, Don Julian de Arriaga, de Esterios had ordered the loggers to leave the Rio Hondo until they could produce written permission from the King of either Spain or Britain. He had enforced his order with a small military force.[3]

Grenville and the Secretaries of State were quickly persuaded that this development should be taken as a serious threat, and Grenville almost immediately began to contemplate the necessity of employing naval forces to cope with the situation.[4] He evidently felt unsure of his colleagues, attitudes.[5] However, not even the Duke of Bedford needed to be persuaded. He was a francophile and had a paternal interest in the Peace of Paris he had negotiated, but he had no special feeling for Spain.[6] The British ambassador in Madrid, the Earl of Rochford, was a willing instrument of Grenville's coercion. He was a career diplomat and a privy councillor who was to acquire such a reputation for hostility to the Bourbons that when Lord North made him a Secretary of State in October 1768, he was given the Northern Department, despite his experience in Bourbon affairs. Had his health, and perhaps his views on North's colonial policy, not obliged his retirement in 1775, he might well have prevented French intervention in the Revolutionary War. He was one of the stronger men of the period, ranking with Sandwich in his professionalism within his department. In his initial meeting with the Spanish government on the subject, Rochford bluntly reminded the Marquis of Grimaldi that "this affair has been the occasion of more than one war between the two crowns."

It is clear, however, that no one in the British government wanted war. The strategy was to intimidate the government of Spain in order to deter them from a course of action which might eventually make war conceivable. For the present the central consideration was the belief that Spain could not risk a resumption of the war which had been so damaging to her. On 30 July Rochford assured the Earl of Halifax, Secretary of State for the Southern

William Henry Zuylestein, 4th Earl of Rochford, 1717-81. Engraving by R. Houston after a painting by Dom. Dupra.
Courtesy of the British Museum (Class II period 4; 53.1.12. 1659) Negative PS 123695

Department: "Your Lordship may be perfectly satisfied, that there is Nothing They will not do to avoid quarrelling with Us at this Time."[7]

Any remaining doubts that may have been entertained about the conduct of their diplomacy were soon dispelled by advice of fresh trouble in the West Indies. The new danger quickly brought the decision to call upon naval force to protect British interests. On 20 June the commander-in-chief of the British squadron in the West Indies, Sir William Burnaby, wrote to the Admiralty Secretary, Philip Stephens, that the French governor of Dominica had used force to expel Bermudan salt pan workers from Turks Island.[8] The governor was the notorious Comte d'Estaing, who had broken parole during the war. This letter was received in London on 1 August, and the next day Stephens forwarded it to Halifax.[9]

The government were even more concerned about French aggression than they were about Spain's. Governor Shirley of the Bahamas wrote to Halifax pointing out the strategic importance of Turks Island in the conduct of wartime operations against French trade.[10] However, the chief consideration of Grenville's cabinet was that the Family Compact should not be permitted to achieve a petty victory which might encourage efforts to reverse the decision of 1763. On 6 August, Grenville wrote to Sandwich that d'Estaing's action was "a business of the most serious and important nature which requires some immediate step to be taken."[11] Sandwich and Halifax agreed on the need for strong measures, although Halifax took the precaution of asking the Commissioners for Trade and Plantations for an opinion on Britain's claims to Turks Island.[12] The task of persuading Bedford of the need to coerce France was entrusted to Sandwich, his political dependent.[13] Again Bedford proved more willing to resort to force than had been anticipated.[14] Grenville continued to be very much in awe of Bedford and was even to manoeuvre his exclusion from a critical cabinet meeting on 5 September. Bedford, however, never wavered in his support of the policy of coercion, although he was generally more moderate.[15]

Because of the proximity of Honduras to Turks Island it was possible for one naval deployment to handle both situations. This circumstance may have encouraged Grenville to adopt the tactic of preparing a naval force to take the law into British hands, forcibly restoring the *status quo ante* should diplomatic means prove slow or unproductive. Since it was obvious to all that Bourbon naval reconstruction had as yet done little to narrow the margin of British superiority, the principal requirement was that the force on the spot should be adequate to discourage any local Bourbon opposition. Local weakness might ultimately lead to an escalation of the force required and thereby create unnecessary international discord. Sandwich, who during his five months as First Lord of the Admiralty in 1763 had experienced the pinch of peacetime economies, had already remarked to Grenville: "I doubt whether Sir W. Burnaby must not be reinforced, as he has no ship of the line with him, unless you so call a bad 50-gun ship with her lowest complement of men; and if you send a reinforcement from hence, I fear it would operate upon our funds, but of that you are the best judge."[16]

Burnaby commanded only *Dreadnought*, fourth rate, and a force of eight fifth rates, frigates, and sloops.[17] On the 17th the cabinet resolved to reinforce him with two guardships. The Admiralty ordered two third rates, *Africa* and *Essex,* fitted for foreign service and victualled for six months. Sandwich immediately wrote to Bedford that the implication of taking a strong stand and employing naval forces was that it was "absolutely necessary to reinforce Sir William Burnaby as he had no ship of the line with him, and without such an addition to his squadron would be liable to an insult."[18]

British diplomatic tactics with respect to France and Spain differed. Considering, presumably, that overt threats would drive the French to resent that which they were in no position to prevent, no suggestion was made diplomatically that they might be obliged to submit to superior British force. Instead, on 20 August, Halifax ordered the ambassador in Paris, Lord Hertford, to present a memorial to the French court expressing astonishment at the action and demanding restitution of the island, reparation of the damages done, and punishment of the responsible French officers.[19] With the Spaniards, on the other hand, every effort continued to be made to emphasize the danger of refusing British demands.[20] Dissatisfied with the concessions the Spanish ambassador in London, Prince Masserano, was prepared to make, Halifax ordered the Admiralty on 29 August to fit out two ships of the line lying in ordinary, further to reinforce Burnaby.[21] He warned Rochford that unless Madrid immediately issued orders to provide redress and reparation, "His Majesty will find himself obliged, tho' with great Regret, to take the proper measures for reinstating & protecting His injured Subjects in the Enjoyment of those Rights & Privileges to which they are justly intitled by treaty."[22] Nevertheless Halifax was not seeking a pretext for war. Rochford believed that the anti-British Arriaga had a great deal of control over formal dispatches to London. Halifax accordingly refused to treat directly with Masserano and channelled his demands through Rochford.

Grenville continued to set the pace for naval preparations. He was afraid that the *Africa* and the *Essex* would be inadequate to ensure local superiority in the West Indies, without which there was too much risk of battle between the British and French squadrons there. He wrote Sandwich on the 31st: "The sending a small force may be attended with very great inconveniences, as it is possible that upon this alarm France and Spain may steal out two or three ships of the line, and it is the highest importance to extinguish this spark of fire at once, lest it should kindle into a blaze, which probably may be the case, if our forces, and that of France and Spain, shall be nearly equal in those seas."[23] On 3 September the Admiralty ordered the *Thunderer* of seventy-five guns and the *Edgar* of sixty fitted for foreign service, and three days later Vice-Admiral Holbourne was ordered to turn over to them men from the guardships at Chatham.[24]

Once satisfied that British forces would be adequate, Grenville seems to have been very willing to employ them. The protestations of the Duc de Praslin that he did not even know where Turks Island was located did not prevent the cabinet deciding on the 5th to order Burnaby to recover Turks Island by force and to be ready to intervene in Honduras.[25] Halifax embodied this decision in a directive to the Admiralty on the 7th, at the same time authorizing them to commission two more ships to replace the guardships destined for the West Indies. This latter was not done, but the Admiralty immediately ordered the *Wolf* sloop to carry to Burnaby orders which they drew up. All dispatch was ordered in the preparation of *Thunderer* and *Edgar*.[26]

Horace Walpole suggested that the decision to send ships was influenced by public resentment with the peace treaty.[27] He was a biased witness who tried to get political advantage from the crisis, but it is true that political considerations reinforced the strategic ones. They may even have distorted them. Earl Gower, who was a Bedford man and Lord Chamberlain of the Household, expressed to Sandwich his approval of the decision: "The measure of reinforcing S:W:B: [Sir William Burnaby] must be right, for tho I believe the appearance of firmness will have its weight with the Court of F[rance] & Spain, the reality will have more & the people of England will like to see that the ministry will not permit this country to be insulted, tho I really think a war at present w[ould] be the destruction of it."[28]

Grenville's resolve was not put to the test. On the 8th Hertford's second letter arrived from Paris with news that Praslin had said that "Nothing can exceed . . . Our desire of preserving a good intelligence with his Britannick Majesty." Without awaiting a report from d'Estaing, Praslin disavowed his action, ordering him to restore British property and to arrange for reparations. Only the promise to punish the offending officer was refused, and it would have been unreasonable to make that the *sine qua non* of continued peace. A copy of the order to d'Estaing to abandon all pretence to Turks Island was included, and Halifax, forwarding Hertford's letter to Grenville, asked Egmont to stop the sailing of the sloop *Wolf*. The orders to Burnaby, signed the day before, were returned to the Admiralty and cancelled. On the 12th Grenville wrote to Bedford to tell him of Hertford's letter. He regretted that the French had not punished d'Estaing, but he expressed the hope that the crisis was past.[29]

London was satisfied with the outcome of negotiations with France. In a cabinet meeting of 21 September at which both Bedford and Egmont were present, it was decided to direct Burnaby to superintend d'Estaing's restitution.[30] Hertford was advised that, "Redress and Reparation being now obtained, it is not His Majesty's Intention that You should formally enter into any Further discussion upon the nature and Extent of the Outrage committed."[31]

The success of Britain's diplomacy with France gave Grenville a free hand with Spain. The cabinet decided to order Burnaby "to take as speedily as may be the most effectual measures for re-establishing His Majesty's Subjects employed in the cutting of logwood in the several places from whence they have been lately unjustifiably driven." Despite the decision to resort to force, however, the intentions remained within the scope of diplomacy. Burnaby's instructions were such as would minimize the likelihood of general conflict. Lyttleton was ordered to supply Burnaby with troops, and on 26 September *Africa* and *Essex* sailed to Port Royal, Jamaica. The orders which they carried, which the Admiralty had drawn up at Halifax's instruction, were that Burnaby was to avoid initiating hostilities.[32]

In the end it was unnecessary to use even this limited force because Spain was eventually persuaded that resistance was useless. On 14 September, Rochford had begun a letter which was a journal of his discussion with Grimaldi: "From the knowledge I have of this Court and from the thorough persuasion I am in, that there is nothing they would not do to avoid a rupture at this moment, I knew the more I frightened them, the easier I should carry my point." Grimaldi had protested about the British refusal to make the peace treaty more explicit, but when he refused to punish the governor of Yucatan, Rochford had said: "I was sorry to find he stopped short at such a Trifle, but that unless satisfaction was given, the King would be obliged to take measures for reinstating his injured subjects, and he must see that this would be the same thing as to *sonner le tocsin de la guerre.*"

The Spaniards quickly capitulated and ordered the restoration of the cutters, only refusing reparation. Rochford formally protested at the latter, and Grimaldi believed that the British would later agree to delineate the area where logwood could be cut. In fact, however, the issue was dropped as it stood and the British government felt it had achieved all they needed.[33] As the guardships had already sailed, Burnaby's orders were forwarded in the *Wolf*, still in England after the cancellation of the second set of orders.[34] Fortunately Burnaby had not been able to act immediately upon the original orders sent him in the guardships. *Wolf* arrived in time to end the risk of accidental conflict.

It had only been "gunboat" diplomacy in intention and as a last resort. The actual naval operations in the West Indies had been noted for their moderation and caution. Nevertheless, Halifax hardly expressed the true nature of the confrontation when he wrote Rochford "It is by no means the Principle of the British Court, as certain Powers in Europe have of late affected to suppose, to be arrogant in Peace, because we have demonstrated a superiority in the late war."[35] The Grenville administration had established its style of foreign relations and was to have more opportunity to employ it.

THE GAMBIA

The success which had met Grenville's first two attempts to exploit Britain's naval strength can only have encouraged him to try to do so again when reports were received of French efforts to assert themselves in the trade of the River Gambia. Basically, Grenville's tactics remained the same with respect to the French: to impose British will firmly while attempting to avoid an overt threat which the French might be forced to resent. This time, however, the government made an ill-conceived effort to dispense with diplomacy

George Montagu Dunk,
2nd Earl of Halifax,
1716-71. Engraving by
Aliamet.
Courtesy of the British
Museum (Class II period 4;
1931.5.5. 23) Negative
191647

entirely; this failed, forcing it back on more classical coercive diplomacy. Part of the interest in this incident lies in the detail which is available of the correlation of naval movements with government policy.

The French had been driven from their factory at Albreda on the River Gambia during the war, but no mention of the Gambia had been made in the Peace of Paris. Consequently when the French returned to Senegal they also reoccupied Albreda, which they began to fortify. The British Company of Merchants Trading to Africa, with a more extensive post at James Fort upstream from Albreda, resented the French return and reported to the government. The Commissioners for Trade and Plantations advised that the French presence at Albreda had always been on sufferance and that, acquiescing in that position, the French had never previously attempted to fortify their factory. Otherwise no action was taken for eighteen months, until 4 October 1764. Immediately after the receipt of Rochford's account of the Spanish capitulation over Honduras, however, the cabinet discussed the situation on the Gambia. A minute was agreed upon: "that a 50 or 60 gun ship and a smaller frigate be sent to the coast of Africa to protect and defend His Majesty's possessions and the rights of trade of His Majesty's subjects and to prevent any encroachments."[36]

The government's object was to stop French encroachment in such a way that the French government would not feel itself challenged. It was usual for a small squadron to be dispatched to West Africa, every year when possible, and the Admiralty were already preparing *Shannon* and *Hound* sloops.[37] Besides patrolling for pirates and keeping an eye on the French and Dutch, the naval officer dispatched to Africa had a supervisory duty over the forts of the Africa Company. On the 18th, Halifax told the Admiralty they could use one of the two ships of the line prepared to reinforce Burnaby in the West Indies instead of the 50-gunner previously ordered, and accordingly the *Edgar* was ordered stored for eight months and sent to rendezvous at Plymouth.[38] Only then, nearly a month after it had been decided to send warships to protect British interests, did Halifax write to Hertford in Paris with details of what had happened and what had been done. He was instructed not to make diplomatic representations. The Admiralty had its orders, and Hertford was only given the information so that he could "reply to any Representations which the French Ministers in Conversation, or otherwise, may hereafter make to you on this Subject."[39]

Initially the expedition remained on the footing of a routine inspection, but the substitution of *Edgar* for a 50-gun ship, although it was ostensibly for reasons of technical facility, suggests an awareness of possible complications and a concern to send sufficient forces to prevent local resistance. The news from Africa continued to indicate the possibility of armed action. In July, the French governor of Goree, Monsieur de Poncet, had arrived at Albreda with a 32-gun frigate and one hundred soldiers. According to Joseph Debat, the governor of James Fort, de Poncet had taken the trade of the "king" of Barra by force. He had told Debat that he intended to run the guns of James Fort and trade in the upper reaches of the river, but sickness had prevented the attempt and he had returned to Goree. There he seized a committee storeship and imprisoned one of her officers for an alleged offence. This news was forwarded on 29 November to the King and to Halifax, via the Commissioners for Trade and Plantations, and was discussed by the cabinet on 12 and 13 December.[40]

By that time the Admiralty had completed its preparations. On 23 November *Shannon* and *Hound* had been ordered to Plymouth, and on 1 December command of the expedition and of the *Edgar* was given to the man who would in 1781 command the British fleet at the Battle of the Chesapeake, Captain Thomas Graves.[41] Two days later he was ordered to sail for Africa in defence of trade, to investigate and prevent any French attempt to force a trade from Albreda.[42]

Realizing the delicate nature of this mission, Graves delayed his departure and requested more precise instructions about what he should do if the French had constructed a fortress. His orders were to prevent French encroachment on British territory, but he pointed out that Albreda was considered to be French and asked whether he should use force.[43] The government was itself concerned about its legal position. At the cabinet meeting on the 12th, it was resolved that Graves should attempt "to obtain from the people of the country a cession of the several places and an exclusion of all other nations." The additional instructions sent to Graves on 28 December from the Admiralty were of an especially secret classification. Even so, they only reiterated that the French had always been at Albreda on sufferance. Receiving his orders on 1 January, Graves sailed on the 4th. He was turned back by contrary winds but eventually got away on the 22nd.[44]

The attempt to obviate diplomatic dispute with France failed. On the 8th the Comte de Guerchy, the French ambassador in London, requested that Halifax inform him of the destination of Graves' ships. When he was put off with a vague answer he reported to Paris and, on the 20th, sent Halifax a formal written query asking whether the public reports that Graves was gone to attack a French fort were true.[45]

A fait accompli was no longer possible. A new strategy was needed, and the cabinet met the next day. Since there could be no hope of avoiding diplomatic complications, it was decided that the threat inherent in Graves' squadron should be used to force rapid diplomatic satisfaction. The cabinet resolved to tell de Guerchy that if he should "be authorized to declare in the name of his court that no such force shall be used by French armed vessels, nor any such fort erected, His Majesty, will, in that case, give fresh instructions to Commodore Graves to abstain from any measure of force on his part."[46] It was agreed that *Hound* should be delayed so that she could carry on to Graves any necessary change of orders.

The Admiralty sent an express to Plymouth on the 22nd, but it arrived too late. Thomas Pye, the port admiral, replied that Graves had sailed that morning on a fair wind and that the only hope was to send the *Spy* after him to Madeira, where he planned to take on stores.[47] He was authorized to do so on 1 February, but the progress of negotiations was very rapid, and order was followed closely by counter-order.[48] On the 29th Halifax had heard from Hertford that as a result of de Guerchy's letter the French ministers had lectured him severely on international etiquette but had also indicated that they were prepared to accede to Britain's demands. Praslin had said: "France might be disposed either from the Reason of the Thing, or for the Sake of Peace, to give up a Claim; and yet not be inclined to suffer an Affront offered to Her in the Face of all Europe, by Force of Arms."[49]

However, he had also said that the governor—"a busy Man who, By his Projects might embroil Matters between the Two Nations"—was being recalled. Choiseul added that Albreda "is not worth disputing, and we shall think ourselves overpaid for relinquishing it, if henceforth you learn to treat us with more friendly trust and confidence." Halifax doggedly repeated that when London received a copy of orders to the governor of Goree in which he was forbidden either to force a trade on the Gambia or to maintain a fort at Albreda, then Graves would be forbidden to use force.[50] It was apparent, however, that the French were not going to be difficult. Presumably in expectation of soon having concrete news for Graves, an express was sent down to Plymouth just in time to stop *Spy* sailing.[51]

Once again the situation had been dominated by the hard fact that the French were in no position to resent British action. London continued to exploit the threat inherent in Graves' orders. When de Guerchy presented Halifax with a written disavowal of forced trading or fortifications and asked that Graves be ordered to abstain from acts of violence so that trade could return to the footing extant before the Peace of Paris, Halifax replied that Graves would be advised to avoid force.[52] The Admiralty immediately drew up the order and sent it, along with copies of the correspondence between Halifax and de Guerchy, down to the *Spy* by messenger in the evening of 12 February.[53] To Hertford, however, Halifax wrote, as he did to de Guerchy, that the French declaration fell short of the British demand to the extent that it had not been possible absolutely to forbid Graves to use force.[54] This silly hair-splitting may have been the result of the government's embarrassment and consequent desire to parade an inflexible determination, but it did serve its purpose. Praslin told Hertford that Choiseul would dispatch orders immediately for returning the situation on the Gambia to normal.[55]

Having achieved its objective, the government made a concession to the French which makes it apparent that it was French aggression and not the trade of the Gambia which concerned London. In the same manner as the minor points in the Honduras and Turks Island settlements had been waived, London was prepared to make a gesture to reduce French resentment over their treatment. Praslin had remarked that the French had no other object in the Gambia than to conduct the same trade as they had before the war. Hertford attempted to persuade the French of Britain's exclusive right to trade there, but Halifax immediately wrote that the King consented for the time being that the trade should remain on the same footing as it was "before the Conclusion of the late Peace."[56]

Halifax instructed the Admiralty on 13 March to forbid Graves to use force. The orders were drawn up on the 22nd, and Halifax was informed that the *Wasp* was to carry them.[57] Perhaps because of the delay at the

Admiralty, the government's method of conducting its foreign relations met with the bad luck to which it was peculiarly liable. The *Wasp* was unable to find Graves and on 25 July returned without having been able to deliver the dispatches.[58] Fortunately Graves was a careful man. Before arriving at the Gambia, he had reminded Stephens that "the doubtful part seems to be in case I should meet with French Merchant Vessels Trading quietly in the River Gambia, whether I am to act in such a manner as to reduce them to the necessity of Trading by an Armed Force; or of not Trading there at all."[59]

In the event he handled the situation well. He had received the orders of 11 February to avoid using force, and when he reached the Gambia on 29 March, he had sent Captain Garnier in the *Hound* to Goree with a copy of de Guerchy's letter. M. de Poncet had already been recalled and the new governor sent a very satisfactory answer. When Graves worked *Hound* upstream to Albreda, the resident was persuaded to give up his guns and ammunition and promised to destroy the palisade. Mr. Debat later admitted to Graves that the French had not as yet, in fact, attempted to use force on the Gambia, although their competition had been prejudicial.[60] Graves had equally avoided the use of force, and in August *Edgar* was reduced to a guardship.[61]

NEWFOUNDLAND

The attempt to minimize unpleasant dispute and to use naval force effectively to protect British interests in the River Gambia had a parallel in Britain's confrontation with France in Newfoundland waters. The problem for the British in Newfoundland stemmed from provisions in the Peace of Paris. Despite France's loss of Canada, French fishermen were to be permitted to continue fishing in northern Newfoundland, and they were granted the Islands of St. Pierre and Miquelon as an unfortified "abri" from whence they could operate. The Newfoundland fisheries were regarded as an important "nursery" for seamen to man the British and French navies, and the French had held out in the last days of the war to ensure they would be able to retain this indispensable element of their naval strength. Pitt's hostile memorandum on the Peace of Paris had specifically criticized that concession, and the Grenville administration felt that it was important that the French fishery be restricted to the terms of the treaty. Another concern of the British was that Choiseul would utilize the legitimate fishery operations to facilitate continued communications with Acadia and Canada, possibly for the purpose of inspiring revolt. A numerous squadron therefore was kept in Newfoundland waters and rigorously enforced the limitations which the Peace of Paris had placed on the fishery. Vicious action was undertaken against French fishermen, which effectively defeated

Sir Hugh Palliser, 1723-96.
Painted and engraved by
J. R. Smith.
Courtesy of the National
Maritime Museum, Negative
218

a major French effort to build up their fishery.

French activities were not confined to commercial action. A small squadron of warships had been sent to St. Pierre to police the fishermen. Captain Hugh Palliser, British Commander-in-Chief Newfoundland and governor of the colony, was alarmed by the implications of this move. He wrote to the Lords Commissioners of Trade and Plantations that the French warships "would render it impossible for the governor and His Majesty's officers to execute the laws."[62] To M. Tronjoly, the commander of the French squadron, he wrote on 8 October 1764: "this liberty of *fishing* carries with it no other Priviledges whatever, and cant be consider'd to extend to a Liberty for French ships of war to Parade about that part of His Majesty's Dominions without his leave for it; their very appearance is sufficient to disturb his Government over his New Indian and Canadian Subjects in those parts."[63]

Lord Hillsborough at the Board of Trade agreed with Palliser's concern, and the government was under pressure in the Commons to resist French encroachment in Newfoundland.[64] General Conway, Rockingham's Secretary of State for the Southern Department, protested to Paris about the French action in Newfoundland, drawing particular attention to the presence of French naval forces. Despite Praslin's protest at Palliser's demands, the latter was formally praised for his action. He was instructed to cease to correspond with the Board of Trade concerning the French forces at St. Pierre and instead to write the Secretary of State via the Admiralty.[65] When Palliser sighted another French squadron in Newfoundland waters, in June 1765 he wrote to its commander demanding he depart forthwith.[66]

The French squadron did withdraw, as they claimed had always been their intention. With the passage of the years it became clearer that the British position in their conquest was secure. The confrontation in Newfoundland died away, although when Earl Harcourt was given his instructions on 30 December 1768 before departing as ambassador to France, he was cautioned to keep an eye out for any clandestine correspondence between the French court and the inhabitants of the areas lost in the war to Britain.[67] British policy with respect to Newfoundland may be considered to have been successful. Nevertheless, the success had its shortcomings. Horace Walpole's belief that the burning of French fishing boats in Newfoundland by the British navy led to the French seizure of Turks Island is incorrect.[68] Nevertheless, the high-handed British action could hardly improve relations with France. Praslin's criticism rings true that Palliser's orders "to the naval officer to depart from St. Pierre and to evacuate those seas, were framed in a style very unusual among independent powers, & fitted to give more offence than even real injuries."[69] The employment of naval forces to protect British interests may have avoided the dangers consequential to threatening France explicitly with armed action, but it was at best an inadequate formula. It did secure the immediate British objectives, but it did not avoid exacerbating relations with France.

NORTH AFRICA

Praslin's complaint was certainly valid. The Gambian and Newfoundland questions had been dealt with in much the way Britain handled her relations with the states of North Africa.[70] British consular representatives in Tunisia, Algeria, and Morocco were not of good quality; and the governments of those states were notoriously difficult to deal with. Britons, as a result, tended to regard naval force as a prerequisite for satisfactory relations with them. The governor of Gibraltar had a special responsibility for conducting British relations in that area, and Lieutenant-Governor Irwin, at any rate, was not adverse to replying to the Sultan of Morocco's demand that the British consul be withdrawn by a threat to send to Mogador "a Fleet of Men of War to destroy the Place entirely.''[71] A warship was in fact used to return the expelled consul to Morocco in 1765, and the navy was used on other occasions for similar purposes, although every effort was made to avoid incidents.[72] In June 1767 Irwin wrote to Shelburne of the necessity to renew ''in their minds fears of a Navy which they have almost forgot.''[73] And in September 1768 Commodore Spry, Commander-in-Chief Mediterranean, wrote to Shelburne: ''it appears very plain to me from all those people's behaviour that nothing but fear keeps them our friends.''[74] The use of British naval force was in fact very controlled and limited, but it did not prove effective in preserving good relations with North Africa. The parallel between British naval action in North Africa and that used with respect to the French was too close for the self-respect of the latter.

THE DUNKIRK IMBROGLIO

Presumably the Grenville cabinet's decision to use the incidents in the Caribbean and West Africa as test cases stemmed from the consideration that their trans-oceanic situation would make a resort to naval force at once possible and more acceptable. As the pre-eminent naval power, the right of British governments to determine the outcome of events at sea was half accepted even by her enemies. The distance from the metropolitan, and the political unimportance of the disputed territories, also reduced the danger that the Bourbon states would feel driven to respond in kind to protect their reputations. Indeed, the odds were so much in Britain's favour that failure to take strong measures could hardly fail to provide the impulse for more dangerous Bourbon adventures, which might only be stopped by war.

Naval strength was less suitable for supporting Britain's European interests, such as the refusal of France to honour the paper money used during the Seven Years' War to finance the defence of Canada. Naval force could hardly have been applied to that issue by any means short of reprisal or general war. More important, and more dangerous, than the ''Canada Paper'' dispute was that which developed when the French failed to abide completely by the terms of the Peace of Paris which required destruction of the port of Dunkirk. Ever since Charles II's sale of Dunkirk to Louis XIV Britons had regretted the French acquisition of their only good port in the English Channel. In every war Dunkirk had been used as a base for raids on British trade, and in the Treaty of Utrecht 1713 the French agreed to demolish it. The agreement had not been carried out, but it had been renewed in the Peace of Paris and provision had been made for an English commissioner to reside in Dunkirk to oversee the demolition. The failure of successive British administrations to ensure that the Dunkirk article of the peace treaty was carried out reflects the very real limitations of a foreign policy based on naval strength.

As early as the summer of 1763 the Bute administration had become convinced that the French were deliberately attempting to avoid the full rigours of their commitment. So soon after the conclusion of the treaty the Secretary of State for the Southern Department, the Earl of Egremont, had been prepared to suggest that the reported refusal to execute one of its important terms could only have been the result of a misunderstanding by local French officers of the orders given them by their government.[75] Praslin claimed that the demolitions were proceeding as agreed, but the British agent in Dunkirk reported that the harbour was still suitable for warships.[76] Choiseul also declared that the treaty was being fully implemented. Nevertheless, in February 1764 the Grenville cabinet decided to accept his offer to permit an admiral and a captain to inspect the works at Dunkirk. Their report substantiated that of the resident British agent.[77] By the spring of 1764 Hertford was reporting that Choiseul was disinclined to proceed with further demolition, but Halifax reiterated the British demands.[78]

A crisis appeared to be imminent just when the Honduras and Turks Island incidents were occasioning moves to use naval force, but the Dunkirk issue never became explicitly involved in that dispute and fell temporarily into the background. It appears that the British appreciated that they could do nothing about it by forceful means short of war. In September, in the same letter in which he urged vigorous action over Turks Island, Bedford cautioned Sandwich: "The affair of Dunkirk, I have long thought has been pushed too far, as I am convinced it can never be of detriment, as it is now circumstanced . . . For God's sake let us take heed not to hurry ourselves precipitately into a War, in order to obtain a popularity which, could it be obtained, would be of no service to us, and which must I fear be the inevitable ruin of this Nation."[79]

Sandwich replied that all the government agreed that no more mention of Dunkirk should be made to the French: "After the King's entire approbation of your Grace's sentiments in your former letter it is not probable that any of his servants and your Grace's friends should wish to stand upon any other foundation."[80] Earl Gower commented to Sandwich that "tho' I believe his Grace is in the right, in publick business the opinion of the populace must, I fear be now and then considered." However, the Grenville cabinet agreed to avoid further trouble with France over an issue which it was apparent the French could never be brought at a reasonable cost to concede.[81]

There was no suggestion that action in the West Indies might influence events in Dunkirk, although that is not a possibility to be entirely ruled out. On the other hand, the naval reaction to events in the West Indies did reflect a need to sustain British prestige, which was at risk because of the inability to protect British interests in Dunkirk.

When the Marquis of Rockingham formed his administration in the spring of 1765 British demands were again pressed, and when the Duke of Richmond was sent as ambassador to Paris he started his mission abruptly enough by visiting Dunkirk. He evidently was deceived by the French. He reported that the port was already unsuitable for warships and that further demolition of the jetties and sluices would risk flooding the surrounding countryside.[82] Others were less easily convinced, but in the end the Rockingham, Chatham, Grafton, and North administrations all tacitly accepted the decision not to pursue the issue by extreme measures. The circumstances were such that a resort to force would have far greater significance to the French than did Turks' Island or the Gambia. This restraint upon British freedom of action was apparently acknowledged.

THE MANILA RANSOM AND THE FALKLAND ISLANDS

Successive administrations also displayed reluctance to threaten war in the discussions with Madrid over the claim of the British captors of Manila for the unpaid portion of the ransom they had exacted in 1762.[83] Colonel Sir William Draper and Vice-Admiral Sir Samuel Cornish obtained the diplomatic support of the Grenville administration, but when it became apparent that Spain would not honour the claim unless it were supported by threats of war, Grenville preferred to accept a loss of diplomatic and political respect. When Rockingham formed his administration, there was a renewed possibility that the issue might be resolved by a resort to force. Horace Walpole, however, writes: "The new ministers were more in earnest than their predecessors had been, the ignominy of not obtaining them lay heavier on the latter."[84] Rochford wrote from Madrid recommending firmness, but his opinion was not welcome in London.[85] Draper later wrote that some of the ministers "were ingenuous enough to own, that they could not think of involving his distressed nation in another war for our private concerns."[86] The Spaniards evidently appreciated that they were under no compulsion; and eventually Rochford was instructed to abandon the futile efforts at peaceful persuasion.

The episode nevertheless dragged on, and when Chatham formed his administration in the summer of 1766 an attempt was made to force the Spanish hand, exploiting the coercive potential of British naval strength while avoiding war. Chatham's policy is obscure, but at a later date Rochford wrote that his zeal to bring the Spaniards to pay the Ransom made him "repeat what I before said to Your Lordship in a former Dispatch, that our insisting on its being paid and menacing an Establishment in the Isles of Falkland would infallibly have its weight."[87] In 1765 Conway had authorized

William Pitt, 1st Earl of
Chatham, 1708-78.
Courtesy of the British
Museum (Class II period 4;
1933.6.26.64) Negative PS
030775

the establishment of a British post on West Falkland Island in order to
ensure that Britain had a well-placed depot from which to exploit any trade
that might be opened with the *terra australis incognita* which scientists
believed must exist in the South Pacific. The post had been kept an official
secret because the French explorer Bougainville had already established a
French colony on East Falkland Island people by émigré Acadians and
because Spain had forced the abandonment of an earlier effort in 1748-49.
Spain claimed all lands known and undiscovered in the Pacific and claimed
the Falklands themselves. Port Egmont in fact proved to be badly placed to
support the series of expeditions the Admiralty sent out in the 1760s to
explore the Pacific. Nonetheless, the Spanish government's concern for the
security of its empire was justified. Chatham forced Egmont's resignation
on the issue of the continued support of the Falkland post, but in the end he
decided to retain it, evidently for the purpose of extortion and barter.

The Spaniards may themselves have contributed to Chatham's decision.
In July 1766 Masserano had speculated to Grimaldi that if the expedition

which was sailing under Captain Wallis, and which eventually circumnavigated the globe, should "seize any islands or countries belonging to Spain and if we should object, I think . . . [the British] will say that as long as our dispute over Manila continues, it is a reprisal for our non-payment."[88] Through intercepted letters the British were made aware that Spain feared that the Flota bringing treasure from the West Indies might be captured to secure the Ransom, and the news on 22 September 1766 that the Flota had been cancelled would have confirmed the belief that Spain could be coerced.[89] The Chatham cabinet, however, contented itself with a circumscribed offer to abandon the British post on the Falkland Islands in return for payment of the Ransom, but it specifically reserved "the right of England to navigate the Atlantic and South Seas," which was the real object of Spanish concern.[90] The proffered *quid pro quo* was inadequate to tempt the Spanish government. The captors of Manila got no more than they had carried away with them.

Of more importance was the effect the failure of indirect coercion, combined with unwillingness to threaten war, had upon the credibility of Britain's deterrent capacity. The weak handling of the matter by Rockingham and Chatham encouraged a growing, if unrealistic, confidence in Madrid that British naval strength was no longer beyond dispute. On 25 February 1768 the Spanish Minister of the Marine and the Indies, Bailly Arriaga, signed an order to Bucarelli, governor of Buenos Aires, to the effect that "no English establishments are to be permitted, and you are to expel by force any already set up . . . You need no other orders nor instructions."[91] Only the difficulty the Spaniards experienced in finding the British post delayed the trial of strength.

NOT SO SPLENDID ISOLATION

If British efforts at conciliation were not adequate to reduce Bourbon hostility, that could be tolerated in London provided the objective military situation remained favourable to Britain. Such, however, was not altogether the case. The colonial basis of mercantilist seapower could be protected by naval forces acting away from the metropolitan areas, but the influence of British naval forces in Europe depended upon their prestige in European waters and upon the relative vulnerability of different continental states to naval attack. The failure to enforce the destruction of Dunkirk or to exact payment of the Manila Ransom undermined the prestige of the British navy because it called into question Britain's willingness to take risks for European concerns. Not only was Spain emboldened to risk a confrontation over the Falklands, but Britain's negotiations for an alliance with Russia were also affected.

Successive British administrations had made assiduous efforts to conclude an alliance with a continental military power to replace, if they could not renew, the wartime alliance with Prussia. The inevitable paradox was that without the influence in continental affairs which a large land army would have produced, the British had little power to attract a continental ally. British naval power was not perceived by Berlin, Vienna, or St. Petersburg as significantly affecting their own positions. What limited benefit they did acknowledge the British navy offered them through its control of Bourbon naval power they could see was a by-product of action the British needed to take for their own security in any case. Hence the states of central Europe had no need to bind themselves with obligations to Britain.

Only Catherine the Great had a significant use for the British navy to further her ambitions in the Mediterranean and the Baltic. Diplomatic discussion of a possible alliance with Russia began immediately the peace was concluded, and both parties agreed that Russia and Britain shared many interests. Some common ground was found in vitiating French influence in Sweden. Sir John Goodricke co-operated with the Russian ambassador in Sweden, Count Osterman, in suborning the Swedish political system. At the end of the Seven Years' War, the aristocratic party, the so-called "Hats," had been in power in Sweden, and Sweden was bound to France by the receipt of a subsidy. Sandwich's minimum goal in 1764 had been to "make the purchase of the Swedish Alliance as burthensome to France as possible."[92] The British and Russians had had some luck. Their friends, the "Cap" party, won the elections to the Diet in 1764 and concluded the commercial treaty with Britain. However, Grafton and Conway were unimpressed and claimed to believe that Russia was its sole beneficiary. In 1764 Sandwich had commented "that Nothing material can be effected but by a proper Application of Money," but Sandwich and every subsequent British Northern Secretary refused to substitute a British subsidy for the lapsed French one.[93] In 1766 Grafton advised Goodricke that only a significant contribution of Swedish naval forces to augment the naval power of Britain would justify the payment of a subsidy to any state in peacetime.[94] Consequently Swedish politics proved to be a divisive issue between Britain and Russia. In Goodricke's view Britain should have spent boldly, "instead of giving out Money like drops of blood." However, the opportunity was missed, if such it was in reality, of using Swedish politics to create for Britain "a solid influence in Russia."[95] When Chatham returned to power he was determined to secure the alliance, but the magic of his name was inadequate to paper over the obstacles. No British administration was prepared to guarantee Russia against a war with Turkey when it appeared probable that war between the two states was imminent. The Russians, for their part, were not prepared to guarantee Britain against a war arising out of Anglo-French colonial disputes.

The decision that Russia was asking too high a price for an alliance indicates that the British were generally confident that their naval strength could provide them with security even if they were completely isolated. In 1766 Sandwich had written: "There is one fundamental error which the Court of Petersbourg seems to have taken up . . . that the exigency of Affairs in this Country makes an Alliance with Russia so absolutely necessary, that we shall be glad to accept it upon their own Terms."[96] Chatham agreed with the King that it would be wrong to accept "the Turkish point" in order to gain an alliance.[97] Conway remarked in 1767: "One many indeed be surprised to find that any Minister, in any Part of the World, even the most remote, needs at this Period to be told of the Importance, nay of the Grandure & Glory of this Nation."[98] The decision not to press the Dunkirk issue to the point of violence also constitutes evidence of confidence that the British navy was adequate to compensate for the weakness of Britain's continental position. Nevertheless London did not lose sight of the importance of concluding an alliance. The pursuit of that chimera was to continue with decreasing hope throughout the years of peace and into those of war.

British weakness on Dunkirk was proof to the courts of Europe that Britain was not prepared to take risks for continental interests and hence would not be a reliable ally. In this respect Grenville's more vigorous response to oceanic disputes was unsound. They could do nothing to build up the significance of British naval force in European affairs, either for the purpose of attracting an ally or to protect Britain's non-oceanic interests. In 1768 the failure of the Grafton administration to prevent the French occupation of Corsica further undermined the significance of the British navy in European affairs. The débâcle also effectively undid whatever good Grenville's handling of the oceanic crises of 1764-65 had done to British prestige in Bourbon courts. The reputation of the British navy was weakened and so was its real capacity to dominate the Mediterranean.

THE CORSICAN DEBACLE

Repeated warnings had been sent to Grafton's Secretary of State for the Southern Department, the Earl of Shelburne, that the Genoese were tiring of struggling against the Corsican patriot General Pasquale Paoli.[99] Shelburne was nevertheless taken by surprise when on 9 April 1768 the consul at Genoa, James Hollford, wrote that the republic had leased Corsica to the French in return for a guarantee that Paoli's insurgents would be suppressed.[100] The initial response of the Grafton administration indicated an awareness of the importance of Corsica. Sir Horace Mann, envoy at Florence, warned that if Corsica were occupied by the French and if "at any time a War should break out, either with England, or in which His Majesty should take a contrary Part to the French, they would be totally Masters of this Part of the Mediterranean, and more particularly of the trade with Leghorn.''[101] Shelburne agreed with Mann: he warned Rochford, who had been moved to the Paris embassy, that ''the Fate of that Island may undoubtedly become an Object of the most serious Nature to Great Britain.''[102]

Rochford remonstrated with Choiseul on the grounds that the aggrandizement of France was a violation not only of the fifteenth article of the Treaty of Aix-la-Chapelle, but also of the balance of power.[103] On 5 and 26 May, Shelburne met the Comte de Chatelet, the new French ambassador; the cabinet met several times to discuss the French action; and on 27 May Shelburne advised Rochford ''that the Extension of Territory, Force or Possession of any of the great Powers of Europe cannot be a matter of indifference to their neighours and may consequently endanger the Peace of Europe.''[104]

Because Corsica is an island it was in the power of the British government to use naval forces to intervene. The advance warning London had of French intentions made it possible to anticipate the actual commitment of French troops, unlike the situation in 1764 when Grenville had had to salvage British interests after Bourbon faits accomplis. A squadron of observation could have been sent to guard the Corsican approaches, making it clear that Choiseul could only send the necessary troops to defeat Paoli if he were prepared to initiate hostilities with Britain. This point of tactical advantage was missed. In 1768 Grafton's cabinet was not capable of making a quick decision.[105] Instead, Shelburne, and later Grafton, dispatched agents to report on the reliability of Paoli and on the state of French preparations for war.[106] Hollford continued to bombard Whitehall with reports from Genoa, but he was never given any instructions as to how he should conduct himself.

Political turmoil in London contributed to the failure to prevent French occupation of Corsica. The Duke of Grafton regarded statesmanship as the duty of the landed aristocracy, but he had little talent for it, and his difficulties were increased by political ineptitude. Shortly after the abortive attempt to extract the Manila Ransom, Chatham had retired to his country seat in a state of mental breakdown. Grafton was left in effectual as well as nominal command. He found himself faced with controlling a chronically divided cabinet, if that term has any meaning in the Grafton administration. Chatham had installed his disciple the Earl of Shelburne in the Southern Department. Grafton brought in the Bedford group, making Earl Gower Lord President of the Council. The newcomers were long-standing opponents of Chatham and were determined to eclipse his influence. Grafton continued to add to his difficulties. In January 1768 Viscount

Augustus Henry Fitzroy, 3rd Duke of Grafton, 1735-1811. Engraving after a painting by P. Battoni. Courtesy of the British Museum (Class II period 4; 53.1.12.1348) Negative 1/2 pl. PS 022051

Weymouth, a Bedford man, was made the Northern Secretary, and Shelburne's own office was divided to give the Earl of Hillsborough a secretaryship for the colonies. Amid this political manoeuvring there was little resolution to confront Choiseul's machinations.

Sir Horace Mann and Lord Shelburne both clearly believed that Corsica in the hands of the French was a great danger to British seapower. Chatham was not at the time capable of expressing an opinion, but he later declared his view to be similar to that of Shelburne. The commander of the Mediterranean squadron, who was also the accredited minister to Genoa, Commodore Spry, felt so strongly about the matter that on his own authority he demanded an explanation from the Doge and admonished the Genoese Secretary of State. He pointed out that in a war French ships could be based on Corsica and cut trade to Genoa, whereas in the past Corsica had been a protection to merchant ships.[107] Paoli tried to persuade Shelburne that possession of Corsica would enable France "to give the law to all the Italian states" and make ineffectual the British squadrons at Gibraltar and

Sir William Petty,
2nd Lord Shelburne,
1737-1805. Engraving
published by
C. Bretherton.
Courtesy of the British
Museum (Class II period 4;
1920.12.11.826) Negative

Port Mahon, which would be unable to protect British trade.[108] Informed naval opinion, however, was divided.

It was naval advice which the government later used to justify its inactivity. On 17 November 1768 there was a call for papers in the Commons concerning Corsica.[109] The Honourable Augustus Hervey, a naval officer of repute who had been in command of the British squadron in the Mediterranean and was to become a Lord of the Admiralty in 1771, initiated the defence for the government. He declared that Corsica was not an important source of naval reserves of men or of timber, which he described as brittle. Captain Lord Howe supported Hervey's principal conviction, although he disagreed in detail.

I can't agree with the Honourable Gentleman in thinking that Corsica in the hands of the French is of no importance, but as to going to war, that is nothing to the point. You suffer'd in your trade in Queen Ann's time.

In a future war with regard to Corsica, it would not lay you under great danger, if Corsica were in possession of the French, for they [i.e., the merchant ships?] must have convoys.

Finally, Admiral Hawke told the Commons that he was of the same opinion. Admiral Sir Charles Saunders declared: "I think it would be better to have gone to war with France, than let them have Corsica," but Hawke replied: "Upon no other ground do I speak than from what I know from experience, & from that experience I differ in opinion from the Hon[oura]ble Gentleman who spoke last."

The government eventually came to the decision that technical naval considerations did not warrant a resort to war. Grafton later wrote in his autobiography:

> I never could think that the possession of Corsica would add to the crown of France, the degree of advantage, which many were industriously giving out. And though, on his side, the French minister may have been rash, or wicked enough to plunge his country into the horrors of war, through a restless ambition, our consciences would never have allowed us to advise on this occasion a re-commencement of hostilities.[110]

However, the issue was not confined to the strategic effect that French possession of Corsica would have on the naval balance in the Mediterranean. Of no less importance was the effect that the loss of Corsica to France would have on Britain's reputation as a naval power and the weight British naval strength was given in the affairs of Europe. In November, Lord North, who had recently been made Chancellor of the Exchequer, told the Commons: "We should be the bullies of Europe, if we were to attack France, wherever she goes: we shall come off with a bloody nose." But Grenville's comment, "For fear of going to war, you will make war unavoidable," was probably a better reading of the international situation.

Even if the loss of prestige were preferable to war, sound statesmanship would have discerned that British interests could be upheld without war. It is possible that Grafton's failure to act decisively before the French troops were committed to the invasion of Corsica was occasioned by a misconception of French strength and of Paoli's abilities. Only after the French had begun their conquest did the reports from Shelburne's agent, John Stewart, and from Grafton's, Captain Dunant, reach England. Grafton then wrote to Shelburne lamenting that ignorance of the true situation had prevented his taking more forceful action.[111] If Grafton was ignorant, however, it was his own doing. The secret service had been sending regular reports of the financial difficulties which had stopped Choiseul's naval construction program, and Rochford reported how unpopular were Choiseul's measures which made war a possibility.[112] Louis XV was known to be averse to a return to war, and Edmund Burke, who did not have to bear the weight of deciding to risk one, asked the Commons in November: "Why is [the invasion of Corsica] unpopular in France?" and answered himself, "Because the French fear to plunge themselves into a war." Paoli recognized France's weakness and told John Stewart that "she [i.e., England] has only to declare Herself the Protector of the Corsican Nation, and France must give way."[113]

The rest of the story is anticlimactic. Sir James Grey, the new ambassador in Madrid, had been asked to investigate whether Spain could be made to see "her own true interests" and join in protesting against an increase in the power of France.[114] This diplomatic support for Paoli had no success, and the only course remaining to London if French chances were to be damaged was clandestine aid to Paoli. The scale on which such aid could be given while keeping it secret was inadequate to stop Choiseul's resolute attack.[115] King George had been impressed by the report Captain Dunant had rendered of Paoli's strength. On 12 August he made his first known intervention in foreign policy to urge the need to thwart France.[116] He soon changed his tune, however, writing to Grafton in September: "I am ready to declare to the whole World, that I cannot think under the present State of Debt that it would be expedient, for the Sake alone of the Island of Corsica, to begin acts of hostility against France."[117] In view of Choiseul's determination these two desires, to stop the French and to take no risk of war, were incompatible.[118] Coercion might still have succeeded by measures short of war, but the point had passed when intervention would have involved little or no risk. Instead, care was taken to keep involvement unofficial and secret, and when Catherine of Russia wished to send munitions to Paoli, she was warned that they must not be sent in a British ship.[119] Finally, in June 1769, the consul at Turin reported that the resistance was over and that Paoli had fled.[120]

In the debate on the handling of the Corsican crisis, Edmund Burke remarked: "France has the advantage of her conquests, & we the advantage of our memorials." To deny the implication of government fumbling would be futile. There is no indication that leaving Choiseul free to annex Corsica improved Anglo-French relations; rather, it had the effect of encouraging further Bourbon encroachments in the belief that the British would no longer defend their interests. This view was evidently shared by Count Bernstorff, the Danish minister. When Denmark mobilized a fleet in March 1769 to prevent French naval intervention in Sweden, and to influence the Swedish election, the British ambassador Sir Robert Gunning was instructed to "assure the Danish Minister, that it is His Majesty's Intention to co-operate heartily with the Courts of Russia & Denmark." Gunning replied:

"I am told that he does not scruple to say that from the Conduct Great Britain has held of late, there can be no sufficient Dependence on a Timely Interposition from that Quarter."[121] It took the Falkland Islands crisis of 1770 to restore the credibility of British seapower with Spain, but even that did not suffice to persuade Catherine of Russia that the British had the will or the ability to defend their common continental concerns. Disregard in Europe for British seapower prevented any possibility of ending Britain's diplomatic isolation. The poor statesmanship and political bickering of the Grafton administration had seriously damaged British interests.

4

The Falkland Islands Crisis

THE FIRST MOVES, 1768-70

The failure to prevent the French annexation of Corsica was the result, essentially, of the disruption of the British government of the time. British strategic thinking continued on the whole to recognize the need for constant restraint upon Bourbon *révanchist* activity. When the Bedford group succeeded in ousting Shelburne from office, the way was cleared for a return to what may be regarded as normal British statesmanship, to which in reality the supporters of Bedford and Shelburne equally subscribed. Rochford had been brought into the administration as the Secretary of State for the Northern Department. His consistent policy of confronting the machinations of the Bourbon states with suasive force was not a good preparation for the complexities of Baltic diplomacy, but his grasp of Britain's relative security and naval strength was a firm basis for negotiations with Russia and Prussia, and he was soon to be moved to the Southern Department.[1] It was not possible simple to write off Corsica, however, and to expect the affairs of Europe to continue on their earlier course. From the summer of 1768 to the summer of 1770 the British gradually became aware of an increase in the tempo of the Bourbon challenge to their position. In 1772 the British ambassador in Paris, Lord Harcourt, reported that the Duc d'Aiguillon, who succeeded Choiseul after the crisis of 1770, "was candid enough to say, that it was from the idea of the bad state of our marine that the Spaniards had lately shown such a readyness to fall out with us."[2] The small growth of Bourbon naval strength at the end of the 1760s may have contributed to the Spanish delusion, but the refusal of the British to risk war in 1768 could certainly be calculated to produce an impression of naval weakness.

In the end the trial of strength centred on disputed claims to the Falkland

Islands, although that issue was never more than the occasion for it.[3] Because Port Egmont had been established to facilitate attempts to break into Spanish proscriptive claims to the Pacific, its existence was a demonstration of Britain's superior strength. Out of concern for Bourbon solidarity Choiseul had been obliged to arrange for Bougainville, the proprietor of the French colony, to sell his post to Spain. The continuation of the British post indicated that the British were more interested in extending their commercial empire than in establishing good relations with Spain. Such an attitude was only possible so long as it was apparent that Spain could not risk war with Britain. The fact that the British presence at Port Egmont was a product of Britain's strength in Europe had been recognized by Chatham in 1766 when he rejected a plan to increase Port Egmont's local defences; and their absence increased the importance of Port Egmont as a symbol of Spanish weakness. A stable arrangement which acknowledged this fact had not been established, however, because the British had kept the location of Port Egmont a secret, apparently to prevent diplomatic representations.

Choiseul found himself much less ready to risk war than he had hoped to be by the late 1760s. It is clear, however, that the Falkland Islands crisis has to be viewed as a general Bourbon challenge to Britain. In October 1766 Choiseul had requested Grimaldi to take no action for two years which would endanger the peace, and in January 1767 he extended his request until the end of 1769.[4] However, the French ambassador in Madrid, the Comte d'Ossun, warned Choiseul that Spain was committed to war within two years.[5] In reality Choiseul's objective differed only in timing. Grimaldi had sent to him for approval a copy of the order to Bucarelli ordering the expulsion of the British before it was dispatched. Choiseul agreed to it. It appears that the Spaniards thought they could enforce their claim without war, or at least that the risk of war was acceptable to them, but Choiseul must have known he was surrendering control.

Immediate British fears for Port Egmont may have been allayed by the interception of a letter from Grimaldi to Masserano in June 1767. When deciphered it indicated that Spanish efforts to locate the British post had not been successful.[6] The first sign of a serious challenge from France came from the east. Shortly before the debate had opened in November 1768 on the handling of the French threat to Corsica, the Secret Committee of the East India Company forwarded to Weymouth, the new Southern Secretary, a report from Madras of the difficulty the company was having with Hyder Ali and of the danger they would be in were the French to aid him. Madras admitted that M. Law, the governor of the French fortress of Pondicherry, had assured them that his instructions forbade him to interfere with the ''country powers.'' But little reliance was placed on such assertions. In any

Etienne François de
Choiseul, Duc de
Choiseul-Amboise, 1719-85.
Engraving by S. Fessard
after a painting by L. M.
Vanloo, 1763.
Courtesy of the British
Museum (French Portraits
1917.12.8.3823) Negative
191800

case, instructions could be changed. Reports had been received that the
French were gathering thirty companies of one hundred soldiers each at the
Ile de France (Mauritius) where they were ideally placed to interfere on either
side of India.[7] The Under-Secretary, Robert Wood, immediately demanded
further information. This was eventually obtained at the end of March 1769
when the East India Company forwarded two reports which it had received
from Paris from Anthony Chamier, who was to be made deputy Secretary at
War in 1772. Chamier calculated that there were 5,300 men at the Ile de
France, including 2,500 of the Légion des Iles de France, but not including
the militia, which enlisted all the fit inhabitants of the Ile de France and
Bourbon and was reported to be first class.[8] A month later confirmatory
reports from Fort William, Bengal, dated September 1768, told of 4,000
French soldiers at the Ile de France, with reinforcements expected.[9]

Initially Weymouth does not appear to have been alarmed at the
possibility of a French attack. He did not trust the East India Company and
his first concern was to end the misrule of the Company's affairs in India

which tempted the French to interfere. It was primarily with this in mind that on 12 June he directed the Admiralty to prepare one of the fastest frigates for a voyage to the East Indies. A few days later he ordered that another frigate and a sloop be made ready for the same voyage.[10] At the end of July, Sir John Lindsay sailed with full powers to negotiate treaties. The frigate *Aurora* was to follow carrying three commissioners to review the Company's affairs, but as the *Aurora* was later lost with all hands, Lindsay was fully occupied with duties ashore. Weymouth's instructions had directed him to discover more about what the French were doing, but he was told that as yet there had been carried to the Ile de France "no more soldiers than are necessary to keep up their Establishment; which does not exceed 4,000."[11]

The immediate threat was eased when a peace was made with Hyder Ali, although in December 1769 Harcourt wrote from Paris that that was "apparently a Disappointment to many People in this Country."[12] Weymouth was more concerned about the men in India embroiling the two countries in a war than he was about the French government's beginning hostilities.[13] Reports had reached London that the French at Chandernagor in Bengal, where they had only been re-established at the Peace of Paris as disarmed traders, were violating the treaty by digging a ditch around the town, ostensibly for drainage. Weymouth only advised Harcourt to "inform" Choiseul about what was happening.

Choiseul's reply to Harcourt was very soothing. Slowly, however, Weymouth awoke to realization of unpleasant facts. On 4 January the Admiralty sent him intelligence indicating that the French had five sail of the line, two frigates, 5,000 European foot soldiers, and 1,000 of horse at the Ile de France. Upon further questioning, Choiseul admitted that precautions were being taken to defend the Ile de France "if ever a new war should break out." In March 1770 Harcourt had further information showing 4,700 foot soldiers of the French Crown in the Ile de France. By then Lord North had replaced Grafton at the Treasury, and perhaps North inspired Weymouth, who had kept his place, to take the bull by the horns. Harcourt was instructed to hint to Choiseul that a stop could be put to international tension if the French were to permit Colonel Monson, who was travelling to India, to visit the Ile de France so "that he might be able to contradict the late reports and bold assertions, that the French were making the most hostile preparations for an attack upon our settlement in India." Choiseul replied "with a good deal of warmth, that it was inconsistent with the dignity of the King, his Master, to submit to such an inspection." The delusions of the British government practically disappeared at this point, but they still hoped to avoid a military confrontation over the French garrison at Ile de France, and instead patient steps were taken to clarify the situation at Chandernagor.[14]

The growing threat of trouble in India threw a sinister light on developments which were threatening to upset British interests in Europe. French diplomacy was vigorous both in the Baltic and in the Mediterranean, and in 1768-69 the threat developed of French naval action in both those seas. In each case Russia was the direct opponent of the French, although the scenes of conflict were Sweden and Turkey. Britain was involved, if for no other reason, because of the hope of persuading Catherine II and her minister Count Panin that France posed a threat which necessitated a defensive alliance that would be brought into force by colonial conflict between France and Britain, but would not participate in Russia's war with the Porte. British efforts continued to be met with rebuff, but British ministers remained hopeful and continued in an ambivalent way to co-operate with Russia in anti-gallican manoeuvres in northern and southeastern Europe.

In the north the focus of attention continued to be control of the Swedish government, primarily by means of corruption. London's refusal to pay a subsidy to Sweden, however, had ensured that the Caps would loose their popular support. In December 1768 the Swedish king Adolphus Frederick was brought by the Crown Prince Gustavus Adolphus to refuse official functions until a Diet was summoned, at the election of which French money would again be influential. London reluctantly co-operated with St. Petersburg and Copenhagen, but Bernstorff's partial mobilization of the fleet in support of the Caps was muted by his belief, following the Corsican episode, that he could not rely upon British offers of support. He avoided an outright break with France, "Cap" economic policies were unpopular, and a "Hat" Diet was elected.[15]

France did not send a squadron into the Baltic in 1769; it was in the Mediterranean that Anglo-French manoeuvres for influence in Europe took an active naval line. The immediate reason for dispute was the long anticipated war which broke out between Russia and the Porte in 1768. Choiseul had tried to use the French minister at the Porte, the Comte de Vergennes, to bring it about, but French diplomacy was hardly necessary.[16] London's first reaction was to use the strength of the British navy to support an attempted mediation, with the hope of gratifying Russia.[17] The Turkish government was too deeply committed to war to be able to accept the offer, however, and Catherine preferred to send her fleet from the Baltic to prosecute the war in the Aegean. London attempted to remain neutral, trying without success to prohibit Britons from serving in the Russian fleet. All the consuls and governors in the Mediterranean, particularly Sir John Dick at Leghorn, where the Russians hoped to establish a base, were cautioned to maintain a strict neutrality.[18] Nonetheless they were biased in favour of Russia. The Russian navy had been built with British assistance and was partly manned and officered by Britons. Bourbon ports were closed to the Russians, but Britain's were not.[19] When the first division of the Russian fleet passed out of the Baltic towards the end of September, provisions were made ready for it at Hull. The Commander-in-Chief Mediterranean, Commodore Charles Proby, was ordered to render all necessary assistance.[20]

The British attitude towards the Russian naval operations in the Mediterranean was ambivalent. The provision of limited assistance to Russia might facilitate the conclusion of the coveted alliance; the Russian navy made itself so objectionable, however, that when the second division of the fleet left the Baltic in December it met with a less enthusiastic reception. It was permitted only emergency repairs in British dockyards.[21] An alliance was speciously attractive, but clearly London did not trust the Russians. As early as September, Rochford had complained to the ambassador at St. Petersburg, Lord Cathcart, that "the jealousy, which may be created in the several powers of the Mediterranean, by an alteration of property, and any new powers being formed in their neighbourhood, is thought no less to deserve the consideration of the Court of Petersbourg."[22] Because British influence in Europe, such as it was, depended to a considerable degree upon the ability of the British navy to protect Britain's friends in the Mediterranean, the permanent establishment of Russian naval power there could only injure British interests. Furthermore, the obvious dependence of the Russian fleet upon British assistance made it easy for the new French ambassador at the Porte, M. Saint-Priest, to convince the Sultan that Britain was a covert enemy.[23] The Russians did nothing to hide Britain's involvement, even taking with them to the Mediterranean three British provision ships equipped illegally with Mediterranean passes certifying they were British and thus immune from Arab attack.[24]

The Russian navy, however, was the lesser of evils. When it was learned from a "usually reliable" source in Paris in October 1769 that Spain wished the Family Compact to send their fleets to sea to prevent the Russians damaging Bourbon interests, London immediately recognized this possibility as a much greater danger to British influence. The first reaction was to advise St. Petersburg, doubtless in the hope that Britain's reflex reaction would earn merit in Russia.[25] Nevertheless London was obliged, even if the Russian alliance were unobtainable, to protect the position of the British fleet as arbiter of the Mediterranean. When the North administration did in fact order the navy to prevent French naval action in August 1770, Rochford remarked to Lord Stormont, on embassy to Vienna, that "nothing but the indispensable duty of Great Britain as a maritime power could have dictated such a measure."[26]

Rochford's intelligence reported that Choiseul had rejected the Spanish suggestion because of the danger of such action leading to general war, and in fact other British sources confirmed this. Sir John Dick, Consul at Leghorn, sent a report that fifteen ships were fitting at Toulon. The Admiralty, when forwarding the report to Weymouth, remarked that it was unsubstantiated. The British intelligence chief in Rotterdam, Robert Wolters, suggested that "the advice received from Sir John Dick . . . is spurious and only the echo of what has been wrote from Genoa above a month since."

Nonetheless London remained vigilant for any sign of Bourbon naval activity. Harcourt was ordered to recruit an agent to visit French ports, and it soon became apparent that active measures might yet be required to prevent French intervention. Harcourt was not often in Paris during this crisis and when he was absent his secretary, Robert Walpole, eldest son of the great prime minister and brother of Horace Walpole the author, was responsible for the conduct of British affairs. He reported on 15 November that Choiseul had spoken of sending a squadron to defend French shipping by attacking North Africa, but he seemed confused about whether the blow was intended against Tunisia or Algeria. It was natural to imagine, as did Walpole, that the African expedition was a blind. He reported that two ships of the line and three frigates were already arming, and remarked: "it is supposed [they] will be sent out to watch the Russian Fleet, and protect their own Trade from being interrupted by those Ships, whose officers *are new* in their Business, and can *know nothing* of *the Marine Laws* as M. de Choiseul expressed himself to me."[27]

Secret orders were immediately given to increase the complements of some of the guardships. The only official orders which survive were to lieutenants to raise volunteers for guardship service, and these were not dated until 23 November.[28] By then the secret was out, and de Francés, the secretary of the London embassy, had reported to Choiseul rumours of war which had affected the funds. On 22 November, Choiseul denied to Harcourt that the reports of a Toulon armament were well-founded and said "That if Such a Measure be thought adviseable for the Protection of their Flag, they would notify it to the different Courts." Weymouth acknowledged in reply that "Rumours of that Sort occasioned Orders here to man some of Our Guard Ships."[29]

The success of Grafton's démarche was short-lived. Choiseul's refusal to permit a British inspection of the Ile de France in April ensured that London was on the alert. On 14 May 1770 Anthony Chamier wrote that Choiseul's "adversaries" believed "he would plunge the nation into a war to make himself more necessary to the King." He reported as certain that Choiseul had "urged the necessity of putting to sea, all the ships they could fit out; it was long debated in council, but determined that only two or three frigates should be sent. I cannot doubt . . . the truth of this account."[30] On 18 May a letter reached Weymouth from Consul Lynch at Turin: "By accounts I have just received from Toulon, I find the French are fitting out in that place one Frigate, two Xebeques, and an armed Polaque. They are, I believe, by this time, ready to put to Sea." On 4 June, Robert Walpole sent to Weymouth unconfirmed reports "that Orders are given to arm at Toulon, Two Men of War, Two Frigates, Two xebecs, and Two bomb Vessells," ostensibly to attack Tunisia. And on 8 June further information was received from Lynch that "the armed Barque is going to the Levant, to take Plans and Soundings of the different Ports," which was an annual occurrence, and that "the Frigate is the Tarantola, a new Ship: She is to go to Corsica, and from thence, it is said, is to go up the Archipelago, to observe the Russians." This account was corroborated by Robert Walpole on 13 June when he reported that Choiseul had advised him "that they were sending some ships against Tunis" and "that some Frigates were going towards the Morea, in consequence of an application from the Department of Marine, in order to enquire into the Truth of what had happened lately at the Morea and in those Seas." British fears that the Tunisian expedition was mere deception were confirmed when on 22 June another letter arrived from Lynch stating that two frigates "are sailed from Toulon; tho it is given out that they are gone to protect the trade of France against the Corsairs, yet I have reason to think they are gone to Corsica, & from thence are to sail for the Levant."[31]

In the midst of these alarming accounts the Admiralty reported, on 6 June, the arrival of Captain Hunt from Port Egmont in the Falkland Islands. He brought news that a Spanish officer, Don Fernando de Rubalcava, had discovered the British post and had delivered a formal protest at the British presence. Hunt had replied by demanding that the Spaniards leave the Falklands. After Rubalcava departed Hunt turned over command to Captain Farmer and sailed for Plymouth with the news that Port Egmont was no longer secure against attack. Rubalcava indicated that he would abstain from further action until he received instruction from Spain, but the Spanish discovery and Rubalcava's protest opened the alarming prospect that the French and Spanish operations might be concerted and that the Family Compact might be prepared to contest the dominant position of British naval power.[32]

Within a few days of Captain Hunt's letter reaching London the act of force took place at Port Egmont. On 10 June Spanish soldiers landed at Port Egmont under the command of Don Jon Ignacio Madariaga. The British garrison surrendered and agreed to return to England. To ensure that Madrid was given earlier warning of the event, the rudder was removed from the station sloop *Favorite*.

Thomas Thynne, 3rd
Viscount Weymouth,
1734-96. Engraving after
portrait by Thomas
Lawrence.
Courtesy of the British
Museum (Class II period 4;
Negative 38.7.14.120)

Although these events were not known for some time in Europe, the warning of imminent danger in the South Atlantic as well as in India and the Mediterranean had to be taken very seriously. The North cabinet were called upon to deploy all Britain's diplomatic and naval resources to protect British interests. As a first move it was evidently decided that the state of naval preparedness should be improved in expectation of the need to make some demonstration of resoluteness. On 20 June, Under-Secretary of State Robert Wood wrote a private letter to Philip Stephens authorizing a secret augmentation of the crews of some of the guardships.[33] The next day the Navy Board was advised by the Admiralty that the guardships should be moved out of the dockyards and be anchored at Spithead and in Plymouth Sound. The third rates *Dorsetshire* and *Edgar* were ordered fitted out for Channel service.[34]

No diplomatic representation was made to Spain, but Weymouth wrote to Robert Walpole in Paris.[35] He warned that Britain could not be an indifferent spectator to French action in the Levant. When Walpole remonstrated with Choiseul the latter indicated that he recognized the objection to French naval action of any sort. To satisfy the merchant community he had decided to send only two ships to observe developments. Walpole thought he was dragging his feet to enable the ships to get to sea before he should be obliged to stop them. In reply, Weymouth sent to Walpole on 6 July a letter to show to Choiseul in which he expostulated on the rashness of dispatching ships which Britain would have the right, and necessity, to follow with others. On 11 July Choiseul told Walpole that de Francés had heard of the arming of the *Dorsetshire* and *Edgar*.[36]

Presumably it was known in London that the secret was out, for on 13 July Wood wrote to Stephens offering to supply formal authorization for mobilization of the two ships. This was done five days later when *Dorsetshire* and *Edgar* were officially ordered brought forward. Still, however, there was no directive made about their destination. *The Gentleman's Magazine* assumed that they had actually sailed for the Falkland Islands, but in fact no direct naval or diplomatic action was taken to ward off the anticipated attack there. In November the government was criticized in Parliament on that account, and a call was made for papers to discover whether the information available had been such that it should have led the government to act. There was no real doubt that the government had been well informed. During the summer de Francés reported to Choiseul that the possibility of a Spanish attack was public rumour. The government's apparent lack of concern about events at Port Egmont can only have been deliberate.[37]

The cabinet's expectation that the Spaniards would not risk the peace may have been encouraged by an intercepted letter from Grimaldi to Masserano, dated 16 July, which spoke of making a protest, but did not mention resorting to force.[38] Whether they were deceived or not, there were many reasons for deferring a confrontation over the Falkland Islands until an attack was actually made. A local defence of Port Egmont was discouraged by the distance, and it would have begged the real question of Bourbon regard for British strength. The fact that Port Egmont symbolized Britain's pre-eminent maritime strength also discouraged diplomatic representations, which would have suggested a weak concern to avert possible dangers.

There were also technical naval reasons for deferring action. When Parliament was opened on 13 November, Chatham, with all the force of his experience as prime minister during the Seven Years' War, declared in the Lords that the delay in preparing for war had been unjustifiable because "it is impossible to equip a respectable fleet within the time, in which such armaments are usually wanted." North, however, told the Commons that mobilization had been postponed because "our fleets cannot be fitted out except when our trade is at home, or just coming home, because sailors are at no other time to be had''; mobilizing in June could not have been effective and would have given the Bourbons an advantage.[39] The British dependence upon voluntary enlistment and press gangs created technical difficulties which the Bourbons with their systems of conscription did not equally share. The fact that the mobilizations eventually came in the autumn reduced Britain's disability. Her far greater naval reserves could then be tapped, which may account for her startling success.

Several members of the House of Commons claimed that the ministry was afraid to risk war because of the public anger over the Middlesex election.[40] Political insecurity may have added to the many reasons for North's wishing to avoid war, but the diplomatic advantages of not anticipating attack and the military advantages of delaying the major confrontation until the autumn were solid reasons for the British reacting first to the Bourbon challenge already made in the Mediterranean. It was a commonplace of British thinking, however, that strong action in one theatre would discourage attack in another. It can only be assumed that the North cabinet's Mediterranean strategy was also intended for the eyes of Spain.

On 16 August, Weymouth ordered the Admiralty to send *Dorsetshire* and *Edgar* with provision for four months to join Commodore Proby's small squadron in the Mediterranean. It was arranged that Proby should receive his operational orders directly from the Secretary of State.[41] Two days later, with the utmost secrecy, Weymouth advised Proby that British intentions were to remain neutral between Russia and Turkey, but that as there was "too much Reason to suspect that His Most Christian Majesty's Councils are not governed by the same Pacific Spirit, it was impossible to look upon the Measure, of sending Two French Frigates into the Archipelago, with Indifference." He was accordingly to "send into the Archipelago a Force at least equal to that of the Four frigates which are said to be sailed from Toulon." The officer given command should be instructed to observe neutrality, but also to watch the actions of the French. If they openly supported the Turks, he was to "exhort them to desist, & if that does not succeed, He is to compel them by force."[42]

Proby sent *Dorsetshire* and the frigates *Niger* and *Montreal* to Smyrna, an adequate force to deter but not so large as to insult the French. *Edgar* had been damaged in passage and was sent to Port Mahon to make repairs and to watch for French reinforcements to the Levant. Little diplomatic representation was made after the departure of the guardships to call attention to their significance. They could be expected to carry their own message, and overt threats might be provocative. The French frigates made no attempt to obstruct the Russians, but this restraint could not be attributed to the presence of the British ships, which did not reach Smyrna until 24 October. The Russians had inflicted a major defeat on the Turkish fleet at the battle of Chesme in July and felt no gratitude to the British. London's attempt to exploit the naval deployment by offering the Russians mediation in the war, with a secret agreement that Russia should gain the lion's share of the settlement in return for concluding an alliance guaranteeing British possessions in America, was to no purpose.[43] For their part the Turks regarded the British ships as virtual enemies, only allowing them to enter Smyrna one at a time. Apparently, however, the British démarche was not entirely valueless. The determination to prevent French interference in the Russo-Turkish war, which the naval movements later emphasized, does appear to have decided Louis XV against a proposal to ally with the Porte.[44]

THE CRISIS

The démarche had been too late to have any effect on Spanish plans against Port Egmont. On 7 September the Admiralty forwarded to Weymouth a letter they had received on that day from Captain Braithwaite of the *Liverpool*, dated in Cadiz Bay, 14 August, reporting that "two days ago arriv'd at this Port a Spanish Frigate of War, last from Buenos Ayres, who brings Accounts, that The Spaniards there were fitting out a small Squadron in order to attack Falkner's [sic] Island."[45] Weymouth's response was immediate. No attempt was made to restore the *status quo ante* by the dispatch of a small squadron, as Grenville had done in 1764. Grimaldi had rather expected the British to react in this way. In August 1766 a minute had actually been drawn up for the Spanish court of a cabinet agreement that the destruction of Port Egmont was bound to lead to a trial of strength and that preparation should be made for war. The greatest danger being that the British navy would operate in the South Atlantic near rather weakly defended parts of the Spanish empire, Madrid should attempt to keep the fighting in the north.[46] Weymouth evidently considered that only a clear demonstration of the inability of the Family Compact to go to war would discourage continual attacks. On the day Braithwaite's letter arrived, he secretly advised the Admiralty to man all the guardships to full complement and to fit out "a number" of frigates. There were at the time eighteen guardships, but the *Dorsetshire* and the *Edgar* were in the Mediterranean and their replacements were only now authorized. Consequently there were only sixteen ships which could quickly be made ready for service, and these the Admiralty ordered brought forward on 11 September. Two others, the *Albion* and the *Prince of Wales*, had to begin their mobilization from ordinary and were not ordered until 21 September.[47]

There appears to have been no disagreement within the British cabinet about policy, although there was to be some dispute about the rate of its development. North and Rochford were both out of town at the time, although the King was within reach for consultation, but Weymouth's orders provoked no protest. Sir Joseph Yorke, the British ambassador at The Hague, later reported that the Dutch minister at Madrid had heard "that if the British Court only remonstrated they [the Spanish government] should pay no Attention to it, but if they took it seriously, equipped, and sent out an Armament, they would be embarrassed & probably desist."[48] This was the very sentiment of the British, both in and outside the government. In his autobiography, Grafton later wrote: "The vigour of our preparations to meet a war was the best means, by which the negotiation then pending could end honourably for this country."[49] The North cabinet was plainly prepared to fight if necessary, but war was an unlikely outcome and, in any case, one little to be feared. Admiral Hawke had himself visited France during the summer, and his observations confirmed the intelligence reports about the inadequacy of the French navy and of the failure of naval finances.[50]

Initially, care was taken to keep the Bourbon ambassadors from becoming alarmed, presumably so that the British mobilization might have a head start. When Rochford came to town on the 8th to meet Weymouth, he wrote to the King that "as it might occasion suspicion if he went to Richmond today," he proposed to delay his seeing the King until the morrow.[51] The secret was kept for a few days, during which time Masserano visited Weymouth. In the hope of delaying any British reaction to the seizure Grimaldi had instructed Masserano to report that "he had good reason to believe, His Cath. Majesty's Governor of Buenos Ayres, has taken upon him to make use of force," suppressing, however, Arriaga's order to Bucarelli of February 1768 and the fact that the deed had already been done. However, Weymouth had already received a letter from James Harris, the British chargé in Madrid, which confirmed Braithwaite's report. Arriaga's orders, soon to be common knowledge, could be guessed at.[52] Consequently, when Masserano expressed

> His Wishes, that, whatever the Event at Port Egmont might be, in consequence of a Step of the Governor, taken without any particular Instruction from His Cath. Majesty, it might not be productive of Measures at this Court dangerous to the Good Understanding which at present subsists between the Two Crowns . . . [Weymouth] told His Excellency, that if His Apprehensions of an exercise of Force . . . were well founded, it was difficult to see how the fatal Consequences of such a Step, could be avoided, by any thing that was left for us to do.

Without informing Masserano of the British armament, Weymouth expressed the hope that if Bucarelli had acted without orders matters could soon be accommodated. After he had spoken with the King, however, he also formally told Masserano that he "had His Majesty's Commands to demand a disavowal of the Proceedings of His Catholick Majesty's Servants settled there, & also to demand, that the Affairs of that Settlement, should be immediately restored to the State in which they were before such Proceeding."[53]

From the first it was apparent that Spain was less important in the dispute than was France and that the pressure of British preparations for war would most rapidly produce diplomatic developments by its effect upon the court of France. On 12 September, the same day that Weymouth had written to Harris informing him of the demands which had been made of Spain, Robert Walpole wrote to Weymouth to report that Choiseul had offered "his service to influence the Court of Spain, if the Court of England should think it necessary." Four days later Choiseul told Walpole "that he could answer for the Court of Spain, that She did not mean to go to War." He expressed the hope "that the Court of England would not make any preparations for Arming of Ships, which would give an unnecessary Alarm; & occasion discredit in different Countries." Even on the 18th, after the news of the British mobilization had reached Paris, Choiseul offered to "recommend it to His Most Christian Majesty not to take any measures for an Armament, and will prevail upon the Court of Spain to adopt the like sentiments."[54]

As the crisis deepened Choiseul became increasingly active in his intervention, but it is possible that his purpose was to provoke hostilities. He did not hide his efforts to restrain the Spaniards, and the predictable result was further to discourage any British tendency to conciliation. Louis XV was determined to avoid war, but Choiseul was politically insecure because he opposed the King's new mistress, Madame du Barry. His diplomacy was so inept that it supports the rumours current in Paris that he thought war might serve his interests, provided he did not appear to have been instrumental in bringing it about. For a while he toyed with the idea of using as a *casus belli* the action of East India Company servants in destroying the French ditch at Chandernagor, but the reality of his precarious political situation obliged him to lay aside that plan. Nevertheless it appears that secretly he continued to hope for war.

No mercy was shown. On 19 September Rochford ordered the Admiralty to mobilize twenty-two more ships.[55] Three days later Walpole was instructed to warn Choiseul that French "measures of the same kind" would further accelerate the British armament.[56] Choiseul was already pleading with the Spaniards to make concessions. On 26 September he wrote to d'Ossun to say that any delay would bring military advantage to the Family Compact, especially as the Newfoundland fisheries would not return until the end of October. He suggested that it would be politic to agree to the immediate

British demands since war could be brought on at a convenient moment on the question of right to the islands.[57] On the 22nd the *Favorite* had arrived in England from Port Egmont with full details of the incident, and Choiseul believed that North would be driven to war out of fear of the opposition.[58] Indeed, on 28 September, Hillsborough, the Secretary of State for the American Colonies and President of the Board of Trade, had secretly instructed the Admiralty to inform the commanders-in-chief of the various stations that the present armament had been occasioned by the occupation of Port Egmont. Unless it was disavowed, it would be considered as an act of war. The purpose of arming, however, remained the restoration of Britain to her rights, avoiding the wastages of war if at all possible. The commanders were ordered to be "much upon their guard on the one hand to prevent surprises and on the other not to give any offense."[59] A suggestion made in the Commons in November that the French Newfoundland fisheries should have been attacked in order to cripple the French navy was wide of the mark. Such action would have precipitated war, and war was not wanted.[60]

Choiseul assured London that "His Most Christian Majesty would certainly not adopt any Intentions of Arming."[61] In such circumstances it was impossible for a British government to rely upon protestations. As early as 22 September Rochford instructed Walpole to report any news of a French mobilization. Neither Walpole nor the secret service, however, had any report of activity in French dockyards until the end of September. When at last it was learned that France was arming, it did not appear that the results need be feared. On 13 October Robert Wolters' agent in Paris reported that there were twenty-one ships and eight frigates ready to be armed in Toulon, but he also estimated that the French mobilization could not be completed within four months. On 31 October the Brest agent reported great deficiencies, stating: "l'Etat du Port est magnifique, et tout le monde y a été trompé; L'Apparence était magnifique c'était tout; on travaille avec vigueur à réparer cette Négligence." Wolters confirmed this report with information he had received from a Dutch sea captain, and he added that the French ships were being docked four at a time to prepare them to be armed. Of the 18,000 French seamen called up only 5,000 had reported. According to the Paris agent, the French were relying upon the Spanish navy. However, Harris, who had been slow to discover that Spain was beginning her naval mobilization, had reported on 18 October that Spain was equipping all the ships she could but expected to have no more than ten ready by the end of November. He reported Spanish plans to be strictly defensive.[62]

This intelligence indicated that British naval preparations had a clear lead. On 17 October the Admiralty reported that thirty ships of the line were being readied for service. When Weymouth asked whether there was any way "to accelerate the Preparations, so as to collect the greatest Naval force in the shortest time possible," the Admiralty explained that dockyard capacity limited to twelve the number which could be made ready at once. Ten ships from ordinary were now completed and the full forty could be brought forward.[63] There was no reason to be concerned about the mobilization of matériel. On 30 October, Philip Stephens sent to Robert Wood a report of answers made by the Navy Board to an Admiralty questionnaire. Beginning by discounting the damage caused by a recent fire in Portsmouth, the Navy Board compared the present state of the navy not unfavourably with what it was in 1759 during the Seven Years' War. There were now eighty-six ships of the line, compared to ninety-seven in 1759.

> In which Account [the Navy Board commented] though the number of ships are less than in 1759 those of the Line are little inferior in strength to those of the Line in that period, as will appear by a comparison of the number and nature of the Guns, the Tonnage and Complements of men; so that the great decrease in strength is almost wholly in the smaller ships under the Line which may be soonest augmented.

This picture was further brightened by the fact that, except in the case of the very largest ships, which required scarce English oak, "the present List of the Line may be increased to the highest establishment at any of the former periods and in the same time. . . . There is no doubt of procuring all other Stores and Materials for equipping and augmenting the Navy in sufficient quantities as in the last War." The Navy Board concluded that up to six ships in ordinary could be made ready from the stores in twenty days and that, except for the largest oak timber, the unwrought stores and cordage were more plentiful in July than they had been in January 1755 (see Table 14).[64]

Manning was inevitably slower. On 14 September the Admiralty had applied for press warrants, and a great effort had also been made to raise volunteers.[65] On 12 October, "there being a great number of men wanting to man His Majesty's ships fitting out for sea," the Admiralty applied for an order-in-council recalling seamen from abroad, and raising bounties to £3 for able seamen volunteers, £2 for ordinary seamen, and £2 and 30 shillings respectively for anyone revealing the hiding places of those who would not volunteer.[66] On the 19th, 20th, and 23rd the Admiralty issued orders limiting the complements of most of the battleships so that some ships which normally had a full complement of 650 men would enter only 600, and other ships of between 64 and 74 guns would enter 500 men.[67] Even those figures were not reached for some time, but apparently the Admiralty did not think the time being taken was untoward. Barring the sort of emergency which intelligence of a French or Spanish fleet ready for sea would create, there was

TABLE 14: Navy Board comparison of British fleet strengths during
the Seven Years' War and in 1770

Ships of the line	1755	1756	1759	1770
Ships	55	69	97	86
Guns	3,804	4,912	6,850	6,168
Tons	73,258	94,957	136,935	134,101
Men	28,420	37,150	51,980	49,930
Ships under the line				
Ships	91	199	180	89
Guns	2,544	3,050	4,238	2,130
Tons	49,163	60,174	100,469	42,735
Men	16,635	21,750	32,885	14,931
Total				
Ships	146	268*	277	175
Guns	6,348	7,962	11,088	8,298
Tons	122,421	155,131	237,404	176,836
Men	45,055	58,900	84,865	64,865

* Given in error as 118

no way of hurrying the great machine into action.

On 28 September Harris had written: "There is not the least reason to doubt their sincere desire here of the continuance of Peace as well from their Inabilities of supporting a war, as from the dread they have of its consequences." When he presented the British demands to Grimaldi, however, the latter protested his desire for peace but made no suggestion likely to restore it.[68] He said that he was sending what he hoped might become an accommodation to London to be negotiated by Masserano. When Grimaldi's messenger to London left a copy of it in Paris as he passed through, however, Choiseul considered it so strong that it was unlikely to be accepted.

In the vain hope of persuading Masserano not to act on his instructions Choiseul wrote on 7 October to de Francés.[69] He also suggested to Walpole on 9 October that he might be able to ease the tension without mediating, a diplomatic form distrusted in London.[70] He told Walpole that Masserano had the fullest powers to make a settlement with the British government. He said that the Spanish court proposed "that after the reestablishment of the English at Port Egmont the two Courts of Spain & England should abandon those islands & that the island should remain neuter." He also admitted, however, that he thought the stipulation would be unacceptable to England and let Walpole know that he had suggested to Masserano that "the epoque for abandoning the islands should be left to the will of His Britannick Majesty.''[71] As Masserano refused to follow his suggestions, Choiseul's conversation with Walpole served only to notify the British that they should hold out for greater concessions.[72]

The failure of the negotiations in September and October made it imperative to bring home to the Spaniards that the time was inexorably approaching when Britain would go to war to defend her interests, even though her objectives were limited. The British parliamentary system increased the difficulty of persuading the Spaniards to submit because, while the Lords and Commons could be expected to demand extreme measures, an unruly House might persuade foreigners that the administration could not risk war. However, the hand of the cabinet was to be strengthened further by parliamentary success. Lord Chief Justice Mansfield suggested that the opening of Parliament ought to be deferred in hopes of receiving a satisfactory answer from Grimaldi, and Horace Walpole wondered why it was not. But North recognized the dangers of this policy and told the King he was "convinced that it would be improper as that [i.e., the Spanish] Court and that of Versailles would upon it augur that we are resolved at all events to accommodate the present dispute, and consequently would encourage them to raise perhaps so much in their demands as would make War absolutely necessary.''[73]

Mansfield apparently came round to this view.[74] Parliament was opened on 13 November, and the opposition was less fearsome than had been expected. Horace Walpole considered that the King's speech was designed to leave a loophole for the Spaniards to make an accommodation.[75] Others criticized the government for not pushing a more forceful line. The King said of the military preparations "I shall not think it expedient to discontinue [them] until I shall have received proper reparation for the injury, as well as satisfactory proof, that other powers are equally sincere with myself in resolving to preserve the general tranquillity of Europe,'' but he was careful to lay the entire blame for the incident on the governor of Buenos Aires.[76] This face-saving formula roused the scorn of Junius.[77] It was necessary, however, if the Spaniards were to be persuaded to agree to the substance of British demands. In the end, to the great satisfaction of the King, the address in reply to the speech was passed without amendment.[78]

This freedom to act as the situation seemed to demand continued to be supported by the rapidity of the mobilization. Manning continued to be a problem, but considering the difficulties progress was very satisfactory. This may perhaps have been the result of North's strategy of delaying the crisis until the autumn, when the British ocean trade was returning home. The severity of the winter which was setting in may also have helped. When the Thames froze the coastal trade could no longer supply London, and out-of-work coastal seamen could be recruited or impressed.[79] On the other hand Lieutenant Robert Tomlinson, in the preface to his *A Plan for a Practicable, Easy and Constitutional Method of Manning the Royal Navy* (1774), remarks that "the impressment, which commenced in September 1770, although short, was so severely felt, as to have occasioned three or four publications." Various civic corporations had responded to the national need by offering supplementary bounties for seamen who enlisted. On 16 November the Common Council of the City of London voted to do so, but Horace Walpole believed that its reason was less one of patriotism than a dislike of press warrants. There had been difficulty over impressment within the City, and John Wilkes, being at the time an alderman, had ordered the release of a man pressed within its limits. Wilkes persuaded the Lord Mayor, Barlow Trecothic, to protest against the issuing of Admiralty protections to citizens. Citizenship of the City should have been sufficient protection. He later sought assurance of the legal validity of press warrants. Consequently the King was careful to remind the Admiralty to thank the City for their bounty.[80] These difficulties, however, did not prevent the Admiralty's being able to report on 21 November that enough men had been collected to man the eighteen guardships to within 785 men of the full complement. The remaining twenty-nine ships and frigates would still be 5,845 men short, but at least one powerful squadron was ready at short notice. The guardships were virtually all ready for sea, and seventeen of the twenty-two ships ordered out of ordinary had been docked and were fitting out for service in the various naval ports of England.[81]

The speed of British mobilization left London with the hard choice of initiating hostilities or being seen to avoid that step, with the risk of undermining the credit of British arms. Weymouth rapidly came to the conclusion that restraint was ceasing to serve national interests. He received a letter from Walpole on 19 November recounting a conversation with Choiseul in which the latter had revealed that Masserano's instructions would allow him to leave out of any settlement a declaration of Spain's claims.[82] It was not surprising that when Masserano presented his proposals, which did include a reservation of Spain's rights, Weymouth did not accept them.[83] Masserano had agreed to present another proposal, but Weymouth said that he could not accept any that did not agree with the British demands. He asked the King to name an admiral for the Mediterranean squadron and to order the augmentation of the army. The King supported Weymouth, but he suggested that the first request should be presented to the cabinet and that the latter should be delayed a few days.[84] On 24 November, however, Weymouth wrote to the Secretary at War, Viscount Barrington, ordering "all officers belonging to His Majesty's Land Forces, to repair to their Posts without loss of time."[85] On the 23rd and again on the 28th he wrote to tell Harris that there had been no change in Masserano's attitude, that war was likely, and that the governor of Gibraltar and the consuls should be warned.[86]

At the end of November, Choiseul sent to London a new ambassador, the Comte de Guines, and instructed de Francés to open direct discussions with the British government. This gave the British an opportunity to make concessions to Spain, which they could not have done directly without giving the Spaniards an impression of weakness. North seized the occasion and told de Francés that Britain would certainly abandon Port Egmont in the long run as it was of little use. He would not agree that this should be publicly included in a settlement, but the ice had been broken and his concession was eventually to constrain the Spaniards to yield to Britain's demands, apparently humbling themselves before Britain's naval might. A few days later Rochford also told de Francés that Britain would gladly abandon the Falkland Islands and that she had no desire to fight for them. However, he would not say so much to Masserano because Masserano had not yet made an acceptable statement. On the same principle, the cabinet would not ask for royal endorsement to a secret treaty of evacuation. There could be no direct bargaining for satisfaction.[87]

North increased the British concession to Spain by declaring that Britain would abandon Port Egmont without insisting on the reciprocal abandonment by Spain of Puerto de la Solidad, the post on East Falkland Island purchased from Bougainville. The Spanish post violated the British claim to the Falklands, but the British were no longer greatly interested in it. North, however, would not enter into an accommodation in which Spain declared her claim to the Falklands, and the negotiations were not permitted to interfere with the rate of mobilization. On 4 December, fifteen additional ships of the line and a proportionate number of frigates were ordered brought forward.[88] This resulted in greater financial needs for the navy. On 25 November the House had been asked to enlarge the vote from 16,000 to 40,000 seamen, but the increase of fifteen more ships added a further 9,282 seamen and cost the navy an additional £482,664. On 12 December North asked the Commons to raise the land tax to 4 shillings in the pound.[89]

Because of the difficulty of sustaining the coercive effect of mobilization if it became apparent that the British government was reluctant to commence hostilities, time was rapidly running out for a peaceful solution. The strains of deciding whether it was diplomatically necessary to make the break or militarily desirable to defer it were enough to split the cabinet. The East India Company was clamouring for advice as to how it should instruct its servants in India, and Weymouth decided that the Company should be encouraged to strike a blow at the French establishment there. This would have made war inevitable. Weymouth, grasping the nettle, demanded the recall of Harris from Madrid. Rochford, however, warned the King on the 6th of the shape events were taking, and the latter immediately expressed his disagreement. He suspected that Weymouth was attempting to prevent an accommodation, and it has been suggested that Weymouth was hoping to force the recall of Chatham as an indispensable war leader. Under-Secretary Robert Wood has been mentioned in connection with these machinations. Rochford asked the King to suggest to Weymouth the need for a cabinet meeting. This took place on the 7th and a compromise was made. Weymouth agreed not to recall Harris immediately and to alter a letter he proposed to send to the chairman of the East India Company so that it could not claim to have been authorized to undertake hostilities. He would not agree to instruct Harris to reopen negotiations, however, and three days later he resigned. He may have had political motives, but he was prepared to accept alternative employment to avoid an appearance of political disunity. He told Rochford that "his Chief complaint is that we are in a state of uncertainty and are taking no measures to distress the enemy."[90]

Rochford's and the King's hesitation was probably occasioned by an accident to several battleships, which raised doubts about Britain's readiness for war. Because of the crisis, the normal relief of the garrisons in Minorca and Gibraltar, which was to have been performed by hired transports, had been suspended. On 2 October, Weymouth had asked that the Admiralty order to Spithead the first six major ships and the first six frigates ready for service. On the 8th, seven ships being ready if not yet fully manned, he ordered five of them to Kinsale and Cork to embark troops. After a month's delay, *Defence, Ajax, Arrogant, Rippon,* and *Achilles* sailed; but on their voyage to Ireland three of the ships were damaged by a storm. When *Arrogant* and *Achilles* put back into Portsmouth the Admiralty ordered Vice-Admiral Geary to replace them with *Centaur* and *Yarmouth,* two guardships. On 30 November the Admiralty informed Weymouth the *Ajax* had sprung a mast and gone into Plymouth where, if repairs could not be effected right away, *Hero* would take her place. But apparently not all the guardships were in fact ready for sea, and on 3 December the Admiralty advised that *Belle Isle* would be going to Cork because *Yarmouth* had been found to be suffering from rot.[91]

The damage sustained by ships supposedly just fitted, not to mention the need to dock a guardship which was supposed to be ready for sea, alarmed Rochford and the King. On the 6th Rochford suggested that another column should be added to the naval reports showing the condition of ships, and the King wrote: "it appears by the Ships that were sent to Corke that their bottoms were not clean of course they ran great risk of foundering at Sea, and if the remainder which are now supposed to be ready should turn out to be in the same condition, the most dreadful consequence may be

Edward, 1st Baron Hawke,
1705-81. Engraving by
J. Hall.
Courtesy of the British
Museum (Class II period 4;
1868.8.8.1654) Negative w/p
24022

apprehended from it.'' On the 9th, however, Rochford was able to tell the
King that Hawke had said that the twenty-two ships ordered out of ordinary
had been both docked and sheathed, although the guardships had only had
their annual cleaning and would have to be docked again in the spring. With
this the King expressed himself satisfied.[92]

Indeed the reaction of the Admiralty was to make light of the disaster,
and the Navy Board supported this attitude. On the 12th, Hawke reassured
the Commons: ''I do take upon me to say th[at] we are forwarder now than
we were then [in 1755].'' Admiral Keppel replied: ''I don't say every ship is
bad, but those you h[ave] tried are bad,'' and Hawke was only able to say
that guardships ''are not intended to be sent abroad, they are a deal
forwarder than the ships in ordinary to be sent out to cruise upon the
enemy.'' The *Belle Isle* was also found to be defective, and the *Yarmouth* not
to have been properly surveyed. Nevertheless, no one at the Navy Board or
Admiralty considered that matériel defects seriously endangered Britain's
naval superiority.[93]

Rochford and the King were satisfied by Hawke's assertion, and Weymouth's resignation did not lead to a change of policy. Rochford had quickly offered his services to the King in the Southern Department, where his experience as ambassador in turn to Spain and France could be put to good use. He was duly appointed, with Sandwich taking the Northern Department. Rochford soon came to the same decision as had Weymouth. The logic of the situation impelled the British government towards a diplomatic break. Choiseul had made one more attempt to draft a proposal acceptable to Britain. He struck out the Spanish demand that Britain disavow Captain Hunt's action in ordering the Spaniards to leave Falkland Island and replaced it with a strict stipulation that Spain not waive the question of right.[94] His proposal arrived in London on 13 December, and since Masserano refused to violate his sovereign's instructions, de Francés undertook to deliver it. He was eventually able to get Weymouth, whose resignation apparently was not immediately announced, and North together on the 16th. It was North, however, who would not accept a declaration in which Spain mentioned her claims to rights by discovery and treaty.

The King urged that the remaining seamen required be pressed as rapidly as possible, and on 18 December when the moon had become dark, the Admiralty ordered the admirals of the dockyards and the regulating officers to institute a general press without regard to any protections save those authorized by acts of parliament.[95] The next day, at a council meeting at which Weymouth was not present, it was agreed that Harris be recalled.[96] On the 21st orders were sent to Madrid, and a warning message was sent to Commodore Proby in the Mediterranean.[97]

PREPARATIONS FOR WAR

The decision to proceed to war had reluctantly been taken, but no detailed plans had been made for immediate offensive operations. There was some thought of reviving General Paoli's partisan cause in Corsica, but Sir Horace Mann's report that the French had virtually suppressed Paoli's troops forced Weymouth to agree that it would cost more than the British wished to spend to reactivate that theatre of operations.[98] Nevertheless there apparently was little real hope of cheap victory once hostilities were begun. It has been seen that Weymouth eventually came to the decision that war should begin by sweeping the French from India. To have effected that might have required little in the way of preparations in Britain, and it might have been undertaken at short notice. In the King's papers is a sketch plan for an amphibious assault on Ferrol which acknowledged the lessons of the Seven Years' War. He sent this, and also a plan for an attack on New Orleans, to Weymouth.[99] Strikes against French India and against Spanish peninsular and colonial cities might have persuaded the French to make peace on British terms, and that against Ferrol, if it had succeeded, would have meant the destruction of an important part of the Spanish navy. With the possible exception of the Indian campaign, they would not have been easy, and in the absence of detailed plans could hardly have been undertaken rapidly. However, it is doubtful that British seapower had any quick way of bringing pressure on France. Moreover, it was winter. Winter naval operations were still uncertain, as the garrisoning of Gibraltar had demonstrated.

The apparent assumption that, if it could not be avoided, war would be protracted had led to the preparation of plans of a general and defensive nature. Operations were generally carried out under Admiralty orders, but it was the Secretaries of State who decided what should be done and frequently how it should be done. By October plans were well advanced for the defence of British trade, which was both politically and nationally an important consideration. The merchants trading to North America had petitioned the Admiralty for protection, particularly for Newfoundland trade bound for Spanish ports. Rochford assured the Admiralty that they already had authorization to make arrangements. When Admiral Lord Howe responded to a petition from his Dartmouth constituents by presenting a plan for stationing three ships at the focal points of Santander, Bayonne, and Gibraltar to warn inward-bound shipping, it was immediately adopted. *Emerald* 32, *Favorite* 18, and *Merlin* 18 were ready on 8 November, and after a reminder to Weymouth, they were ordered to take their instructions from the Secretary of State. Apparently, however, there was little real concern for the trade. Although the normal cruises in defence of trade were dispatched, and insurance rates for outward-bound ships rose from 4 to 10 per cent, *Emerald* was diverted to carrying officers to Gibraltar and Minorca, while *Favorite* and *Merlin* never sailed. Special arrangements were made only for the protection of the homeward-bound East Indiamen, which were alone a sufficiently tempting bait to have precipitated war. They were ordered to await convoy at St. Helena whither the *Portland* 50 was later sent.[100]

If war did follow upon mobilization, defence of trade and of those outposts most likely to suffer attack were equally important. On 18 September, when the guardship squadron was ordered to carry troops to Gibraltar, Weymouth had written to warn Lieutenant Governor Boyde of Gibraltar, Governor Johnson of Minorca, and Commodore Proby. The garrison was built up at Gibraltar and funds were belatedly voted to strengthen the already elaborate defences.[101] Johnson complained of the inadequacies of the Minorca garrison, sending his letter by the common post of France, but Weymouth coldly replied that "the military men, whose opinion I have asked on that subject, think differently from you."[102]

General Cornwallis, Governor of Gibraltar, had noted in 1768 that:

Gibralter has its faults, but, with them, [is] as tenable in my opinion as any place in Europe; where it is vulnerable, is, to the sea. And I think the strictest attention should be paid to that; I mean on no account to suffer a Fleet of the Enemy to get the start of ours upon an approach of war, for tho' it has often been said, that Gibralter was impregnable, which no place is according to my notions, it is always understood, "while you command the sea."[103]

The same could be said of Minorca. Proby had been placed directly under the command of the Secretary of State to facilitate control of naval operations in the Levant. On 16 October, Weymouth ordered him to concentrate his forces as near to Gibraltar as possible. Three days later he wrote to the Admiralty instructing them to order the five ships of the line carrying troops to Gibraltar to remain there under Proby's command. However, Admiral Hawke disagreed with weakening the battle fleet by detaching a squadron which would not be strong enough to defend itself. He later told the Commons that "he did not understand sending ships abroad when, for aught he knew, they might be wanted to defend our own coast." Consequently, Robert Wood wrote on the 26th, probably to Philip Stephens, that Weymouth agreed to rescind the previous instructions and further to order the recall of *Edgar* and *Dorsetshire*. Proby was left with five frigates and sloops dispersed on various duties. Later, further efforts had been made to organize a Mediterranean squadron. On 23 November, having virtually despaired of preserving the peace, Weymouth had urged that a commander-in-chief be appointed for the Mediterranean. Hawke gave the post to Lord Howe. He justified this promotion of a comparatively junior officer to the Commons by crediting the King with the selection. The *Warwick* was ordered to be prepared as Howe's flagship, and all 74-gun ships were ordered fitted for foreign service. This force never assembled, however, and even the five ships carrying troops to Gibraltar were delayed until the new year.[104]

The weakness of the naval forces in the Mediterranean was a major criticism of the government's handling of the crisis. The opposition, led by Chatham, dwelt upon the obvious failure. During the debate on the increase in the land tax, Admiral Sir Charles Saunders argued that the presence of a squadron capable of cutting French trade with the Levant, an important source of French naval reserves, would be a strong inhibition on her actions.[105] He was probably right. Bourbon strength in the Mediterranean, however, did not permit more than a defensive policy. The best had to be made with what was available. On 31 December the Admiralty suggested to Rochford that Proby be ordered to leave Minorca and concentrate his forces on Gibraltar. This had, of course, already been done unknown to the

Admiralty, and Proby had already sailed there, taking with him two companies of artillery from Minorca. On 5 January, Cornwallis sailed to take command at Gibraltar, and on 14 January Proby was ordered to make the best defence he could of the fortress. If confronted with a superior fleet, he was ordered to land what seamen he could to assist the garrison and to flee to the Tagus, if possible, or to Port Mahon.[106]

Although the fleet was not sufficiently operational to spare forces for the Mediterranean, the mobilization was well under way. On 25 December the Navy Board reported that of the fifteen ships ordered on 4 December, five would be ready for men in five weeks, five in six weeks, and five in seven weeks. Manning was still slow, and on 21 December the Admiralty went so far as to request an embargo of the ports, but as the Bourbons were no further advanced there really was no urgency to send the battlefleet to sea in mid-winter. To increase the number of men available for sea duty, Rochford ordered that special arrangements be made to guard the dockyards so that the marines could be employed at sea. His letter to the Secretary at War, ordering two regiments of foot to be stationed at each of the naval dockyards, has a minute on it that there were already two regiments at Chatham and Plymouth and three near Portsmouth. By 4 January, Philip Stephens was able to forward to Rochford a report that the guardships could be fully manned should their recruiting parties be called in. The remainder of the fifty-five ships ordered in the emergency were still 7,000 men short of complement, but the muster-books show that at the beginning of 1771 the first forty ships ordered were 61.5 per cent manned, so that it would have been possible to fully man twenty-four ships (see Table 15).[107]

At the end of the first week of January, Hawke was forced by increasingly bad health to announce his resignation to the cabinet. His colleagues in government had found him a difficult man to work with and were not sorry to see him go, but his resignation did not indicate a failure in his department, and it did not lead to a change of policy. Sandwich quietly accepted the office which North had promised should be his whenever it came vacant. When he inspected the dockyards in the spring he reported eighty ships of the line fit for service, and forty-three others reparable. Accounts of the total manpower raised in the emergency differ. The official Admiralty list-books show that in August 1770 there had been 14,611 men in the fleet, which number increased in three months to 35,472, and at the peak in February 1771 had risen to over 44,812 men. The year-end abstracts prepared for Sandwich give lower overall manning figures (see Table 16).[108] Sandwich's papers also contain an abstract dated 13 February 1771 which showed only 36,805 seamen and marines to man the fleet, the full complement of which called for 44,491 men. The muster-books of the ships themselves show that by May, forty-eight ships were 75.2 per cent manned.

TABLE 15: Abstract of the state of manning derived from the ADM 36 series of muster-books

	Oct.	Nov.	Dec.	Jan.	Feb.	Mar.	Apr.	May
18 guardships ordered 7 September								
Ships reporting	9	14	18	17*	17	17	12	14
Complement	5040	7680	9980	9380	9380	9380	6640	8020
Men borne	2173	4963	8382	7903	7946	7830	5045	6124
Percentage	43.2	64.6	83.9	84.2	84.6	83.4	75.9	76.3
22 ships ordered 19 September								
Reporting		10	17	19	18	19	19	18
Complement		5640	9630	10580	10060	10580	10580	9920
Men borne		689	2456	4682	6091	7373	8595	7812
Percentage		12.2	25.6	44.2	60.5	69.6	81.6	78.8
15 ships ordered 4 December								
Reporting					6	8	8	6
Complement					3490	4330	4330	3210
Men borne					323	944	1936	1970
Percentage					9.2	21.8	45.3	61.3
The 55-ship fleet ordered in the emergency								
Reporting	0	24	35	36*	41	44	39	38
Complement	5040	13320	19610	19960	22930	24290	21550	21150
Men borne	2173	5652	10838	12585	14360	16147	15630	15906
Percentage	43.1	42.4	55.2	61.5	62.1	66	72.4	75.2

Marines and supernumeraries for wages are included as men borne, and the complements are those established before the emergency reductions ordered in October 1770. The figures refer to the first muster of each month. Seven of the last 15 ships never returned musters; otherwise the ships missing muster were different each week.

*An account of the state of manning of the guardships dated 7 January 1771 in the Sandwich Papers reports that 19 ships (including one which was not a guardship) mustered 1,116 short of complement, but with more than enough supernumeraries to equal full complement.

TABLE 16: Manning abstracts prepared for Sandwich

	Seamen borne	must'd	Marines borne	must'd
1770 Aug.	12,639	12,625	3,763	1,689
Sept.	14,922	14,749	3,812	1,734
Oct.	21,260	21,067	3,938	1,737
Nov.	24,924	24,899	4,011	1,766
Dec.	27,855	27,276	4,185	1,725
1771 Jan.	31,127	30,919	4,077	1,725
Feb.	33,048	32,887	4,241	1,852
Mar.	32,057	31,568	4,384	2,246
Apr.	31,267	31,682	4,565	2,731

This degree of success certainly surpassed the expectations expressed in the paper prepared for Chatham in 1767 embodying the lessons of the war, that "39 ships of the line, and 474 men over, is all that can be raised in the first year."

Far from Hawke's mobilization being a failure, the reports from British intelligence indicated that it had already left the Bourbons far behind. On 7 September the Brest correspondent had reported that in fifteen days eighteen ships and twelve frigates were expected to be armed, but it was not until 17 December that he could report that they were ready. Twenty other vessels were being worked on by 10,000 men. The intelligence from Toulon was incomplete, but the Admiralty had information through the consuls in the Mediterranean of twenty-two ships and six frigates at Toulon. As late as 30 October, however, these were reported to be "unrigged and unmann'd and by what I can learn they are not all fit for present service." Wolters' agent in Toulon reported on 8 November that two 80s, eight 74s, and seven 64s were ready to be armed. In fact, however, progress was very slow. At the end of the year the French were still not far advanced preparing their fleets totalling thirty-five ships and had been seriously disappointed in the condition of their ships in ordinary. In January 1770 a copy had been obtained of an official French fleet-condition report listing fifty-two ships in good repair and only six out of repair. Early in 1771, however, it was reported that during 1770, while nine ships were newly built, purchased, or under construction, another nine which had been considered in good condition had had to undergo heavy repair or even rebuilding. Even more dramatic, no fewer than ten ships had been condemned as unfit for service.[109]

The Spanish fleet did not appear to be any more ready for war. Harris had somewhat underestimated its size, and the Rotterdam espionage net did not bring in as useful information about it, but finally, on 7 January, the Madrid correspondent forwarded detailed information. It appeared that twelve ships were fitting at Cartagena, eight at Cadiz, and twenty-four at Ferrol. The eight at Cadiz, with four from Cartagena and three from Ferrol, were to form a squadron to sail under the Marquis de Cassa Tilly to protect Spain's restive empire. This disposition left only twenty-nine ships for war in Europe. At the time of writing, moreover, only thirteen of the twenty-four ships ordered at Ferrol were ready for sea, a state of affairs which did support Harris' general contempt for the Spanish navy.[110]

THE CRISIS RESOLVED

The British cabinet felt able to go to war if necessary to secure their minimum demands, but it proved to be enough just to reach the point of crisis. A contributing cause to the backwardness of the French mobilization had been Choiseul's political weakness. Rather than face war, Louis XV exiled him to his estates on 24 December, and asked Charles III to make concessions needed to preserve the peace.[111] Charles complained that the exile of Choiseul would convince Britain of Spanish weakness and make her more obdurate, but Masserano was instructed to follow French directions.[112] Grimaldi told him to accept North's secret promise and to reduce Spain's claim of rights to a minimum. In order, perhaps, to lessen Spain's diplomatic humiliation, Masserano was not to continue negotiations. They were to be conducted by de Francés until an agreement was reached, when Masserano would reappear.[113]

Harcourt and Harris both recognized the implication of Choiseul's dismissal, but that did not remove all the dangers from London's coercive diplomacy.[114] Reversal of the decision to recall Harris to London would give the obdurate Spaniards further opportunities for delay or evasion. It was necessary to make it clear that war was still a possibility if Spain refused to be reasonable. This difficulty threw Rochford off balance. When Masserano said that it would be impossible to proceed with the agreement unless Harris returned to Madrid, Rochford pretended that Harris was needed for consultation and that his leaving Madrid had no hostile import. Masserano had a tactical advantage and refused to continue in a diplomatic role until Harris was reinstated. He suggested that the recall be obliterated by appointing a new ambassador to Madrid, a solution for which de Francés also pressed. The King, however, felt that it would be wrong to re-establish relations until an agreement had been reached. Instead, Rochford placed a time limit of 22 January, the latest that the parliamentary Christmas recess could be extended, and declared that if no concession had been made by then he would advise the King to proceed to war.[115]

The Spanish position was so poor that really all that remained to be found was a face-saving formula. With Masserano cut off from St. James's, it was de Francés who carried the latest Spanish plan to North, who for his part had promised that if it was acceptable Harris would immediately be redirected. After some discussion and a little alteration it was accepted and Rochford instructed Harris to return to Madrid. The order was antedated to 18 January to save Spanish honour. The eventual declaration made on 22 January was moderate in reserving to a later date any discussion of whose was the prior right to the islands, a reservation Rochford did not acknowledge when he accepted the declaration. North's secret agreement to abandon Port Egmont could be interpreted as conceding Spanish sovereignty over the Falkland Islands, but because the agreement was secret, it did not affect British freedom to operate in the South Atlantic and Pacific. On the contrary, that freedom was clearly implied in the Spanish declaration, which amounted to an admission that the Family Compact could not dispute British seapower.[116]

On 23 January the Admiralty was still preparing to send warnings to Cadiz, Gibraltar, and Minorca, but the next day Rochford was able to permit the Secretary at War to grant leave to officers and to stop recruitment of invalids. A few days later all military recruiting was ended. On 22 February the land forces were reduced to the peace establishment.[117] Although no reduction was made in the naval armament until after the formal agreement had been made, the crisis was passed. On 24 January the Admiralty Board received advice of the dénouement with Spain from Hillsborough, who asked that the commanders-in-chief of the foreign stations be notified. On the 26th Howe was given leave to resign his Mediterranean command.[118]

The exchange of declarations was not the end of the issue because the Spanish government attempted to obtain a formal agreement that Britain would abandon the Falkland Islands even before Spain had restored them. They maintained their armament, hoping to force British agreement. Rochford and North, however, would take no step which appeared to make the secret arrangement instrumental in the exaction of the Spanish submission. They would only discuss the eventual abandonment after the nations had disarmed and Port Egmont was restored. The Spanish attempt to apply pressure was rendered futile by the common knowledge that France would not fight. Eventually Grimaldi realized that there was no alternative to trusting King George's honour.

Consequently it was agreed, on a proposal of Rochford's, that the three powers disarm simultaneously.[119] He announced at the same time that the British peace establishment would be raised from 16,000 to 25,000 men, an increase the Bourbons were welcome to match. Steps were also taken to restore Port Egmont to its condition before 10 June 1770. A small squadron was dispatched under the command of Captain Stott. It arrived at Port Egmont on 13 September 1771, where a Spanish officer had arrived in time to return the fort and the captured stores officially.[120] Port Egmont was garrisoned for several years, the men suffering great privations. In February 1772, distressed by the cost of maintaining it as it was, the government reduced the garrison to fifty men. There was no attempt to make the fort defensible, but only to retain a mark of possession.[121] The reduction was reported to the Spanish government.[122] Eventually the fort was left without even a warship guard, a small prefabricated shallop being assembled at the island to take its place.[123] In 1773 it was finally decided to abandon the colony altogether, and North justified the step to the uninterested Commons on the grounds of economy. The Duc d'Aiguillon, who had succeeded to Choiseul's position after a few months, nearly prevented the quiet withdrawal by insisting that Britain had promised the abandonment. That statement had to be denied.[124] Fortunately not even d'Aiguillon's unpolitic action was able to prolong the affair.

Samuel Johnson well expressed the natural exasperation of the historian when he wrote his *Thoughts on the Late Transactions respecting Falklands Islands:* "What continuation of happiness can be expected, when the whole system of European Empire can be in danger of a new concussion, by a contention for a few spots of earth, which, in the deserts of the ocean had almost escaped human notice."[125] Horace Walpole considered Johnson's pamphlet the most servile of government panegyrics, but in a letter to Sir Horace Mann on 4 October 1770 he had written:

> England that lives in the north of Europe, and Spain that dwells in the South, are vehemently angry with one another about a morsel of rock that lies somewhere at the very bottom of America, for modern nations are too neighbourly to quarrel about anything that lies so near them as in the same quarter of the globe. . . . By next century I suppose we shall fight for the Dog Star and the Great Bear.[126]

Johnson's principal motive was profound disagreement with war *per se*, heightened by the pettiness of the immediate objectives. He did not consider the establishment of Port Egmont as a base from which to carry British commerce against Spanish will into the Pacific, and to the ports of South America, a just or necessary national objective. When he revised his text in 1776 he did not quarrel with the decision to abandon the British post. He had no doubt, on the other hand, that the North administration had obtained what was necessary for British security and did not dispute that what was gained was the result of British strength. He set himself to demonstrate that the country would not have benefited by exacting further demands, which, if they did not immediately provoke war, could only have built up a dangerous fear of British power throughout Europe.[127]

It is certainly true that the immediate issue was hardly worth a war. The reward for defending British interests would have been greater in 1768 when Grafton failed to prevent the French annexation of Corsica. In 1770, however, North's cabinet had been faced with a deteriorating situation not of its own making. In the circumstances they had coped adequately with the demanding task of using force to support diplomacy.

5

Business as Usual:
India and Sweden

The crises in the Levant and in the South Atlantic had taken attention away from the problem of the forces France was reported to be building up on the Ile de France.[1] The resolution of the Falkland Islands crisis demonstrated that Britain retained the capacity to punish her Bourbon enemies and provided some security for British possessions. The threat of retaliation, however, was an inadequate defence for British interests in India. They were in a precarious state owing to the misrule of the East India Company and to the interest of the Indian "country" powers in exploiting the divisions between European states. A local defence was needed to supplement the general deterrence value of the threat of war. Port Egmont had had little more than symbolic value, and that had been strengthened by the crisis. In contrast, a French attack on India could do a great deal of long-term damage to British interests before any diplomatic or military action in Europe could force the French to withdraw. When the Admiralty presented its proposed peace establishment on 1 March 1771, it included provision to increase the force in the East Indies to three ships of 70 guns, one of 50, one frigate, and two sloops. By the 25th the four heavy ships were on their way under the command of Rear Admiral Sir Robert Harland.[2] Rochford made it clear to the French ambassador that this additional strength had been occasioned by the size of the French squadron in the Indies.[3]

After the departure of the East Indies Squadron, further reports reached London which revealed the scope of the French plans. In August Harcourt sent to Rochford intelligence from the Dutch commanding officer at Cape Town that 7,000 French soldiers had gone to the Ile de France that year.

Later reports also said that the French were garrisoning the Seychelles. Rochford's only response was to warn the East India Company to watch the potential allies of France among the Indian rulers.[4] Reports continued to arrive during the autumn of 1771, however, and on 30 December Colonel Blanquière wrote to warn Rochford that the Chevalier de Ternay, on his way to the Ile de France, had orders to embark 3,000 men and take them to Pondicherry to rebuild the fortifications. A note of this letter is the last entry in a careful account of intelligence received in 1770 and 1771 from France and India which is among the King's papers. The great build-up of ships and men in India is clearly noted, and at the end is a computation of the maximum and minimum number of French ships reported in India. The minimum reckoning was one ship of 60 and another of 64 guns, two of 54, two of 36, one of 30, one of 22, and two of 20 guns. The maximum computation included seven of 54 to 70 guns and six smaller. Eight private ships were added to the royal squadron.[5]

No further naval or diplomatic action was taken by the British government until January 1772. Presumably the outcome of the Falkland Islands crisis was thought to have dispelled any immediate likelihood of France choosing war. However, on 17 January 1772 additional intelligence was received from the East Indies that there had been in the previous summer at the Ile de France 6,000 regulars, 2,000 creoles, 1,000 kafirs, six East Indiamen armed with up to 60 guns each, five royal frigates, sixteen large transports, and six smaller Indian vessels. Four men of war, twelve transports, and provision ships from the Cape were expected.[6] This was an enormous force and a threat to be taken seriously. To guard against possible trouble two 64s were sent to reinforce Harland.[7]

When the Commons debated the increase in the strength of the navy to 25,000 men on 22 January, there was considerable criticism of the government's policy of meeting the possibility of a French attack in India by building up the East Indies Squadron. Sir Charles Saunders declared that the forces in the East were at once too large and too small. He said: "if there is a peace it is too much, if you suspect the French it is too little, you are liable to dishonour there, you are liable to lose your force by retail." Lord North agreed that it was undesirable as a "general principle" to maintain "foreign squadrons in time of peace." However, as Lord Palmerston, one of the Lords of Admiralty, pointed out, it was impossible to dispatch guardships to so distant a station. Threats had to be anticipated if they were to be parried. North's policy was to have foreign squadrons "in case of intelligence."[8]

On 4 March, Harcourt forwarded from Paris intelligence that Chevalier Law, the governor of Pondicherry, was urging that immediate steps be taken to profit from the ferment in British-ruled India. He had asked for troops

George Simon, 1st Earl
Harcourt, 1714-77.
Engraving by Edward
Fisher after a painting by
Robert Hunter.
Courtesy of the British
Museum (Class II period 4;
1885.12.12.79) Negative 1/2
pl 38700

and warned that in two years it would be too late to salvage anything in India
for France. Monsieur de Boynes, who as Minister of the Marine was
responsible for Indian affairs, was reported to wish to take the opportunity,
but he also hoped to avoid a maritime war for one or two years until he had
time to complete his naval reforms.[9] Among Sandwich's papers is a précis of
intelligence from the East Indies showing the build-up of ships since 1769
and of the steady outward movement of troops. The last entries are dated in
April.[10]

As a result of this obvious threat, further steps were taken to ensure the
safety of India and to persuade the French that they could not succeed with
a *coup de main.* Rochford's concern was that "the opportunity which they
may think they see of ruining our Affairs in that Country may tempt the
Court of France to act sooner than they would otherwise wish to do."[11]
Harcourt was instructed to inform the French government that the British
would be obliged to match any French forces sent to the east. On 1 April the
Admiralty informed Rochford that *Intrepid* and *Prudent* were ready to

proceed on their voyage, and two days later Rochford wrote again to Harcourt.[12] While there was no treaty to prevent it, the French fortifications at Pondicherry being "designed against other enemies than the Marattas" was a circumstance which added weight to the fears occasioned by the 7,500 regulars Sir John Lindsay reported there to be at the Ile de France: "It is plain [he wrote] that such a body of Men cannot be maintained there, but must either be brought back to Europe, or carried on to other parts of India, and Your Excellency is aware in case the 6,000 Marines should be sent out to relieve the Regulars as is pretended, what a great Force together [they will have?] to act with."

Harcourt was directed to advise d'Aiguillon that, "from his general Instructions to protect our Settlements and Allies," Harland would probably feel obliged to intercept any troop convoy sent to Pondicherry.[13] On 7 April, Rochford directed the Admiralty to send *Prudent* and *Intrepid* on their way, and soon after he wrote to Harland specifically authorizing him to use force if necessary to prevent the French building up dangerous numbers at Pondicherry.[14]

The Anglo-French confrontation over India was complicated by other conflicts of the global political systems of Britain and France. Intelligence was at the time being received in London of further efforts of the French to establish themselves on the north bank of the River Gambia despite the confrontation with British forces there in 1764-65. On 10 April, Rochford directed Harcourt to enquire of d'Aiguillon whether that was indeed the case, whether they were attempting to interfere in the gum trade, and most particularly, whether the report that three frigates had already sailed to Gambia, to be followed by more, were correct.[15] Hillsborough agreed that a serious situation could develop there.[16]

Britain was also involved in a show of force with Denmark as a result of the imprisonment and disgrace of Caroline Matilda, Queen of Denmark and sister of George III, after Bernstorff's fall from power. On 16 April a squadron of eleven ships of the line was ordered brought forward for four months' Channel service; the Danes bowed to the menace; and on 30 April two frigates and a sloop were ordered to carry Caroline Matilda from Elsinore to Celle, where she was to be allowed to live in exile.[17]

The battle squadron had been countermanded on 18 April, but international affairs are complex.[18] British determination to enter into hostilities with Denmark if necessary may have helped to carry Rochford's meaning to the French.[19] At any rate on 21 April, d'Aiguillon told Harcourt that the report of 7,500 men at the Iles des France et Bourbon was false and that, while the garrison was to be relieved by the Légion des Indes and part of the Marine corps, the new force was not to exceed 4,000 men. There were, he said, no plans to send troops to Pondicherry, and he said that the frigates sailing to Africa were carrying stores for Goree and would not interfere with British interests. He further undertook to send no more ships until the commander of the first force sent his report.[20] On 3 May, Harcourt reported that "in Consequence of some Altercation between the Duke D'Aiguillon and Mons. de [Boynes?] an Order was sent two Days ago to Brest, to stop the Sailing of the French Squadron" to the Ile de France. The "Expeditious Equipment" of the British Squadron "seems to have had a very surprising Effect here."[21]

Rochford remained very suspicious of the French. Harcourt confirmed that d'Aiguillon and Boynes had quarrelled in council over whether the necessary steps should be taken to preserve French interests in India. D'Aiguillon had stated decisively that France could not afford to give umbrage to Britain. "For that Reason," wrote Harcourt, "he opposed the Sailing of the whole Squadron as was first intended, but, he said that he should not be against the sailing of three Ships of the Line, with as many Frigates, to cruise and exercise the Seamen." In a further "Secret and Private" letter, Harcourt reported that "the Provisions of three or four Ships of the Line, and as many Frigates, have been landed"; "such has been the uncertainty that has attended all their measures of late, that the Provisions have been landed, & reshipped five or six different times."[22] Only a few frigates and soldiers were, in the end, sent to Africa.

This report appears to have reassured London. The French squadron continued to cause concern, but in a European rather than an Indian context. The immediate threat having apparently passed away, on 21 August Rochford directed the Admiralty to reduce the size of the East Indies squadron. In consequence Harland was ordered to send home two of his ships, those in the worst condition.[23] Worried about the national debt, North wanted to reduce the fleet in commission yet further.[24]

Not only was North disappointed in his hopes, but also Rochford's decision to recall two of Harland's ships was soon found to be premature. A few days before Rochford authorized the recall, the Chairman of the East India Company had forwarded to him a startling account which bore out Harland's revelation. The governor of the Ile de France had carefully kept all British ships outside Port Louis harbour and restricted the movements of visitors to keep secret the build-up and destination of forces. In this he had been assisted by the prevailing wind, which made it necessary to warp ships into Port Louis. In February, however, Captain Lockhart Russel was sent by the Company to obtain information. He was able to take advantage of a hurricane which, although it nearly wrecked his ship, and did strand or sink most of the shipping at Port Louis, also set up an unseasonably favourable wind. He crashed his way through high surf into the harbour. Perhaps because Choiseul's plan had already been set aside, or perhaps for other reasons, he was able for the first time to give an exact report of how the French had built up the garrison ever since 1768, received a shipload of specie from the Spaniards at Manila, and arranged alliances with Hyder Ali and other Indian princes: "The result of these Politics [he wrote] was the forming of an Expedition, which aimed at totally extirpating the Company from their possessions in India, by landing twenty thousand Europeans about July or August 1771 at Pondicherry, who were immediately to take the field."[25]

It appeared that the plan of operation had been laid aside, but there was no guarantee that it would not be taken up again. On 11 September 1772 Philip Stephens received from Harland a report from Captain Johnson, who had in fact visited Mauritius in November 1771 and whose account agreed with Russel's.[26] Clearly the French had been planning something really big and it would be inadvisable to reduce British forces until there was no possibility of the assault taking place. On 7 October the cabinet decided to retain all the ships of Harland's squadron in the East Indies.[27]

THE SWEDISH CRISIS

The reports from India might not have persuaded the cabinet to take action had it not been faced at the same time with a renewed crisis in Europe. The constraints on Britain's ability to use her navy to influence European affairs made London jealous to ensure that the capacity of the British navy to act as exclusive arbiter of the Mediterranean and Baltic should not be undermined. In 1773, when the Russian problem returned in a new form to trouble the British cabinet, North was obliged to use naval force to demonstrate British commitment to European interests. London resorted to the most sophisticated use of "gunboat" diplomacy to be attempted between the Peace of Paris and the commencement of hostilities in America. French exercise of naval power was forestalled, but the outcome was not wholly satisfactory for Britain and demonstrates the very real limitations there were to the ability of naval forces alone to protect British interests.

Concern that Russia's naval power in the Mediterranean might become a permanent feature is most evident. Especially unwelcome were hints from Russia that it might like to take possession of an island in the Aegean, obviously for use as a naval base. Rochford informed John Murray, ambassador at the Porte, "that the Idea of acquiring an Island in the Archipelago, or even a Communication from the Black Sea to the Mediterranean has been hinted to Lord Cathcart to be disagreeable here, as necessarily giving Jealousies to all the Nations in possession of the Trade of the Mediterranean."[28] The Earl of Suffolk, who succeeded to the office of Secretary of State for the Northern Department when Halifax died in 1771, denied to Cathcart that the increased coolness of the British towards Russia proceeded "from a jealousy entertained here of the progress of the Russian arms on the coast of the Black Sea. They know the falsehood of the assertion."[29] Such a denial only serves to confirm that London was suspicious of Russian intentions. In July 1772 Suffolk wrote Sir Robert Gunning, who had replaced Cathcart in St. Petersburg, recounting that the Russian ambassador Mr. Pushkin had "for the first Time, explained the Navigation of the Black Sea as applied to the Pretensions of His Court, into a free Passage thro' the Dardanelles, to & from the Mediterranean. This is so new a Construction of that Object, & so material, that I must recommend you to give immediate and Accurate attention to it."[30]

The concern about the growth of Russian naval power did not diminish the alarm felt at the prospect of the French navy being used to obstruct Russian expansion. This fact was made evident in the late spring of 1772 when intelligence reports reached London that a small squadron had sailed from Brest supposedly to exercise in the Mediterranean. Orders were sent to Sir Peter Denis, the British commander-in-chief Mediterranean, to ensure that the Brest squadron did not join one which the Spaniards were reported to be preparing, and form an allied fleet of observation in the Mediterranean.[31]

The continued hope in London of creating common ground with Russia and the reflex gallophobic reaction had persuaded the British to continue to support Russian efforts to ensure control of the government of Sweden. London did not exhibit much professionalism in its handling of Baltic affairs, being obsessed by the conviction that every state must, of course, equally feel a French threat to its security. Suffolk brought with him no new insights, and he conducted his business in a relaxed way, spending much of his time in the country. In 1771, believing that Russia was getting all the advantage from the Swedish intrigues, North severely restricted British funds for that purpose. His timing was unfortunate. The Crown Prince of Sweden, Gustavus Adolphus, was in Paris when news reached him of his father's death. He immediately presented himself to Louis XV and it was agreed that he would work to bring about a palace coup which would set aside the constitutional restraints on the Swedish monarchy. In return the arrears of the French subsidy should be paid. It was also agreed that the French embassy in Stockholm should be put in the capable hands of the Comte de Vergennes, who had been ambassador to the Porte until his reluctance to foment war had led Choiseul to replace him with St. Priest. On 19 August 1772 the young King Gustavus III, with funds Vergennes somewhat apprehensively provided, set in motion the coup.[32] It succeeded, and at a stroke France gained decisive influence in Sweden. That put the fat into the fire.

London very rapidly decided to accept the Swedish revolution as a fait accompli. Panin turned to Britain for assistance in reversing the coup, but the partition of Poland among Russia, Prussia, and Austria in 1772, and especially the anti-British behaviour of Russia's ally, Prussia, in Danzig, was doing little to support British warmth towards Russia. On 30 October 1772 Suffolk wrote to Gunning "that after all the Reserve & Inattention which we have experienced from the Court of Petersbourg, We don't wish to be dragged into a War from which this Country has much to lose & nothing to gain."[33]

It was not really possible, however, for London to be content with watching events from afar. Suffolk had earlier observed that he did not think the Russians were in a position to intervene in Sweden by force, writing that "if Russia attempts any thing in Sweden, She must make some sacrifices elsewhere, & patch up a peace with the Turks upon different Terms, than She might otherwise have insisted on."[34] It was an immediate advantage that Russia's embarrassments in the south should prevent her from undertaking military operations in the Baltic. Nevertheless, Britain could not be indifferent if a French success in the Baltic forced Russia to make peace with Turkey.

The worst of it was that if and when Russia did attempt to intervene with military force in Sweden, the inevitable French response would be naval. Suffolk had pointed out to Gunning that "France is too deeply engaged not to support her own work," and, as d'Aiguillon later complained, a subsidy would not be adequate to sustain Sweden. Neither could France risk sending military transports through the Danish straits unless they were escorted by ships of war. The significance of a French naval deployment to the Baltic would be Europe-wide. That London was sensitive to all the implications had been made abundantly apparent when intelligence was received in March 1771 that France might be going to send a squadron to support the King of Sweden. Rochford advised Goodricke and Cathcart, "that altho' the principal Intention professed by France in making this Offer, was to convince the King of Sweden of their Disposition to give Him every possible Succour, it is certainly combined with a Design to oblige Russia to keep back Part of that Naval Force which she may have destined for the Mediterranean."[35]

Control of the Mediterranean was important to enable the British navy to influence continental affairs. Naval control of the Baltic was a more fundamental defensive necessity to ensure access to naval stores from Russia in the event of war. London was prepared to write off the French success in Sweden, but was not prepared to see the French use their navy against Russia. Apparently no comfort could be taken from the thought that such action would embroil France in a war with Russia; the French could certainly be expected to win a war at sea.

The problem for London was complex. The only means available to discourage a Russian act of force was to warn that Britain would not prevent the French intervening in defence of their client. At the same time, the only way to discourage the Swedish king from attempting a vainglorious attack on Russia was to let it be known that Britain would indeed prevent French intervention in the Baltic. In any event, the British were unquestionably determined to prevent the French from using naval force in the Baltic, and if actual war was to be avoided, the French had to be warned of this determination. The outcome was that at the meeting of cabinet on 7 October at which it was decided to retain Harland's forces in the East Indies, it was resolved that Harcourt should be instructed "to declare to the French Ministry, that if they mean to send a fleet either into the Mediterranean or the Baltick for attacking the Russians, we shall in consequence thereof certainly send another, & not suffer the Neutrality, hitherto preserved, to be broken through."

Rochford, forwarding the cabinet minute, wrote Earl Gower: "we are determined to let France knew that we will not be bambouzled, I hope we shall not shew our teeth without biting, 'though I believe it will not be necessary, for I am sure if we are *firm & temperate* we may yet keep all quiet."[36] On the other hand, a month later, on 10 November, Suffolk informed Gunning of "His Majesty's determination not to join in the declaration to the Court of Stockholm." He commented that "Mons. Panin must be devoid of reason to expect the King's concurrence."[37] Both positions had to be maintained simultaneously.

The possible need for a naval confrontation over Sweden, as well as the decision to leave the force in the East Indies intact, led to the decision that the navy vote, which had stood at 25,000, should not be cut to below 20,000. In January, North had been very sympathetic when opposition members had called for a reduction in the vote. To a member's comment, "I hope this expense will be reduced another year," North had shouted "hear hear" and said he did not "consider this augmentation as a peace establishment. God forbid."[38] In September he had tried to persuade Sandwich to agree to a reduction in the strength of the guardship squadron, saying that he did not "recall to have seen a more pacific appearance of affairs than there is at the moment." Sandwich, however, had used the Swedish crisis to justify resistance to the demand.[39]

Especially after the partition of Poland, Russia was an increasingly odious potential ally. The King was disenchanted. Nevertheless, as he wrote to Suffolk on 5 November, "if Russia is attacked by France views of general policy [will] not permit our remaining idle Spectators . . . if France sends a fleet into the Baltick the English Ships cannot remain at home."[40] He added, "indeed, I wish to keep off a war as long as possible," but his ministers were beginning to think that sooner would be better than later if war was inevitable. Rochford circularized the cabinet on the question of whether the opportunity should be taken of fighting a preventive war against Bourbon révanche in circumstances when Russia would be an ally.[41] Sandwich was clear what the decision must be: "I dread the consequence of too long an acquiescence in suffering other great powers to take considerable strides without our interfering."[42]

The eventual cabinet decision was against preventive war. A diplomatic line was adopted which succeeded in the objective of immobilizing France and Russia, but at the expense of all hope of a Russian alliance and also at further cost to Anglo-Turkish relations. The démarche was so brilliant and devious that it is open to question how great a part accident played in the outcome. At the same time that the French were formally but secretly warned against undertaking naval action, informal and even more secret negotiations were begun towards a tentative rapprochement between Britain and France. King George mooted the idea in a memorandum on the partition of Poland. Rochford made overtures to the Comte de Guines and sent a merchant by the name of James Bourdieu to France as a go-between. D'Aiguillon sent the Chevalier de Martagne back to Rochford. Rochford communicated a part of his negotiations to North and the King, but to nobody else.

An accord with France might have been a very sensible way out of Britain's problems, had it been possible. Politically, however, it was not. The English public would not support it. Neither was it practical international politics so long as the French remained dissatisfied with their humbled status. Nevertheless, the rumour of the negotiations, which was fostered by vociferous and unnecessary denials of them by Rochford, alarmed the Russians and may have contributed to their decision to abandon their plans against Sweden. In December 1772 the London Post Office deciphered a letter from de Guines to d'Aiguillon recounting his conversation with Rochford. Rochford protected himself by writing noisy disclaimers to Colonal Horace St. Paul, who was the new secretary of the Paris embassy, and to Lord Grantham, the ambassador who had been sent to Madrid after Harris' recall. This advertising was hardly necessary. On 11 December Gunning reported from Petersburg that the British resolution not to support the Russians in Sweden had the effect of "confirming this court in every suspicion, however unjust . . . of the influence France has over our Councils, of our large Politeness." In January 1773 Goodricke reported that the Russian ambassador at Stockholm, Count Osterman, had warned that, unless the impression of Anglo-French accord were corrected, Russia would be unable to achieve the reversion of the Swedish constitution by threats and would be obliged to attack. Osterman, however, was only posturing. On 10 April Panin showed Gunning a paper in which the Russians disclaimed any intention of assaulting Sweden.[43]

The problem of deterring French adventures remained. In the new year Rochford wrote St. Paul to warn d'Aiguillon that the dispatch of a French fleet to the Baltic "not only could not be seen with indifference by His Majesty, but that we should find Ourselves under the necessity (disagreeable as it would be) to send a Fleet also to the Assistance of Russia."[44] There is a suggestion that Rochford, as part of the secret negotiations, went so far as to offer France a collusive bargain to allow it a head start on a mobilization at Brest of ships intended for the Baltic. However, the offer, if one was indeed made, was apparently limited to seven days and hedged with a warning that the head start would only be illusory because the British would make secret preparations for a counter-mobilization. If he did actually make the offer, Rochford cannot have intended it to be taken seriously.[45] Its real significance can never be known, for the French chose to ignore it. Instead, orders were given for arming a squadron at Toulon.

The first news of this determination reached London from Mme Wolters' agent in Paris, who reported the rumour that a training squadron would be mobilized at Toulon in March. International relations were too strained for it to be possible to believe that the purpose of the squadron was to train seamen, especially as the Admiralty had received intelligence in December 1772 which pointed to a Spanish naval armament of fourteen or fifteen ships to oppose the Russians in the Mediterranean.[46] Lord Stormont, who had just arrived to replace Harcourt as ambassador to France, believed the Toulon squadron was to consist of twelve ships of the line and six frigates: "It seems clear to me [he wrote to Rochford] that there were not only equal objections to a French Fleet in the Mediterranean as to one in the Baltic, but that they were even infinitely greater."[47]

London had an intelligence report which claimed that the Swedes actually preferred money to French troops, which suggested that the French objective was to flaunt their naval power. Rochford wrote to Stormont:

> the Fleet is the object, and the Duke d'Aiguillon's Administration would be for ever glorious, if He could prevail with us to suffer a French Fleet to be parading in the Baltick, and We remain idle lookers on, & see the Powers of the North held in subjugation. . . . We cannot stand upon better ground in our present situation, than by declaring that if France stirs but an Oar, that We will instantly unbend our Sails, the consequence of which must be obvious.[48]

On the 9th he wrote to Grantham in Madrid to inform him of the events of the past week and to say:

Sir Charles Saunders, 1713-75. Engraving by J. McArdell after a portrait by Joshua Reynolds.
Courtesy of the National Maritime Museum, Negative 1057

I need not tell your Excellency that the King can never see the french or Spanish fleets at Sea separated or united without sending out a Force at least equal to theirs . . . from Principles of national Policy, and for the sake of His own Dignity, as well as security, His Majesty must always make as respectable an Appearance at Sea as his Neighbours, and the Consequence of such Armaments are too obvious to need be mentioned.[49]

London intensified the pressure upon d'Aiguillon by making it clear that if it became necessary to mobilize, it would be difficult to prevent war. Stormont cautioned d'Aiguillon that "when the fleets of two great high-spirited nations were near each other, it was a dangerous neighbourhood indeed."[50] Suffolk was more direct when he wrote to Stormont on 14 April: "it is not right that the Duke d'Aiguillon should deceive himself by imagining that a British Fleet when once out, in such a crisis as this is, can parade about the seas doing nothing, and that His Majesty can long continue without taking a decisive part."[51]

This interpretation of the significance of sending ships to sea is borne out by the assertion of Sir Charles Saunders, who was later made commander of the British squadron when it was eventually brought forward for service. "Upon its being said, that our equipment would be only a fleet of observation [Mrs. Hood wrote to Lady Chatham] Sir Charles said, 'If I sail, it will be a war'."[52] Besides the danger involved in confining two admirals in the same sea, there was also the obvious likelihood that once Britain was forced to make an open move to counter any French one it would become apparent to Russia that she could count on Britain's support. On 10 April, Gunning had reported to London that Panin had abandoned any intention to use force against Sweden, but this letter was not received until 4 May, and even then it could not be known for certain whether British action to check France might not bring the Russians to change their plans yet again.[53]

It was believed in Britain that the implied threat of war would be sufficient. On 8 April, Rochford bluntly assured Stormont: "we have all the reason in the world to believe that the French Ministry will be bullied."[54] On the 14th Suffolk wrote to the King that it was pretty clear that d'Aiguillon would not stand up to Britain's firm demands, and he asked "whether some Ships shou'd not be ordered to Spithead" immediately.[55] Two days later, however, he suggested that, as the British navy was always in a state of preparedness, a few days' delay in ordering mobilization would make little difference.[56] The King was encouraged by an intercepted letter saying that d'Aiguillon would not go to war. He wrote to North that he wanted all the guardships ordered fully manned and sent to Spithead, while another twenty ships were brought forward from ordinary. Stormont should be instructed to "remain silent."[57]

On the 21st the government reached its decision. Instead of twenty, fifteen guardships were ordered into service and fifteen ships were brought forward from ordinary to replace them. A proportionate number of frigates were also ordered.[58] A bounty was proclaimed for seamen who volunteered, and Sir Charles Saunders was appointed commander-in-chief of the squadron which was intended for the Mediterranean.[59]

On the very day the British began to mobilize, d'Aiguillon said casually to Stormont that the armament at Toulon had been suspended, using as the reason the apparent decision of the Russians not to intervene in Sweden.[60] When Rochford informed de Guines of the British armament, the latter seemed to intimate that the result would be the countermanding of the Toulon squadron.[61] Neither of these statements could be relied upon completely. When the news of the British armament reached Paris, however, it seemed to have the desired effect. Stormont wrote:

It seems to be, My Lord, that the only Difficulty at present is, to have sufficient Security for the armament at Toulon's not going on, without *demanding* any such Security, the insisting on which as it would carry, at least in their Eyes, the appearance of our *awing* them into this Disarmament, would be very painful, and by hurting their National Pride might make them from the Passion of the moment, resume a Design which their Reason condemns.[62]

Grantham reported from Madrid that Grimaldi had news that d'Aiguillon was willing to reduce the fleet of twelve ships at Toulon to a token squadron of five. Spain would fight in support of France, but Grantham did not think it would go to the aid of Sweden.[63]

The cabinet seems to have come to the conclusion that their tactics had already been successful. On the 25th King George wrote to North that he had always believed that when M. de Martagne, d'Aiguillon's emissary, returned to Paris the French fleet would be countermanded. As a result of d'Aiguillon's declaration, the King directed the Secretaries of State to say publicly "that the letters arrived from France this day give reason to think the fleet will be countermanded, that therefore it is hoped we may do the same in a few days." He ordered Sandwich not to commission any ships besides the fifteen guardships, and he delayed demobilizing the guardships pending the return of a messenger from Versailles giving confirmation of the French concession.[64]

This, however, was not to be the end of the confrontation. London was confused because de Guines said that the Toulon armament was cancelled but d'Aiguillon would not, as yet, admit to more than its suspension. It was felt necessary to be tactful. Rochford wrote the King on 27 April to say that, as ordered, he had conferred with North and Suffolk and had decided to ask de Guines to meet him. It had been agreed that he should "talk to the French ambassador, as if this contradiction in his language and the D'Daiguillon's [sic] must be owing to a mistake."[65]

Four days later he reported that "the French Ambassador said [to a confidant] he did not know what to think of this business for one party in France informed him they were disarming whilst another Party told him the contrary."[66] The next day de Guines waited on Rochford to assure him that he had received advice from d'Aiguillon that the armament was suspended and, further, that the French ships would not sail at all, even on exercises. Rochford was confident that this was the end of the business. Nonetheless he recommended that no order be sent to the Admiralty until official statements were received from Paris.[67]

The secret service had kept the progress of the French armament under observation, but owing to the time it took for letters to cross Europe, London was two weeks behind on reports from Toulon. The secret service had discovered, and reported on 12 April, that at Toulon a squadron of two 80-gun ships, three 74-gun ships, three 64s, one 50, and two 32-gun frigates had been ordered to prepare for sea under the command of the Comte d'Estaing of Indian and Turks Island fame. A 74 and two 64s were arming at Brest and seven other frigates were ordered to be ready by 10 May at Toulon.[68] The governor of Minorca, Mr. Johnson, had also reported that orders had been sent from Madrid to fit twenty men of war at Cartagena.[69] On 26 April intelligence reported that it was now thought that the twelve ships could not be ready before 15 May despite the six months of preparation which apparently had been going on and the adequate number of seamen.[70] Consul Cook at Turin in Savoy even reported that the squadron could not be ready until June.[71] Later information, however, suggests that the Toulon squadron would have been ready soon after 10 May, when it was ordered suspended, although it might have been smaller than originally thought.[72]

Not surprisingly, the belated arrival of this intelligence, in conjunction with the uncertainty about d'Aiguillon's intentions, created some alarm in London. Such was the success of the reorganization of the British guardship system, however, that the French got no benefit from their head start. As early as 28 April, Vice Admiral Pye at Portsmouth was able to report that the squadron only needed a few days to complete its three-month bread supply.[73] Rochford told Grantham on the 30th that the British force was within ten days of being ready in all respects for sea.[74] On 6 May, when definite word came from Paris of the French intention to disarm, the British preparations were suspended,[75] and orders were given for the discharge of the supernumeraries recruited to man the guardships. Rochford was proud to report to Stormont that "the same Expedition will be used in executing these Orders for the Reduction, as was employed in the Preparations for arming, which were carried on with such extraordinary Activity that the whole Fleet destined for foreign Service, if the Occasion had required it, would be at this instant entirely ready to sail."[76]

Once again British rejoicing was premature. On 12 May Rochford was jolted by a report that the French had not in fact suspended their armament. Later secret service reports were to bear out this suspicion, as it was not until 9 or 10 May that definite orders were given to stop the mobilization, and not until the 17th that orders for disarming ships were received in Toulon.[77] Naturally London, a few days behind on Paris news and two weeks on that from Toulon, feared treachery. Rochford hurriedly wrote to Stormont, and in a private letter he described the problem which he faced.

> I cannot conceive what the Duke d'Aiguillon means by this Duplicity, every pains must be taken to convince him that we are in earnest, for I

am under apprehensions he believes we are not so from a notion we wish Russia should not attack Sweden—To be sure we do but still if Russia does we shall *bon gré mal gré nous* be engaged—Convince him of this. . . . I am just come from Portsmouth, the Tars are ready more so than the most sanguine expectations could lead me to believe, & if the thing grows serious we shall have the start of them—There is not a diversity of opinion in councel but my own private opinion is, that if Russia does resolve to attack Sweden France is too far dipt to desist.[78]

On the same day Philip Stephens sent off an express to Admiral Pye forbidding him to discharge the supernumeraries manning the guardships.[79] The order was made unostentatiously and possibly with an unusual degree of secrecy. Pye received the letter at 7 A.M. the next day and promptly suspended the demobilization. Unfortunately, the supernumeraries in *Barfleur* had already been paid off, but the remainder were kept in service.[80]

In the end the misunderstanding, if that is the proper term, was corrected. On 18 May, Stormont wrote to Rochford that d'Aiguillon had told him definitely that the Toulon force had been countermanded.[81] King George passed the news on to North on the 21st with the comment that the Admiralty could now reduce to peace conditions, although the guardships should remain at Spithead.[82] On the 25th, at a meeting of cabinet at Lord Suffolk's house, it was resolved to carry out the orders to reduce to a peace establishment.[83] For a while a watch was kept on the Spanish armament, reported to number twenty-nine ships ready for service.[84] Even that threat passed. It was known that the Spaniards would have aided the French if attacked but were not interested in Sweden.[85] On 9 June H. M. sloop *Pomona* looked into Cartagena and saw that that squadron had been dismantled.[86]

There was and still is considerable disagreement concerning the effect of the British mobilization. On 11 June Suffolk wrote to Sir Joseph Yorke, ambassador in The Netherlands:

> Your Excellency will have heard of His Majesty's intended Visit to his Fleet at Portsmouth. The Copy d'Oeil will not be quite so sublime & interesting as if the Preparations at Toulon & Ferrol had gone on; But there will still be sufficient scope for the fine Feelings both of the Imaginations & the Heart, at the Review of an Armament to which Europe is certainly indebted for the Preservation of Peace & the Blessings which attend it.[87]

The King's review of the guardships was made a great spectacle of British power.[88] Horace Walpole was not impressed. ''Our [naval armament] being so formidable will, I suppose, be towed overland to Warsaw and restore the

Polish Constitution and their King to his full rights—how frightened the King of Prussia must be.''[89] However, there was no doubt in most British minds that the fifteen-ship mobilization, by indicating a British determination to risk war, had frustrated d'Aiguillon's intention to assist Turkey and Sweden in one move and to present Britain with a fait accompli which only war or the explicit threat of war could have reversed. This belief was essentially correct; d'Aiguillon admitted as much to M. Saint-Priest, the French ambassador at the Porte.[90] Peace had been preserved by abandoning Russia and by the apparent collusion with France, and the French were restrained by the obvious resolve of the British to go to war rather than let a French squadron alter the course of European history. The threat had been used in a restrained manner which had allowed d'Aiguillon to bow to it, and when d'Aiguillon had later appeared to be contemplating resisting British demands, the threat had been kept in the background. There could and can be no doubt that the British fleet, admittedly on a small scale, had beaten the French in the race for mobilization. Considering the turmoil de Boynes' reorganization had caused in the French navy, this is not surprising.

Britain had defeated French efforts to use naval forces to influence the events of Europe, but victory had proved to be elusive. French influence remained supreme in Sweden and powerful in south central Europe. Britain had finally lost her one hope of an ally, and because Saint-Priest had little difficulty in persuading the Turks that the Toulon squadron had been intended for their assistance, British interests with the Porte had suffered another blow.[91] It is difficult, however, to see how the British could have handled the Swedish crisis better. Had they abandoned Russia to her fate the French might well have converted the Baltic into a source of strength dangerous to Britain. To have gambled on the French becoming embroiled in a Russian war would have been a risky venture, as the French were believed to be more than a match for the Russians. Had the Porte obtained the assistance of a French squadron it is possible that Russia might not have obtained the right to navigate the Dardanelles, as she did in 1774 in the treaty of Kuchuk Kainarji. For London, however, the Russian navy was by far the lesser of evils.

The resolution of the crisis did at least make possible the reduction of the naval establishment. The first of a stream of reports telling of arrangements being made at the Ile de France for the withdrawal of some of the royal troops had been received in London on 15 October, a week after the decision had been taken to leave Harland with all his ships. Five homeward-bound French ships were reported passing the Cape, two of them carrying troops.[92] After the dénouement of the Swedish crisis, on 16 August 1773, Rochford directed the Admiralty to recall Harland. Only the *Dolphin* and the sloop *Swallow* were left in India, to be joined later by a 50-gun ship and a frigate.[93]

In January 1773, Buller, a lord of Admiralty, told the Commons that it was expected that the East Indies squadron would be home by Christmas. North promised that that would allow a reduction of the vote from 20,000 to 17,000 men.[94] The promise was not kept exactly, but the vote for 1775 was reduced to 18,000 men.

6

Minimal Deterrence: French Intervention in the American Revolution

THE IBERIAN IMBROGLIO AND THE EFFECT OF BUNKER HILL

The Boston Tea Party in December 1773 had focused attention on the revolt in America, but the style of British foreign policy was not immediately affected. In early 1774 the North administration was warned of a possible Swedish-Bourbon manoeuvre to oblige Turkey to accept French mediation. Although the King thought ''The Conduct of our Colonies make Peace very desirable,'' it is probable that the British response would have been up to form had the Bourbons actually attempted such a démarche.[1]

The succession of the nineteen-year old King Louis XVI in May 1774 led to the formation of a new administration of the French government headed by the Comte de Maurepas, the Comte de Vergennes taking the Foreign Ministry. The new king was not eager to court international trouble and his concern to re-establish the royal treasury was manifested by his appointment of M. Turgot to the office of Comptroller General. So long as Turgot retained office expenditure on the French navy would be severely restricted, although Louis XVI was receptive to the need to repair the damage done by de Boyne's ill-advised reforms of the navy administration. Gabriel de Sartine, who was transferred from the command of the Paris police to fill the office of Minister of the Marine, which Turgot had briefly taken from de Boynes, was able in November 1774 to obtain the repeal of de Boynes' *ordonnances*.[2]

London was not alarmed by the changes in French leadership, although it was ominous that on his return to Paris in July 1774 Stormont was faced with a French resolution to resume work on the Dunkirk quays. Rochford's reaction was firm. He wrote to Sandwich: ''it is clear to me they will never quarrell with us solely on the account of Dunkirk, & therefore if they push it

Rt. Hon. Frederick Lord North, 2nd Earl of Guildford, 1732-92 Engraving by I. Burke after a painting by N. Dance.
Courtesy of the British Museum (Class II period 4; 1920.10.11.459) Negative 1/2 pl. P.S. 004217

now it will be in vain yielding."[3] A measure of the confidence felt by the North administration can be gained by the decision which was made to reduce the strength of the fleet by 4,000 men in December 1774, although 2,000 of those were restored to the naval strength in February 1775, probably because of the need for crews in American waters.[4] Whether or not Sandwich was really satisfied by the return of 2,000 men, he felt able to give the House of Lords a very reassuring account of the state of the navy.[5]

The decision to impose a naval blockade on North America to enforce the excise law made a collision with France a possibility, although Vergennes offered no objection when advised in January 1775 of the Admiralty order to intercept all ships in North American waters. He claimed that no French vessels were engaged in the contraband trade.[6] In November and December, and again on 25 February 1775, Sandwich was able to forward to Rochford intelligence received from an agent he had established in the Brittany town of Morlaix, indicating that there was very little activity at Brest dockyard.[7] Rochford, however, also advised Stormont to be vigilant about any activity in French dockyards, as the only reliable indicator of Bourbon intentions: "at this juncture it will be very proper for Your Excellency to watch narrowly the Motions of the French in their Ports."[8]

It may have been in the hope of keeping the French amenable that it was decided in the spring of 1775 to accept liability for the losses French fishermen suffered in 1772 when they were wrongfully evicted from Bonavista, Newfoundland.[9] However, it is evident that the North cabinet was not yet dominated by the need to avoid hostilities with France. When a report was received that French traders were again operating in British-claimed African territory, two frigates were sent "to stop and seize any Vessels that were carrying on a Contraband Trade."[10] Perhaps it is not surprising the French did not agree to reciprocate the concession over Newfoundland by paying the long overdue claim of the East India Company for the maintenance of French prisoners during the Seven Years' War.[11]

London's continued self-confidence was further demonstrated when, perhaps largely because of Horace St. Paul's injudicious reading of evidence, there was a brief war scare in April 1775. The Under-Secretary of State, Sir Stanier Porten, was given a nasty shock when an extraordinary messenger arrived posthaste from Paris with a report that Versailles had ordered nineteen ships of the line brought forward.[12] Suffolk was puzzled, but complaisantly commented to Earl Gower: *"c'es[t] le Tem[p]s qui dé couvre le vent!* as was said you know when the Figure of Time was represented in a Desert looking up a pretty Girls Petticoats."[13] Rochford lost no time in making it clear that Britain would match any French squadron.[14]

The military adventures of the Spanish government were the principal cause of concern in London in the first half of 1775, and were eventually to form the context for the development in London of a new defence policy which minimized confrontation with the Bourbon powers. At the end of July 1774, Grantham warned that Madrid had ordered the preparation of a few ships for an expedition to Vera Cruz. There was good reason to believe that the Spanish government might be contemplating sending forces to South America. The failure of Spain to satisfy Portuguese claims in Paraguay after the conclusion of the war there in 1764 had led the Marquis de Pombal, in the name of King Joseph I, to send troops to enforce Portuguese pretensions. Britain was necessarily involved because Portugal constituted an important element in Britain's naval strategy. Portugal was a long-established ally. In the Seven Years' War it had been necessary for Britain to defend her, and Portuguese armed forces had not flourished under Pombal, but Portugal was important as a sleeping partner. The use of the port of Lisbon was nearly indispensable to British naval operations in the Mediterranean, and the denial of Portuguese harbours to Spain made the latter more vulnerable to British attacks on her trade.

The Portuguese problem was complicated, and obscured, by Spanish ambitions in other directions. Grimaldi had been elevated in 1773 from Foreign Minister to President of the Council in place of the unpopular Conde d'Aranda, who was sent to Paris as ambassador. To mark his enhanced station by a spectacular foreign policy success, he ordered a military expedition to destroy the great corsair port of Algiers. The plan was soon known in Algiers, where it was accepted at face value. Suitable precautions were taken to thwart it. London, however, had to view the alleged objective with suspicion. A diplomatic line was taken with Madrid which was comparable to that taken throughout the decade and more since the Peace of Paris. When Morocco declared war on Spanish Ceuta, making it improbable that Madrid would seek trouble elsewhere, the British ministry relaxed somewhat.[15] Nevertheless, on 20 March 1775 a letter was received from Robert Walpole, who was now ambassador in Lisbon, which made it clear that there was no foundation for the belief that an accommodation had been reached between Spain and Portugal.[16] The reports of Spanish armament continued to flow in and they had to be watched closely.[17]

Alarm was increased when the Spanish embassy chose this moment to raise again the question of the East India Company's post at Balambangan in the Sulu archipelago. Obviously it could be the intention of Spain to find a pretext for war. Rochford wrote two letters to Grantham. In a cipher letter by messenger he wrote: "We must soon know whether Africa is the sole Object of Spain or only a Pretext for deeper views," and he explained: "My Separate Letter No 11 of this date is purposely sent out Cypher, that it may be seen in France or Spain." In the unciphered letter which thus served as an indirect warning in the Bourbon Courts he wrote that he hoped "Balambangan will not turn out another Falkland Island business."[18] Sandwich took the opportunity to declare in the House of Lords that the British fleet was in admirable condition, and could be at sea "on a few days notice."[19] However, Madrid did not on this occasion want war with Britain. Grimaldi assured Grantham that no orders had been sent to effect a dispossession of the British post at Balambangan.[20] On 28 July, three days after the arrival in London of news of Bunker Hill, it was learned that the Spanish armada had indeed attacked Algiers, where it had been decisively defeated.[21]

The temporary release of anxiety about Spanish intentions did nothing to reduce the psychological impact in London caused by the news that General Gage had suffered heavy casualties making a frontal assault on rebel positions on Bunker Hill. London became obsessed with the problems of the North American campaign. On 23 August a *Proclamation of Rebellion* was issued forbidding all intercourse with the rebel colonies and authorizing the seizure of colonial shipping. Attention was turned to securing the position in North America for the winter. Five Irish regiments were ordered to stand by to proceed to Boston, and Hanoverian regiments were hired to garrison Gibraltar and Minorca to release British regiments. General Gage was recalled and General Howe given command with orders to transfer his force from Boston to New York.

During the summer of 1775 the campaign in North America began to put heavy pressure on the navy. Thirty ships, including two second rates, were in North American waters, and in the second half of the year twenty more ships were sailed. Sandwich said that "it was the intention of administration to complete the number, by the time that operations were commenced [in 1776], to seventy vessels."[22] In order to man this number, the Privy Council had agreed on 16 June to authorize impressment for North American service.[23] On 27 September it also agreed to enlarge the navy estimates to 26,000 men from 18,000, at a cost of £1,352,000; and on 27 October it agreed to increase the fleet further to 28,000 men, which it was subsequently estimated would cost £1,456,000.[24]

Vergennes was convinced that a British army could not recover America. After the news of Bunker Hill he wrote to de Guines: "It will be vain for the English to multiply their forces there . . . no longer can they bring that vast continent back to dependence by force of arms."[25] British observers on the whole, however, believed that the rebellion could only be sustained so long as the Americans could hope for support in Europe. After his retirement Rochford urged a treaty of guarantee among the European colonial powers which would "make the Americans despair of that foreign aid which their Congress has hung out to them," declaring that he was confident "it would Conquer America sooner than 20,000 soldiers."[26] The attitude of France was clearly of the utmost importance.

St. Paul's opinion, for what it was worth, was that "a weaker Ministry than the present cannot be formed; and I am persuaded, that at this moment they have not any plan whatever." Maurepas he disparaged as "more a man of Pleasure than Business" and Vergennes as "merely the Ostensible Minister." Turgot was "solely taken up with his projects for the Reestablishment of the Finances of this Country." So long as King Louis retained his aversion to Choiseul, St. Paul could foresee no danger from France.[27]

This opinion of the French government had to contend with the evidence which reached London of French military preparations and suspicious activities. On 12 July, Frazer wrote from Dunkirk warning that four batallions had been ordered to Brest to reinforce Martinique and Guadeloupe.[28] On the same day, St. Paul wrote that he had reason to believe that the French were supplying the American rebels via St. Domingo.[29] Two days later the Admiralty forwarded to Rochford warning that there appeared to be plans to smuggle military stores into North America from St. Croix.[30]

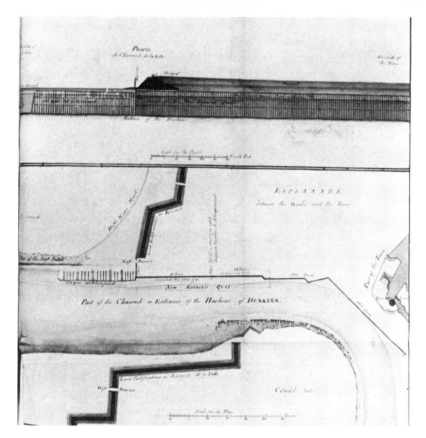

Plan and elevation of the engineering works at Dunkirk Harbour,
prepared by the British agent Andrew Frazer, 7 August 1775.
Courtesy of the Public Record Office, ref. no. SP 78/296

From Turin, Lynch warned, in a letter received 23 June, that "a
Commission arrived at Toulon last week to inspect all the Ships of War
there, and to put in Repair all such as may want it."[31] Three weeks later he
wrote again that all the ships at Toulon were being cleaned and that biscuit
was being baked.[32]

It really began to appear that London had misjudged the pacific intent of
Versailles when de Guines made a formal complaint to Rochford about
threats allegedly made by the frigate *Aldborough* to a French warship. He
also urged an agreement on the Newfoundland fisheries and said that the
settlement of the East India Company claims would be undertaken, but
only, as Rochford advised St. Paul,

provided we would adjust the Affair at Chandernagore at the same time. This is so dirty a way of getting off the payment of a Debt in which their honour is pledged, and this kind of Language at this very critical time is so unpleasant that I thought it incumbent on me to tell Mons de Guines that however critical our Situation was with the American Rebels, his Court must not expect to find us in the least disposed to yield the smallest of our Rights or Pretensions.[33]

A week later news was received from Frazer that not four but six battalions were being sent to the West Indies. When pressed for further information he said that although October was the normal time for relief of foreign garrisons, on this occasion there was no word of any battalions ordered to return to Europe. He also advised that although there was no evidence of intention to exceed the terms of the peace treaty with respect to Dunkirk, the assurance de Guines had made that the new quay would be restricted in extent was misleading because technical terms had been misused.[34] On 14 August a letter was received from Lynch warning that four ships of unknown force were preparing for America, and, on 12 September, Frazer reported that a ship belonging to Americans had landed a cargo at Dunkirk.[35] Finally, on the 13th, St. Paul forwarded the rumour that the squadron of evolutions, when it returned to Brest, would immediately refit for sea.[36]

Despite his belief that containment of the French was fundamental to the outcome of the rebellion, Rochford did not risk putting French good faith to the test. The pattern of British diplomacy from 1763 to 1775 indicated that London could be expected to respond vigorously to French machinations, using naval forces to frustrate them even at the risk of war. In the aftermath of Bunker Hill, Rochford did nothing of the sort. He instructed St. Paul to make discreet enquiries about the West Indian reinforcements which were now rumoured, despite de Guines' assertion there would be no more than three, to number ten battalions. He was instructed, however, to make no formal complaint about French supplies being sent to the rebels.[37]

Instead of confronting France, Rochford adopted a policy of seeking French co-operation. There is a sympathetic echo with Rochford's secret approach to France during the Swedish crisis, but Bunker Hill produced policy changes which went well beyond anything attempted in 1773. On 27 October, Stormont, who had returned to Paris, was instructed to ask Vergennes to drop for the moment consideration of a Newfoundland settlement because in the circumstances it would be "construed by the World a compulsory one."[38] When Pombal precipitated another Iberian crisis by preparing reinforcements to be sent to South America, London sought French support for mediation. On 21 September, Grantham warned that Spain was unlikely to tolerate new attacks in Paraguay, and Hardy wrote from Cadiz of preparation for sea of ships in the arsenal.[39] When Stormont told Vergennes that Britain was bound to support her ally, Vergennes replied that "the great Point to be aimed at now, is to prevent things coming to that Extremity, and to use our Good Offices either jointly, or separately to hinder a Rupture."[40]

Rochford was uneasy about making common cause with the French. He wrote Stormont: "We must not be made use of to intimidate an Ally, especially as We avoid encouraging Them to take any risk or offensive Step."[41] On the other hand, there was great suspicion of Pombal and of the two Souza brothers, who were ambassadors to Madrid and Versailles. Walpole reported that Pombal had said Spain was offering an alliance which obviously would be anti-British, but Walpole suspected that the offer was an invention of Pombal to put pressure on Britain to provide support.[42]

In one of the last dispatches before ill health and possibly disgust with the way things were going in America brought his resignation, Rochford impressed upon Walpole that

> there can be no doubt of the Court of Spain's assembling a prodigious Force and preparing for something early next Spring. If against Portugal, and I have no doubt of it, the War will soon become general. Surely Mons. Pombal will reflect a little on our present embarassed [sic] situation, which I hope and believe another Campaign will put an end to, and that he will not be so unwise as to precipitate measures at this unfavourable Juncture.[43]

Indicative of the extent to which British foreign policy had changed from the palmy days of 1764 is the concern that was felt in London that Weymouth could not return to the Southern Department without a personal quarrel he had had with Masserano bringing about a breakdown of relations with Spain. Weymouth, however, made every effort to defuse the Iberian crisis.[44] He wrote repeatedly to Walpole, instructing him "by every argument [to] enforce the propriety that all hostilities should cease during the Negotiations."[45] In Paris, Stormont earnestly warned Souza of the danger of courting war with Spain.

> It was well known [he told him] how much of our Naval Force, was necessarily employed in America, that tho' our Zeal for the Interests of Portugal would be ever the same, tho' I was persuaded, that no Difficulty of situation would hinder us, from fulfilling our Engagements to the utmost of our Power, yet it was very clear, that our Support must be less Efficacious, at a time when we had so much untoward Business of our own, upon our Hands.[46]

Pombal attempted to demonstrate to Walpole "how unable those two Courts [i.e., France and Spain] are to carry on a war." He was convinced "that a proper Language of His Majesty's Ambassadors at Paris and Madrid held at this time at those Courts, would compel the Court of Madrid to come into the terms desired by this Court."[47] His suggestions were not welcome in London. At the end of 1775 the North cabinet were determined to isolate the American revolt from European politics. The policy was to buy time, and the prerequisite for that seems to have been a measure of wishful thinking. Rochford's proposal from retirement that France and Spain might enter into a treaty of guarantee of colonial territory indicates that he was as eager as was Weymouth to hide his head from facts which ten years earlier would have convinced him of French designs. The arrival of news on 23 December that American forces were besieging Montreal and Quebec could only serve to reinforce the wish to avoid hostilities in Europe. In February 1776, Stormont unwittingly summed up London's suspension of disbelief:

> France does, & must see our difficulties with that Secret pleasure, with which it is natural to behold a Rival's distress, and tho' I believe it highly probably, that she does, and will [continue to] contrive to give the Americans such secret assistance, as may tend to feed the Rebellion, and waste our strength by a long and difficult war; yet I must say, My Lord, that I do not think it likely that the present French ministry will take a bold and open part against us.[48]

AN ARMS RACE IN SLOW MOTION

In the months following Bunker Hill the only evidence of French hostility which London could not ignore were the intelligence reports from French dockyards. At the beginning of January 1776 Weymouth had alerted Lynch at Turin to watch for activity at Toulon, and at the end of February Lynch reported solid intelligence of the preparation of a *flotte d'évolution* to be commanded by no less a personality than the Duc de Chartres, a cousin of the King.[49] By then Stormont had his own intelligence of the armament which he thought would number sixteen ships taken from the Atlantic as well as the Mediterranean dockyards.[50] In the following weeks London received a continuous stream of intelligence concerning preparations for the exercise and revealing the especially ominous news that the Brest division under Admiral du Chaffault was to meet the Toulon division at Cadiz, where the Spanish Admiral Don Gaston was preparing his forces.[51] Finally Lynch wrote to inform London that the Duc de Chartres had sailed 3 May and that the remaining ships of the line at Toulon were being put in condition to be fitted out on short notice.[52]

Charles Gravier, Comte de Vergennes, 1771-87. Engraving by Vangchoti after a painting by Calles.
Courtesy of the British Museum (French Portraits 1891.5.11. 275) Negative 145581

At first no very great alarm had been taken at these naval preparations. London was far more concerned by the problem of the Hispano-Portuguese dispute, and continued to rely upon France as an ally in its settlement. A French suggestion that a congress be held at Paris was accepted with alacrity. Quite unlike the more normal refusal to permit France any part in mediation, Paris was actually preferred as the site for the congress because it was believed that there was a better chance of a settlement if the meetings took place in France. Stormont intervened to dissuade Souza from seeking to transfer the location to London.[53]

By the time Lynch's notice of the sailing of the *flotte d'évolution* was received, however, news had also been received from St. Paul, who was in charge again at the Paris embassy, which made the sailing of a training exercise at a time of crisis between Spain and Portugal appear ominous. He believed that France had ordered the immediate armament of twenty ships in response to the Conde d'Aranda's insistence that whether Britain won or lost in North America she was bound to become more dangerous.[54] When questioned indirectly about the report, Vergennes uneasily answered that they were *not arming*, but that, *nous ne devions pas être étonnés s'ils travaillaient dans leurs Ports,* that every body did right to be prepared, & that tho he was persuaded of the honour, and sincerity of Our Friendly Professions, yet that Our ministry was not always *le maître*, and that the nations voice might force them to take measures to which they might themselves be very averse; that We had once done them a great deal of harm when they were not prepared.[55]

This last was a reference to the orders given before the formal declaration of war in 1756 to the Channel commanders to seize French shipping.

Four days later, on 12 May, St. Paul sent further news which might have warned London that the French had embarked upon a new policy; Turgot had resigned. The reason then unknown to the British was his objection to granting the American revolutionaries a subsidy (which Spain matched) and to the secret supply of arms to the rebels. The decision to do so had followed protracted debates between February and May, during which Vergennes had urged Louis XVI to seize the opportunity to debase British strength and Turgot had argued for retrenchment and domestic fiscal reform. Repair of the navy was seen by Vergennes as necessary to deter British reprisal, but Turgot had recognized that arming the fleet would itself be provocative. His disgrace, therefore, ensured support for the Americans, although Louis at first only allowed limited funds for that purpose. When he agreed to supply the rebels he also confirmed a decision, rumour of which had led St. Paul to question Vergennes, that besides continuing the frigate patrols and the overhaul of ships, twelve ships should be brought forward and held in readiness at Brest and eight at Toulon. The stocks of supplies were also to be built up. These provisions were to give Sartine an effective lever for obtaining increased appropriations for the navy.[56]

London could not know all the implications of the political changes in France. In the King's speech on the opening of Parliament on 23 May, he stated that "no alteration has happened in the state of foreign affairs."[57] Vergennes' advice that the discussion of a settlement between Portugal and Spain should be transferred to Madrid was accepted, and Weymouth wrote Robert Walpole to put pressure on Pombal.[58] Horace Walpole, however, noted in his journal: "The Comte de Noailles was named Ambassador to England, a poor security to us, when two such pacific men as Turgot and Malesherbes were removed."[59]

If there remained any illusion in London about the need to watch the French, it was soon dispelled. On 5 June, St. Paul was able to forward a list of the fleet in Brest which included twenty-three ships and eleven frigates.[60] On 8 June, Sandwich forwarded to Weymouth intelligence from Morlaix, dated the 1st, saying that the squadron which had sailed had been "armed, victualled, as, in War time.'' And on 15 June he had further information from Morlaix that eighteen ships and twelve frigates had been ordered prepared to fifteen days' notice.[61] In fact, only twelve ships had been so ordered, but the authorities in Brest had advised Sartine on 22 May that sixteen ships could be ready by September and another six by the end of the year. Because only twelve had been authorized, Sartine had to stop work on four ships, but three of them were by then nearly ready. British intelligence had not been so far off.[62]

At the same time, reports had been coming in from Spain. On 7 May a letter had been received from Grantham in which he said he thought the Spanish armament was intended ''to influence the Answer of the Court of Portugal by a Shew of Preparations.''[63] Hardy advised that there was substantial military activity on the borders of Portugal and said that it was believed that there would be formed in Cadiz a fleet of nearly thirty sail of the line besides frigates and two bomb ketches.[64] A month later the fleet was believed to be no more than a squadron of five 70s, two 26-gun frigates, two sloops, and a chaveque of 30 guns.[65] Nevertheless Grantham reported the arrival of the Toulon squadron at Alicant.[66] On the 14th was received the news from Hardy that Gaston's squadron had sailed on 21 May. Reportedly it sailed with only forty days' provisions and half-manned. With or without French assistance, it was a potent factor in the Portuguese dispute.[67]

In Sandwich's view the time had now come for Britain to take steps to improve the state of her defence. On 20 June he had a ''Précis of Advices and Intelligence'' drawn up, at the end of which it was noted ''that France and Spain have, or will soon have a larger number of Ships in Commission in Europe than we have, and that they may have double the number unless we immediately take proper measures to keep pace with them in our Equipments.'' It was particularly worrying that a 64 and two frigates had already sailed for Ile de France with troops and ammunition and that with the reinforcements recently sent to the West Indies, there were 7,000 men of the French army in the islands. Accompanying the précis was a paper in which Sandwich outlined the present condition of the British forces in home waters and presented his recommendations to cabinet. He said there were nineteen guardships which might be ready, ''with the aid of a press'' for sea in a fortnight and one other ordered fitted as a guardship. ''All our Frigates (that do not want considerable repair) including Ships of 50 guns, and two of 64, are in America, or appropriated for the American Service, so that we have nothing left for our Home Stations except two Frigates of 32 Guns, and 8 Sloops, and 9 cutters.'' Those, with twenty tenders, were to be disposed for raising volunteers and to be ready to conduct a press. Above that number ''there will seldom be less than 5 or 6 Frigates in England fitting out for America, or of those that from time to time will be coming home to refit.''

There were about 15,000 seamen in the American service and 8,000 at home with 7,000 on other stations. "In case of war [he continued] 80 Ships of the Line may be depended upon as ready for sea (if there is no difficulty about getting men) within a year from the time of them receiving orders to fit out; but it must be observed that it will usually require a month to prepare each Ship for receiving men, and at least two months more before she will be manned and ready for sea."

To contain the threat from the Bourbon mobilizations, Sandwich recommended that the guardship strength be brought up to twenty-four and that twelve other ships of the line be "got in readiness to receive men, which would put them in the state we suppose the Fleet at Brest now to be in, as far as the preparation of the Ships in the Dock Yards; for it is to be apprehended that they can raise Seamen to a certain number much faster than we can." The workmen in the dockyards would have to be permitted to work double tides, and to facilitate a sudden mobilization, should it be necessary, marine companies were to be increased from 90 to 100 men, more volunteer seamen raised, and preparations made for an efficient press.

Copies of the précis and paper are to be found in both the King's archive and in Weymouth's papers at Longleat. Their content was evidently presented at a cabinet meeting held that same day, 20 June, at the Admiralty office. Agreement was reached to increase the number of guardships and to step up the recruitment of men. However, the cabinet did not sanction Sandwich's additional twelve ships. The matter was apparently strenuously debated: a sentence in Sandwich's record of the cabinet minutes which stated "that til further intelligence is received any further preparations are unnecessary" was crossed out and did not appear in the copy sent to Weymouth. Sandwich did without the ships themselves for another month.[68]

The need to increase Britain's naval preparation was soon emphasized when St. Paul, in a letter received 23 June, forwarded the intelligence that of ships and frigates together, twelve were to be made ready at Brest, three at Rochefort, two at l'Orient, and sixteen at Toulon.[69] This intelligence was extremely accurate. Only eight ships had, in fact, been authorized for Toulon, but Sartine knew that an additional eight could be made ready for another one million livres.[70] St. Paul further reported that it was believed Count d'Estaing would command any large force which might be sent out "for the safety of the French Colonies." When asked about the report that biscuit was being made at Brest, always a sign that it was intended to send ships to sea, Vergennes had replied that only a small quantity was being baked. St. Paul's discoveries were confirmed by Frazer, who reported from Dunkirk that all the signs suggested a considerable armament. He wrote "that an uncommon demand has been made for workmen. In the department of Flanders alone, (beginning with Dunkirk & ending with St.

Vallery,) orders are received to send off to Brest a hundred Carpenters or Caulkers and a hundred Sail makers, and we hear on the whole, no less than fifteen hundred workmen are demanded for Brest."[71] On the other hand, Frazer was fairly confident that no immediate war was contemplated. The workmen were to go by land to Brest, which would delay their arrival there for a month, and he reasoned that the present activity could "justly be attributed to the neglected state of the Navy for some years past."[72] Lynch for his part denied that there was an armament taking place at Toulon. There, too, the objective seemed to be to place the fleet on short notice for mobilization.[73] Furthermore, although the agent at Morlaix said the work at Brest was the greatest since the Falkland Islands crisis and that troops had been ordered, still he had also heard that the fishermen bound for Newfoundland had been allowed to depart without restriction.

Even if war was not an immediate danger, preparations for it could hardly be ignored. The intelligence reports were too consistent to be doubted. On 5 July they were added to, and reinforced, by the receipt from the intelligence agency of the late Robert Wolters of what appeared to be a master plan for French rearmament. Whoever it was who drew up the account also repeated that there seemed no immediate danger of war, but he said that six million had been set aside to pay for eighteen months' work in the dockyards. By August, one 90 and one 80, five 74s, one 70, four 64s, two 50s, and six small vessels—twenty in all—were to be put in armament. They were to be followed by the end of 1776 by a further 80, three 74s, four 64s, and five smaller vessels. In 1777 a third group consisting of one 100, one 80, one 76, five 74s, and five smaller vessels was to be taken in hand. In 1778 the repair was to be completed by work on a similar number of ships, but with only four small craft plus the addition of two 66-gun ships.[74] This plan does not appear to have originated in the French Ministry of the Marine, at least not in the form sent to London, but whatever the source of the intelligence, it proved to be a remarkably accurate forecast of the work undertaken in the French dockyards in the subsequent years.[75]

This naval activity made St. Paul apprehensive "that there may be some hostile design."[76] Weymouth too was concerned, writing Stormont that "the quantity of bread that is baking, and the Wine that is said to be procuring would seemingly indicate a further intention than is at present avowed by M. de Vergennes."[77] The Portuguese were convinced that they were in danger. On 8 July a month-old letter was received in London from Walpole saying that the Portuguese foreign minister

> Monsieur de Mello acquainted me the other day, that the *Duc de Chartres* has joined Monsieur de *Chaffaud* at *Lagos* and the French Ships have, since their quitting *Lagos*, been joined at Sea by several

Spanish Ships, at least equal the number of the French.

Monsieur de Mello talked to me of this Junction of the two Fleets, as
a designed Bravado by the Court of Spain and that this latter continues
to march Regiments towards the Frontiers of Portugal.[78]

Grantham felt confident that the Spaniards, at any rate, had no immediate
designs against Britain. He wrote to reassure General Boyde at Gibraltar.[79]
Weymouth, however, cautioned Grantham:

The very great Naval preparations that are making in the several ports of
France is an object of the most serious attention. The present minute is
extremely critical, and His Majesty commands me to require from you
the most vigilant attention, and the fullest information you can by any
means obtain of the views of the ministry where you reside. This is the
more essential as all accounts from Paris indicate that M. d'Aranda
seems to have been very earnest that the several preparations should take
place, and it is even said the Court of Spain contributed largely towards
the expence.[80]

On 11 July Sandwich forwarded to Weymouth a report of an encounter
between the *Enterprise* and the French squadron, in which both parties
seemed to have displayed some truculence.[81] The next day a letter was
received from Lynch saying that two ships and two frigates were to fit at
Toulon to sail to an unknown destination.[82] This French activity was much
more alarming to Weymouth than were the manoeuvres of Spain. The
French mobilization might be intended to encourage "Hopes of a Support"
among "His Majesty's rebellious Subjects . . . or at least a Diversion in
their favour." He did not go so far as to suggest that the French would resort
to force; rather he thought that the French, by making a "greater Shew of
Preparations," hoped to bring about a reduction of the British effort in
North America and make "the submission of the Colonies more tedious as
well as more difficult."[83] Vergennes was profuse with his assurance that no
armament was planned, only repair. Weymouth could not be content with
such assurances, since the French work ensured that "there shall be little
interval betwixt the intention, and the execution of any hostile designs."
The only comfort was Stormont's advice that the provision of six million for
fleet repair was inadequate, that Sartine wanted four million more, and that
unless he got it work would be slowed.[84]

Stormont was convinced that Aranda was exerting pressure upon the
French government to arm against Britain.[85] In any case, whatever the
intentions of France or of Spain were with respect to Britain, fighting
between Spain and Portugal could precipitate a general war. Accordingly it
was very worrying when Grantham learned at the end of June that the

Portuguese had attacked Spanish forces near Buenos Aires.[86] Grantham managed to get word to London by 15 July, and it was followed by a flood of reports of Spanish preparations. Consul Hardy reported that four ships were preparing at Cadiz for Buenos Aires, or to join Rear Admiral Gaston, who was maintaining station at the Tagus. Consul John Marsh reported two 80s and seven 74s plus frigates fitting at Ferrol, and Consul H. Katenkamp reported that a packet boat had been sent to Buenos Aires and that two ships and a frigate were to follow.[87]

All these alarming reports drove Sandwich once again into attempting to obtain a cabinet agreement for some increase in British naval preparations. On 21 July he wrote urgently to North

> that 23 ships of the line are preparing at Brest, and 7 at Toulon; the Spanish have at least 10 sail of the line in commission and many more in readiness to be commissioned; and I own that I dread the consequences, and cannot help thinking we shall have much to answer for, if they are allowed to have a fleet of 50 sail in Europe ready to receive men, when we have not above half that number in the same degree of preparation.[88]

North was not particularly receptive, asserting that both Suffolk and Weymouth "seemed to think the assurances of M. de Vergennes satisfactory," but he did offer to call a meeting of cabinet for the evening of Tuesday the 23rd or for Wednesday morning. If Sandwich thought it profitable to meet earlier, North would change his plans. He admitted: "I think that the situation of public affairs on all sides requires immediate consideration."[89] Sandwich replied that in his opinion Vergennes' declaration only said France did not mean war. It did not rule out "an armed negotiation in case of any untoward events in Portugal." "If they have a fleet ready for service double to ours," he wrote, "their advantages and our danger will be such that I tremble to think of it." Returning to his earlier demand, he urged that twelve ships of the line be made ready to receive men, sweetening the pill by saying it "would occasion no apparent expense, as that would be done in our own dockyards with the men now in annual pay." The real expense would occur if the crisis did not blow over, since private yards would have to be hired to undertake the new construction which could not be done in the royal yards when they were engaged in fitting out.[90] It will be remembered that in 1770 the Navy Board had explained that no more than twelve ships could be made ready at any one time. If the crisis did pass, Sandwich reasoned, the twelve could be laid up again or used to replace guardships which needed refitting.

The next day Sandwich sent to Weymouth the latest report from Morlaix, which confirmed that work was being undertaken at the French dockyards with great energy.[91] There is no record of the cabinet's decision, if indeed it did meet, but at any rate this time Sandwich apparently obtained consent for his demand. Between 24 July and 2 August the Navy Board was ordered to fit nine ships of the line as guardships. By the time the cabinet was ready in October to commission more ships for home service, the full twelve were ready for men.[92]

POMBAL SUGGESTS PREVENTIVE WAR

The reluctant decision in London to go some way towards matching the naval activity of the Bourbon states was not intended to have any effect upon the Spanish-Portuguese impasse, nor could it have had. Every day the news from that quarter was getting worse. On 9 August a report was received from Hardy that a general embargo had been placed on all the Spanish ships in Cadiz Harbour, and quarters ordered for seven regiments, which with the garrison could amount to 15,000 men. In the circumstances he thought their destination would most likely be Buenos Aires.[93] Ten days later Grantham confirmed that "the Destination of the Naval Armaments now preparing, is generally understood to be for Buenos Aires." He believed its orders to be conditional, but he guessed that Buenos Aires was to be made a viceroyalty.[94]

Grantham agreed with Stormont that Aranda was pressing for strong action against Britain, but he thought Aranda would not have his way. "I am clearly of Opinion that Mons D'Aranda takes a great deal upon himself at Paris, and I apprehend that he goes beyond the Instructions which he received. [H]e is very warm in the expressions which he uses against the very Minister whose Office it is to lay them before His Catholick Majesty and the Prince of Asurias."[95] If there was a division within the Spanish government, it obviously would be well to exploit it and to use any delay before the Spanish force sailed to bring about a change in Portuguese policy. Weymouth wrote to Walpole on 20 August and 3 September urging Portugal to restore the captured territory before Spain sent out her forces.[96]

Pombal had grander plans. On 4 September there arrived from Walpole an account of a conversation with Pombal in which he claimed that Spain's intentions were to conquer all Brazil, while those of France were clearly antipathetic to Britain. Pombal let Walpole read a letter meant for the Portuguese ambassador in London, the Chevalier de Pinto, which pointed out that the French efforts to raise a loan in Amsterdam of 70 million livres tournois could not be intended simply to promote Spanish power in South America. He expressed a belief that the French and Spaniards were determined to support the Americans and declared that the means to prevent this, is, for the Court of Great Britain to require of France & Spain to declare whether the great Armaments going on at Toulon & at Brest and at Cadiz are designed against Great Britain or its Allies, or against its National Interests: and that in case France & Spain should hesitate to give an Answer to this embarrassing inquiry, as probably they would; that then His Majesty should order Brest and Cadiz to be blocked up by His Fleets.

At the same time, Portugal would make a diversionary attack on the Spanish border. In this manner, Pombal argued, Britain could be victorious in America because the rebels would lose all hope of supply and support.[97]

Weymouth dismissed Pombal's suggestion since it "would necessarily throw Europe into a flame," and he told Walpole, "The preparations making in the french Ports are such as we are assured are not designed for Armament."[98] Considering the concern the British did feel for the French naval preparations and Weymouth's own conclusion that they were intended to influence the American war, this letter was disingenuous. Pombal's policy of fighting the American Revolution in European waters before France completed her rearmament and on the borders of Portugal has in retrospect some appeal. However, London was probably influenced by the consideration that there was no more reason to think Portugal was capable of defending her frontier without British assistance than she had been during the Seven Years' War. At any rate London clung to the hope that a European war could be avoided altogether, and Weymouth wrote to Stormont clearly disassociating himself from Portuguese machinations.[99] It is only too probable that Pombal was engaged in the time-honoured manoeuvre of securing his own position, which was threatened by the growing infirmity of Joseph I, by fomenting a war which would make it hazardous to dismiss an experienced minister.

THE STRATEGIC IMPERATIVE

Repeated remonstrances to Pombal during the next month had no evident effect, and intelligence from France had become so threatening that the North cabinet was obliged to take further precautionary measures.[100] At the end of September, Stormont had obtained a report that Aranda was being listened to in the French council. He wrote:

My informer tells me my Lord that on Sunday last, M d'Aranda made a formal demand in writing "that a sufficient Number of French Ships should be ordered to join Don *Gastons Fleet of Observation in order to*

intimidate Portugal and engage Great Britain to force the Portuguese to
make an immediate Restitution of all they had taken. And likewise to
give such satisfaction as the Injury required." The next Day an
Extraordinary Council was held to consider of this Demand, all the
Members of the Council except M de Maurepas were for joining Six or
Eight French ships to the Spanish Fleet.[101]

Maurepas evidently urged that no decision be made until 4 October, but in
the meantime d'Estaing was sent to Brest to hurry the work. On 1 October,
Sandwich forwarded to Weymouth intelligence for Morlaix, dated 14
September, which contradicted earlier reports of slackening work and
indeed said that short of a general levee and troop movements, every
preparation was being taken as for war.[102] On the 2nd Stormont wrote that
by the end of the year France would have thirty ships and thirty frigates
ready to be manned, that twelve ships were to be laid down, and that Sartine
had been given an additional twelve million for extraordinary expenses.
Orders had been given for the immediate fitting out of six ships of unknown
force. Du Chaffault's *escadre d'évolutions* had returned to rest but had not
been disarmed.[103] These last two reports were soon confirmed from Morlaix,
with the additional information that there was a levee of sailors and troops
expected.[104]

Once again British intelligence had been first-rate. In August, Vergennes
had at last adopted a policy of deliberate preparation for preventive war
against Britain, while continuing to cool Spanish demands that it be begun
on the Portuguese frontier.[105] Louis XVI authorized a supplementary grant
of nine and a half million livres, which enabled Sartine to order the
dockyards to continue their work beyond the twenty ships called for in
May.[106] When de Chaffault's squadron ended its cruise, Louis authorized
the commissioning of six of the new squadron in order to be able to continue
to provide protection for outward-bound gun-runners.[107]

The alarming nature of the intelligence led Weymouth to instruct
Stormont to seek "fresh Assurances," which, he wrote, "I cannot omit
observing . . . have not been very lately repeated."[108] Stormont was only
able to report that d'Estaing had taken command in Toulon and Comte de
Roquefeville in Brest. Du Chaffault was to command the six ships and four
frigates being readied to short notice. Subsequently, in a letter received 20
October, he advised that the ships were probably to convoy troops to St.
Domingo and that du Chaffault was to command because the Duc de
Chartres had refused a post in which he risked capture if there should be a
war.[109] The next day a letter was received from Deane Poyntz, who had
replaced Lynch at Turin, reporting that the Duc de Chartres' squadron had
arrived at Toulon, where it was being held in readiness.[110] On 22 October,

Weymouth wrote to Walpole in despair: "The great Armament by Spain will probably obtain by force what they were entitled to by negotiation, and it is not probable that they will limit their Operations to the Recovery of what ought now to be restored. The Conduct of Mons. de Pombal is inexplicable."[111]

Again it was Sandwich who led the demand for countervailing British preparations. By this time the evidence of hostile French armament was clear enough to obtain strong cabinet agreement. On 23 October, Sandwich sent the King a memorandum suggesting a general press, manning the guardships to their war complement, concentrating them at Spithead, commissioning the twelve ships of the line that were ready to receive men, preparing others, and generally raising the guard. Twenty-three guardships were in commission, and four other ships on service. Twelve were ready to receive men, twelve others would be ready before the end of the year, and there were twenty-seven ships in ordinary on the serviceable list with five others capable in an emergency of going on foreign service. The total effective force was eighty-three ships of the line.[112] The cabinet met on the 25th, but it only agreed to increase the bounty offered to seamen.[113] It was apparent that Weymouth shared Sandwich's concern, for he sent instructions to Stormont to warn Vergennes that the French armament, and especially the dispatch of troops to St. Domingo, obliged Britain to make preparations.[114]

Any hesitation there may have been in the cabinet was evidently brought to an end by the receipt of another letter from Stormont, which reported that a meeting of the committee of the council had agreed to ready from fifty-seven to sixty ships and frigates and to reinforce St. Domingo and Martinique, for which purpose du Chaffault's ships were to be employed.[115] The imminence of the opening of parliament may have helped to precipitate a cabinet decision. The report had indicated that France would not participate in Spanish action against Portugal unless Britain became involved. London, however, could not stand aside from Bourbon machinations if they included the dispatch of French forces to the West Indies, where they could influence the outcome of the revolution or make an attack without warning. The only way the British navy could protect the British empire was by containing the Bourbon threat near the naval ports of Europe.

On 25 October *Thetis* was ordered to cruise in company with a sloop and a cutter off Brest, ready to send a warning if the French sailed.[116] Three days later the cabinet agreed to a general impressment of seamen, which was carried out that night.[117] The next day the Admiralty, presumably on cabinet authority, instructed the Navy Board to prepare twenty-seven guardships for four months' service with full complements. The men in the dockyards were ordered to work as many tides extra as was necessary, and the ships being built at merchant yards were to be finished without waiting for seasoning.[118] The new French ambassador, Comte de Noailles, was, according to the dispatch he sent to Vergennes, informed by North that the cabinet had agreed to add fifteen guardships to the twenty.[119]

Having once satisfied the minimum strategic needs of the navy, the administration felt it was necessary to diminish the diplomatic impact of the naval orders. The King's speech from the throne on the 31st expressed a strong hope for conciliation between Spain and Portugal. Later, in the Lords' debate on the speech, Sandwich was at pains to minimize the extent of the French armament and to give reassurances that Britain was in no danger. He also took the opportunity to express his opinion on the importance of deterrence. "An early and timely preparation on our part would have the effect of *substantial oeconomy* it would probably be the last expense; for, by incurring it in time, it might, perhaps prevent a much greater."[120] In reality, London's response to French support for the revolutionaries had been so much weaker than had come to be expected that its capacity to deter French activity was definitely limited. Diplomacy was used to ensure that it was understood on the continent that London intended no more than to make minimal preparations to prevent a strategic imbalance at sea.[121] Any coercive purpose was exclusively directed against the French plan to build up forces in the West Indies.

Despite the French armament Grantham was advised that the influence France had over her ally "has tended to soften their resentment towards Portugal."[122] Not surprisingly, this attitude prevented the British mobilization from having any perceptible effect on the Iberian situation. Grimaldi simply expostulated that the French preparations could hardly warrant the British response, saying he would more readily have understood it "if we had given for reason, that Spain was arming." Grantham was left with the impression that both France and Spain were determined to follow through on any consequence of the action to be taken by the Cadiz squadron, although he repeated Grimaldi's assurances that it would be sent to Buenos Aires to regain Spanish territory but would not go beyond that limit or go to Brazil or to Rio de Janeiro.[123] In early December it was known in London that a squadron of six ships of the line and a troop convoy had sailed under the command of the Marquis de Cassa Tilly for Buenos Aires. It was also known that Don Gaston's squadron, which had returned in sickly condition, was refitting for sea. In September, in response to French pressure, Grimaldi had agreed to retain fourteen ships of the line ready at Cadiz.[124] Clearly the Iberian dispute remained a menace to world peace.[125]

The French armament intended for the West Indies was the target of London's minimal deterrence. On 1, 4, and 15 November letters were received in London from Poyntz in Turin telling of the preparations at Toulon.[126] Eighteen ships of the line under the command of the Duc de Chartres were reported ready for sea and only awaiting their orders. This report was followed next day with one from Morlaix which said that at Brest 12,000 to 15,000 sailors had been called up, that there was great activity, and that "in short every Ship will be fit by the end of the year to go to sea and all the Store Houses filled."[127] Stormont reported in a letter received on the 11th that the training squadron was disarming, but that there were 15,000 to 16,000 sailors in Brest. Du Chaffault was in Paris for his orders. Sartine, he wrote, "admits that there is a great number of sailors assembled at Brest, but says, that they are intended to Mann M du Chauffaults [sic] Squadron, and to form a sort of Corps de reserve, for any Event that may arise."[128] The news was so alarming that on 8 November it was agreed to ask the Commons for a navy of 45,000 men, and on 15 November Sandwich wrote a personal note to Admiral Keppel advising him that the King expected "having shortly an occasion for your Service to command the fleet that is now equipping for Sea."[129] The same day Weymouth wrote to Stormont urging him "to use every means in your power" to impress upon Vergennes that the dispatch of a squadron to the West Indies would be a measure "dangerous in its consequences."[130] After two weeks of strenuous representations Stormont was at last able to report that Vergennes had agreed to review the orders to du Chaffault with Louis XVI.[131]

The view from London certainly began to look rosier from then on. Nevertheless on 4 December the naval commanders in American waters were sent a circular warning them of the possible appearance of the French squadron. "You may rest assured," they were told, "that if the French fleet sails, a British Fleet of at least equal force, will soon sail for the security of His Majesty's Islands."[132] It took the better part of a month before London could feel reasonably confident. On 19 December in reply to a private letter from Sandwich, Weymouth was only able to say "that I have received no certain account that Mons du Chaffaults Squadron will not sail."[133] Poyntz sent a reassuring report, however, that the Duc de Chartres' squadron was in harbour, allegedly to be disarmed.[134] It soon became evident that General Howe's defeat of the rebels in New York, news of which had reached France, had impressed the French court with the need for caution. Stormont on 11 December wrote to Weymouth when it appeared that the French would be increasing the size of du Chaffault's squadron to "twelve ships of the Line, and six or seven Frigates." It would be kept at Brest, with three frigates at Toulon, to "wait to see the final Issue of the Campaign in America."[135] On Christmas Day, however, Stormont was finally able to report that M. de Maurepas had stated definitely that du Chaffault's squadron would not be sailing.[136] Providing the Brest squadron did not sail for American waters,

Weymouth was prepared to accept the more or less permanent anxiety generated by its existence in preference to preventive action.[137]

THE DISARMAMENT PLOY

At the beginning of 1777, thanks to the ships ordered made ready in British yards in the second half of 1776, the problem of French naval preparations seemed to be under control. Weymouth was confident that "proper steps have been taken here to be prepared against every event."[138] By mid-November a total of thirty-seven ships had been ordered brought forward for service. Some appear to have been ordered by the Admiralty without specific authorization from a Secretary of State.[139] By 30 December 1776 there were 18,366 seamen in ships in British ports and depots, of which 7,816 had been raised since the general press of 28 October. Excluding five of the 64s which were at sea, and five ships which apparently were not yet ready to receive men, the remaining thirty ships of the line in home waters required 16,640 men to fill their complements, which in the case of the 74s had been reduced to 600 men from the preferred level of 650.[140] Men were also required for frigates, sloops, and small craft, so that the thirty ships were 7,564 men short of complement if the supernumeraries who were drafted to some of them and were paid by the ship are considered as equivalent to crew. On the average they were 55 per cent below complement, although obviously it would have been possible in an emergency to draft all available seamen into the seaworthy battleships.[141] With the return of ships from abroad, however, and with the results of the impressment, the weekly musters showed a satisfactory increase of 3,699 men in the first six weeks of 1777. The muster book for 24 February shows twenty-nine ships fitting in British ports and ready for men, including five of 90 guns, with a nominal complement for the whole of 17,910. These were short by 2,588 seamen and 1,997 marines, but with 249 supernumeraries slightly reducing the deficiency this amounted to a general increase in readiness in the capital ships in port to 75 per cent manned. A total of 22,542 men were available in British ports or depots, and the overall world-wide total was somewhere between 46,231 and 46,503 men.[142]

Part of this fleet was actively employed at sea. From late December 1776 the Admiralty began to supplement the regular frigate patrols with third-rate ships of the line cruising in the Channel approaches, off Capes Finisterre and Ortegal, down into Biscay, and convoying the Iberian trade. On 25 December 1776 *Southampton* was ordered to cruise for a month north of Cape Ortegal between latitudes 45° and 47°, on 2 January 1777 *Ardent* was ordered to cruise for a month between Capes Ortegal and Finisterre, and *Arethusa* was sent to cruise for two months between Cape Finisterre and Lisbon. On 1

February *Belleisle* was ordered to cruise between latitudes 46° and 47° thirty leagues west of Penmarks Point, and *Augusta* was sent to cruise within thirty leagues of Capes Ortegal and Finisterre. A week later *Culloden* and *Torbay* were also ordered to those stations, although no orders were given for the ships to act together. And so it continued. In May the capital ships suddenly disappeared from the "Foreign Cruiser" section of the Admiralty "List Books," but that was nothing more than a change of nomenclature. The list-book for June (by which time the guardships were all fitting for active service and no longer appeared as a separate category) showed six second-rate and thirty-one third-rate ships in British waters, of which no fewer than thirteen were at sea on patrol. Even in the middle of the following winter the capital ship patrols continued with ten third-rates at sea in January 1778.[143]

There appears to be no record of cabinet discussion about the advisability of capital ship patrols as a move in the diplomatic offensive. Frustrated by North's opposition to full naval mobilization, Sandwich may have acted independently. In August he was to be criticized by John Robinson, Junior Secretary of the Treasury, for conducting war "in Departments."[144] The shortage of frigates in home waters was probably the principal reason for the capital ship patrols which were needed to protect trade, discourage gun-running, and provide training for the crews of the newly fitted ships. Whatever their intended function, however, they provided Versailles with a justification for the armament at Toulon, needed to ensure du Chaffault's ability to protect gun-runners from the patrols.[145]

Intelligence from Deane Poyntz showed that there had been no abatement of the work in Toulon dockyard, and there continued to be clear evidence of French support for the American rebels.[146] It was soon known in London that Benjamin Franklin had arrived in Paris to represent the Continental Congress, and in mid-January 1777 the *Amphétrite* sailed for St. Domingo with a number of French officers to serve in America. At the end of January, Stormont spoke very strongly with Vergennes about ships loading ammunition and American privateers selling their prizes in French ports. However, it was evident the French were not going to do more than observe some of the forms of neutrality. In February, Stormont learned that an order had been given to arm ten ships of the line at Toulon. They were to join the twenty at Brest where twenty battalions of troops were being sent, ostensibly to repair the fortifications but no doubt also with an eye to a possible swift embarkation. Sandwich's agent at Morlaix was no less convinced that "Affairs begin to have a serious aspect." Stormont later modified the reported number of battalions sent to Brest to eight, or maybe twelve, but in any case it was evident that France had not eased the pace.[147]

At sea there was increasing tension between the British and French fleets.

There is no evidence that the British were using the ships of the line on patrols in order to intimidate the French, but it is evident that the effect was escalatory.[148] In March du Chaffault sent out his first ship-of-the-line patrol, which had encountered one British ship of the line. Later that month the *Robuste* encountered the *Exeter* on patrol and Captain La Motte Picquet used strong language which Vergennes later was obliged to excuse. La Motte Picquet was reprimanded for exceeding his instructions, and for the time Vergennes felt constrained to tolerate the British inspection of French merchantmen once clear of the French coast. In April the 80-gun *Foudroyant* was sighted on patrol, and du Chaffault responded by ordering his ships to patrol in groups. He was given instructions to maintain two 74s and a 64 on station.

In December, Maurepas had hinted to an unavowed intermediary, probably a Mr. Nathaniel Forth, that both France and Britain should reduce their forces. He had followed the first hint with a direct suggestion to Stormont that "we both put ourselves to great Expense, by our unnecessary Armaments."[149] At the end of January, Maurepas renewed his soundings, again making his approach unofficially through an intermediary, probably Mr. Forth, who is known to have played a part in later negotiations of this sort. Maurepas' idea, apparently, was for an informal agreement.[150] The possibility of a mutual disarmament was raised once more in February by Grimaldi. Grantham guessed, correctly, that the French had put Grimaldi up to it in order to save their face when they saw the size of Britain's armament, or as a result of the success of British arms in North America.[151] Soon thereafter Grantham noted that, consistent with Grimaldi's warning that Spain would have to put herself on guard, it had been ordered that the defences of Cadiz be strengthened. Nevertheless Grantham thought "the measure of putting Cadiz in a state of defence seems rather designed for the sake of appearing to do something than for any other purpose, as it is in itself a step which can give no umbrage or offence." He continued to believe "that France was desirous of a pretence to lay aside her preparations."[152] Weymouth wrote Grantham on 7 March agreeing to Spanish participation in any negotiation for disarmament.[153]

The Spanish initiative was short-lived, and nothing came of Maurepas' suggestion. Grimaldi had never, in fact, been enthusiastic about the plan, which he had only taken up at the request of Vergennes.[154] At the end of February, Grimaldi retired and his place was taken by the Conde Floridablanca. This development, which had been expected since November and was inevitable following the disaster at Algiers, was fairly welcome in London. It was known that there were some who had wished Aranda to have the office. Furthermore, Pombal mistrusted Grimaldi and might be more co-operative with another.[155] Floridablanca did speak of the armament as unfortunate.[156] In the following weeks, however, no more was heard of Spanish mediation.

Instead the British government had to turn its attention to deflecting Spanish plans to reinforce their garrisons in the West Indies and to the French government's continued armament and support for the rebels, which they hardly attempted to disguise. Vergennes did not scruple to throw the blame for French naval preparations upon Britain.[157] Nevertheless he discussed with Stormont a memorial Pombal had sent to London, and they agreed in their opinions of Pombal's schemes. Vergennes also "readily assented" that it contained "many Striking Proofs" of Britain's "sincerity and good faith" and "repeated and earnest endeavours to bring it to a happy issue." His attitude, however, certainly was not satisfactory. Stormont, as he said, "did not attempt to lead him further into the Subject being very doubtful whether any proposal for a partial *Desarmament* or even for a Limitation of our Respective armaments could be accepted by us in the present critical Moment. When I say this, I do not mean to insinuate that M. de Vergennes discovered any Intention of making such a Proposal."[158]

By the middle of March 1777 Sandwich was convinced that the armaments authorized in October were no longer adequate, and that it was now necessary "to proceed immediately in a further armament." He had a memorandum drawn up which showed that France and Spain had in commission at home nineteen ships of the line at Brest, fifteen at Toulon, and fifteen in Spanish ports. Against this forty-nine, Britain only had thirty-six ships in home waters, of which four were under orders for North America.[159] North was approached through John Robinson, who, besides holding the office of Junior Secretary of the Treasury, was a confidant of the King. It was suggested to North that if he agreed to keep thirty-six ships in home waters and only send to Howe two additional ships, the King would undertake to obtain the concurrence of the rest of the cabinet. Robinson, however, had to advise the King that North was not convinced.[160] He wrote King George that he was "so far from thinking a foreign war certain, that he considers it as most probable that we shall not during the course of this year have any contest with any European power."[161]

London was clearly uncertain how to proceed. North himself was virtually incapacitated by the tensions of office. He was so far from coping with the exigencies of the situation that, at the same time that he refused further naval expenditures, he suggested the need for a review of the landward defences. The King rejected that idea with contempt. It would have created panic among the public and accordingly would have had powerful diplomatic implications.[162] Nevertheless, the "wait and see" school prevailed, and Weymouth sent to Stormont a disingenuous and not very useful assurance that "our Armaments appear larger than the immediate circumstances seem to require, owing to the particular exigency of Our Affairs in America, as some Ships of the Line are going on that Service."[163]

This lame account was sent off on the same day, 21 March, that Sandwich sent to Weymouth a report from Morlaix that eleven ships and ten frigates of du Chaffault's squadron were in the road at Brest. Two days later Sandwich sent him another report. Reinforcements were expected to augment du Chaffault's squadron to eighteen ships by the end of the month, and it was expected that d'Estaing was to be given command of the combined Toulon and Brest fleets. Twenty thousand stand of arms and a large quantity of cannon, power, and ball had been put on board du Chaffault's squadron. It was expected that they were intended for the West Indies. The agent reported that there was no talk of more troops, but of course those expected in Brest to repair the fortifications were enough.[164] At the same time Poyntz was reporting that six ships of the line and two frigates, in fact those ships Sartine had ordered in February for the protection of the gun-runners, were at Toulon. There had been a large purchase of hemp.[165] Stormont reported that Le Comte de Grace had taken a 64 out to Ushant to chase off British frigates thought to be there, but had returned without seeing any.[166]

There is no record that this evidence was adequate to convince North, but nevertheless it was decided to bring forward replacements for the five ships sailing to join Admiral Howe. Stormont believed that this decision was the reason for the renewal in early April of the idea of a mutual disarmament of some ships. He was himself about to reintroduce the idea, but Maurepas forestalled him, and together they drew up a proposal for the disarmament of eight ships.[167] Maurepas and Vergennes tried to put some pressure on London for an early conclusion of the agreement by indicating that otherwise they would count seven ships they said were about to be brought forward as part of the eight to be disarmed. Furthermore, Maurepas' real intentions were not clear, for he also said France was going to have to comply with Spanish demands that a fleet be sent to the West Indies. However, he hastily retracted when Stormont replied that "if a French fleet does appear in those Seas an English Fleet must and will follow instantly" and that he "thought it better, if he had such an Intention, to give up all Idea of this Desarmament [sic] We had been Planning."[168]

Two days after the arrival of Stormont's letter, Sandwich forwarded to Weymouth intelligence from Morlaix, which was confirmed by a report from Turin, that du Chaffault was expected to sail on the 8th or 9th with twelve ships and six frigates to join six ships and two frigates at Toulon.[169] In the same week, on the 11th, a letter also arrived from Cadiz warning that Rear Admiral Don Gaston had been ordered to take four ships and one or two frigates to Havana.[170] Presumably these reports more than the verbal warnings from Maurepas influenced London. On the 16th Weymouth replied to Stormont agreeing to the partial disarmament.[171] He also wrote two days later to Grantham instructing the latter to advise Floridablanca that Britain had no ships of the line in the West Indies. It was hoped that Spain could be dissuaded from dispatching Don Gaston.[172]

Vergennes put an end to the idea of formal disarmament by the device of laying the blame on Spain. Stormont was able to report on 16 April that the French government had permitted the Newfoundland fishermen to sail without convoy and that orders had been sent to Brest to slow the preparation of the seven ships just ordered.[173] He soon learned, on the other hand, that France would not accept an early date for a disarmament after all. His speculation that it was pressure from Spain which occasioned the French change of heart was apparently confirmed by Maurepas, who read to him a letter from Floridablanca apparently urging that as many as fourteen or twenty battalions and six or eight ships be sent to St. Domingo.[174] Weymouth was prepared to agree to a later date for the disarmament, but he advised Stormont on 2 May that "A positive Assurance on the part of Spain that her Armament shall cease is to be made a previous condition sine qua non of the *desarmament.*"[175] Weymouth had earlier written to Grantham instructing him, while avoiding any menace, to speak strongly to Floridablanca.[176] However, it was a little strange that Maurepas should have read to Stormont a letter purporting to be from Floridablanca. London began to entertain suspicions, which the receipt of a letter from Hardy reporting that Don Gaston's ships had been immobilized confirmed, that "the *Desarmament* was delayed on other considerations than those respecting Spain." "It is not improbable," Stormont was told, "that the french Ministers may think such a measure may cast too much despondency on the American Rebels."[177]

If it had become evident in London that Vergennes was the real enemy of the peace, however, it was also soon to receive evidence that he was hesitant. When Frazer warned that the privateer Cunningham had captured the Harwich packet and brought it back to France, Stormont was able to secure its release and learned that Franklin had been informed that the action was too glaring to be winked at.[178] Intelligence from Morlaix dated 1 May also indicated indecision, or at any rate a decision for caution. The agent wrote: "the movements at Brest have been so fluctuating, that no fixed judgment could be formed of them: At present the general opinion is a continuation of the Peace, as the Embargo at St. Malo & Nantes is taken off."[179] The reports from Poyntz did not speak of any reduction of tempo at Toulon, as yet. Indeed a report received on 28 April spoke of eight more ships ordered, and another on 5 May said the "Toulon 1st division [was] in the Road ready to sail." These letters, however, had taken two weeks to cross France and could be expected to reflect an earlier phase in the thinking at Versailles.[180] On 24

May, Poyntz wrote that orders had been given, cancelled, and reissued for the arming of three ships. "Whatever may be the Design of the French ministers in the mystery & confusion they endeavour to throw over their present Preparations, [he wrote] I am at a Loss to account for."[181] However, no attempt was made to increase the pressure on France. The King, for one, felt it wisest in his speech proroguing parliament to avoid any mention of foreign affairs.[182]

BUYING TIME

In April 1777 King Joseph died, and Pombal fell from power. That, and a Spanish victory at the Island of St. Catherines, put an end to the threat of an Iberian war and also ended Spanish interest in military preparations against Britain.[183] This development was of very great strategic importance. By it the naval threat to Britain was greatly reduced. London, however, continued its policy of avoiding confrontation.[184] For both London and Versailles the second half of 1777 was dominated by hopes and fears for the success of General Burgoyne's attempt to reconquer New England, pending which neither court wished to take unnecessary risks.[185]

British response to the open assistance given by the French to the Americans, and to Bourbon naval preparations, was no more than strong words.[186] Stormont objected: "it is to the Vigilance of our Cruizers [he wrote], that we must finally trust for the stopping of these Succours [to the rebels], *that* will be more efficacious than any Representations that can be made."[187] A confrontation with Maurepas and Vergennes was followed by a short-term improvement in French observation of neutrality. When Stormont demanded that American privateers be denied the use of French ports, however, Vergennes acted with such duplicity that there was some change of mood in London.[188] Weymouth advised Stormont that, because of the Spanish decision to send two ships across the Atlantic, probably to Havana, and because of the French decision to send a 74 to the West Indies, "His Majesty . . . must think Himself at liberty to send a reinforcement to the Squadron in that part of the world, if His Majesty shall think proper."[189] Nevertheless, this warning remained "strong words." Stormont did not pass it on to the French government because he was afraid its imprecision might panic Maurepas into the immediate dispatch of a superior squadron to the West Indies.[190]

Military realities eventually brought London in the late summer of 1777 to recognize that the policy of avoiding provocation of the French, while pursuing the war in North America, had to be modified. *Mars* and *Monarch* had been held back from their projected cruise in the Channel in order to complete stores for foreign service. But Palliser, now a Lord of Admiralty,

King George III of Great
Britain, 1738-1820.
Courtesy of the British
Museum (Royal Prints
1841.4.3.71) Negative 42264

doubted the wisdom of dispersing home forces. *Mars* in fact spent the
summer on Channel patrol, while *Monarch*, having gone aground on
returning from patrol in August, was sent to be refitted at Portsmouth.[191] At
the beginning of August, North again sounded Palliser on the desirability of
sending ships to the West Indies. Palliser forwarded the suggestion to
Sandwich, but advised that no detachment should be made without bringing
forward more ships at home.[192] Without a superior force at home, he
pointed out, there would be nothing available for detachments to foreign
stations at the beginning of a war, should it come. An inability to send a
squadron after du Chaffault, should he sail to New York, "might give such a
blow to the English fleet that it would be difficult ever to recover. The loss of
America would in such an event be by far the inferior consideration." Even
more serious would be the lack of ships in the Channel to contain the French
fleet in Europe. In the end it was decided to dispatch one ship to the West
Indies, and Stormont was instructed to request the French to advise London
if they intended to send any more ships "as their proceedings in that
particular will govern ours."[193]

Hard-mouthed threats from Stormont that the use of ships of the line to escort troops being sent to the West Indies would lead to war—that public opinion would demand it—were again necessary in early August.[194] The French government was displaying "such fluctuation of Councils" that Stormont reiterated his opinion that "security must depend upon our constant watchfulness and the having a respectable Fleet ready to sail at the shortest warning." He was right to be sceptical. Within four days he was writing that the French appeared to be again entertaining thoughts of sending ships of the line to the West Indies. "It was very obvious to me My Lord, that Momentary Fear and agitation prompted that Declaration which M. de Maurepas made on Saturday last, and that He was particularly anxious for the Newfoundland Fishermen who in Case of an immediate Rupture would in all Probability fall into our Hands. That Danger must in a few weeks cease of course."[195] Despite his desire for war, Vergennes was constrained to await the outcome of the campaign in America. On 23 and 24 August, however, he dispatched orders to du Chaffault to recall isolated ships, and to port commanders placing an embargo on all sailings, and he ordered the immediate recall of the Newfoundland fishermen.[196]

At last Stormont's advice struck a responsive chord in Lord North, who himself took the lead in urging that it was again necessary to increase the state of naval readiness. Summoning the cabinet for 25 or 26 August, he wrote to Sandwich: "We ought to have as full a Cabinet as possible, as our resolutions are likely to be material and may be attended with important consequences to the nation."[197] Presumably for the consideration of the cabinet, Palliser drew up on 25 August a state of the British fleet. There were thirty-six ships of the line in commission, mostly dispersed to various stations, some not due home until October and November, and a minimum of a month's notice required to assemble a large squadron. Six other ships were ready to receive men, but for all purposes the fleet was short 12,300 men. It was also short of frigates to accompany the battle-fleet.[198] The next day Sandwich wrote North outlining the balance of forces:[199]

Spain has 21 ships of the line in commission in Europe	21
France has at Brest	13
At Toulon	6
Mr. Poyntz in his letter of the 2nd of July says 4 more are to be commissioned at Toulon	4
	44
Spain has 20 ships in commission out of Europe	64

England has in commission in Europe   36
   Out of Europe   <u>8</u>
                         43

King George thought diplomacy should be tried again and suggest that Stormont be instructed to make representations directly to Louis XVI.[200] The preliminary soundings made with Vergennes, however, were not encouraging. Stormont failed utterly to stop France from sending the soldiers to St. Domingo and Martinique. Vergennes reasoned that troops without ships could not endanger the British islands, any more than British ships without soldiers to make a landing could hurt French interests.[201] On 27 August rigid orders had been sent to the French ports restricting the entrance of privateers, and Wickes' squadron was ordered to sea, where the *Lexington* was captured and the *Reprisal* lost. By 6 September, however, Vergennes felt confident enough to order the resumption of du Chaffault's patrols.[202]

There was nothing for it now but further naval mobilization. The policy of minimal deterrence and marginal preparation for a European war, however, was much less impressive than the "considerable augmentation of the fleet" with which Stormont had threatened Maurepas. On 18 September the Admiralty sent Weymouth a minute listing six ships it was proposed to commission, and the next day Sandwich also forwarded an intelligence report from Morlaix reporting a great build-up at Brest, men called up, and four ships of the line preparing to convoy troops to the West Indies.[203] Immediately Weymouth instructed Stormont to advise the French that "as the French Court persist in the measure of sending the reinforcements intended to their islands; his Majesty has thought proper to order six more Ships of the line to be put into commission."[204]

This letter crossed one from Stormont saying that he had received reliable intelligence that Vergennes "has in the Course of This Month signified to Franklin and Deane that this Court has now taken its Resolution for war which Resolution will shew itself soon."[205] It was to be another six months, however, before France and Britain were actually at war. London remained convinced of the necessity of buying time, and the decision to bring forward no more than six additional ships amounted to reassurance to the French that Britain was not going to set the pace towards war. On the face of it the British administration was uncertain whether the French were telling the Americans their true intentions or were still playing a double game while avoiding war. The King went so far as to declare that all the intelligence received from France was untrustworthy, because the agents were hoping to make a profit on the stocks by inspiring panic.[206] This is not the mood in which the arts of deterrence flourish.

At the end of September, Stormont informed the French court of Britain's intention to send ships to the West Indies, and to commission others, and he was able to report to London that restrictions had been placed upon the activity of American privateers. Franklin and Deane were apparently much discouraged.[207] Stormont could not find any reason to give any confidence to French assertions, but for the moment London continued to cherish even a nominal peace.[208] The French reinforcements for the West Indies were permitted to sail in early October, under the escort of nothing more than three frigates, without any reaction from the British navy.[209] On 26 October, however, Weymouth instructed the Admiralty to intercept a convoy which was believed to be loading supplies for the Americans in French and Spanish ports. Should the ships be suspicious, even if they had cleared for West Indian ports, they were to be brought in for inspection. Stormont was told to advise the French government.[210] Apparently it was felt that a fine line could be drawn between acceptable and unacceptable behaviour.

Meanwhile intelligence continued to report the intense activity in the French navy. On 30 October Sandwich forwarded to Weymouth intelligence from Morlaix, dated 7 October, that 6-8,000 men were being embarked at Brest for the West Indies, and that twenty ships were ready at Brest, but that there was no levee of seamen. Du Chaffault's squadron was due in to clean, at which point another squadron would sail.[211] Poyntz's intelligence also indicated that the Toulon squadron was regularly sending out ships on training exercises. To contemporary naval observers such extensive training was indicative of belligerent intentions, since it did not take long to turn a merchant seaman into a warrior. A letter from Poyntz which arrived on 28 November reported that at Toulon a 74 had been launched and three more laid down, two frigates had also been laid down, and two ships were on cruise. There was talk of disarming the six ships which had been made ready at Toulon, and arming six others.[212] This last, of course, would be a manoeuvre to permit the preparation of six additional ships while claiming to be avoiding provocation to the British. The French, on the other hand, were also thought to be having problems; 5,000 to 6,000 sailors at Brest were reported to have died of disease.

When Parliament reopened after the recess, the King's speech was as optimistic as possible, but it also warned of a determination to be "a faithful guardian of the honour of the crown of Great-Britain."[213] In the debate that followed Sandwich gave a clear account of the state the British fleet had then been put into, with forty-two ships in commission, of which thirty-five were virtually fully manned. Of their complement of 20,890 men, 18,240 were actually on board. The others were either on board the remaining seven ships as supernumeraries, or were marines training ashore. Only 2,400 seamen and 700 marines were required to man the remaining ships fully. Later in the debate Sandwich made his famous, and unfortunate, boast: "I should, My Lords, be extremely sorry, as presiding at the Admiralty-board, if I permitted at any time the French and Spanish navy united, to be superior to the navy of this country; I should, indeed, be wanting in the discharge of my duty."

This self-satisfied statement was later to haunt him. At the time, however, Sandwich was justly more concerned to prevent Chatham's denunciation of French duplicity from precipitating war. On the 28th the Duke of Richmond called for returns from the ports, and moved that the Lords be summoned on 2 December for an enquiry into the state of the nation.[214] The debate proved to be rather a damp squib, however, and Sandwich was able to satisfy most of his listeners by saying he had fifty-four ships fit for sea, including those in America. By the end of the year he could have ninety ships, if those ready for service in ordinary were included. He was able to fend off demands that the condition of ships in the ordinary be revealed.[215]

FAILURE OF MINIMAL DETERRENCE

News of the surrender of General Burgoyne's army at Saratoga in October, which was received in London at the beginning of December, put an end to the period of equipoise. Vergennes' prediction was wrong: the defeat in North America did not lead the British to choose a European war as a means of recouping their losses. North's cabinet were incapable of such a plan, and King George would not permit North to resign so that Chatham could be brought in.[216] It was the French who set the pace towards war. Vergennes' belligerence was made urgent by his concern that Saratoga would lead to a compromise peace which would preserve for Britain the exclusive navigation to North America upon which the strength of the British navy depended. On 14 December, Stormont wrote that there was word in Paris of an intention to increase the mobilized naval force, and by the 17th he knew that ten additional ships were to be brought forward at Brest, five of them with all speed. This news was denied by Maurepas, who also denied to "a friend" of Stormont's that any treaty had been concluded with the Americans. Stormont, however, no longer believed such claims and wrote on the 28th a very long account of French duplicity which led Suffolk to comment that he seemed "to have summon'd up to settle his year's account, all the bad appearances he had discovered in the course of it."[217]

As late as 18 February, King George did not believe that the French "minister" desired war, but he feared he would nevertheless "run so near the Wind that most probably the two Nations will be involved."[218] The apprehension of war was great enough, however, to impel North and Lord George Germain, the Secretary for the American Colonies, each to send a secret agent to treat with the American commissioners in Paris. The arrival of Paul Wentworth and William Pulteney was put to good use by Franklin. He was able to hasten Vergennes into concluding, on 6 February, treaties of commerce and alliance. In a paper Vergennes had had prepared on 13 January, it was argued that "France must undertake the war for the maintenance of American independence, even if that war should be in other respects disadvantageous."[219] The treaties were for the moment kept secret to give the French navy some further advantage and to give Vergennes additional opportunity to urge Spain into participation in the war.

Sandwich had been asked immediately after receipt of the news of Saratoga to prepare for the cabinet a paper on the naval situation, and this he forwarded to North on 8 December. He expressed his concern that the forty-two ships Britain now had in commission at home, "which may fairly be considered as ready for service," would be no match for the combined Bourbon fleet, which he expected would be undertaking offensive operations from the outset of war. He added:

> It will take a twelvemonth to get 25 more ships of the line ready for sea; 7 of these 25 (including the Victory) are now ready to receive men, and if they were commissioned would be ready for sea early in the spring; and 7 others would be immediately taken in hand, and ready to be commissioned in about two months. If we are in imminent danger of a foreign war (which in my opinion is the case), a day ought not to be lost. What shall we have to answer for if we are taken unprepared, and reduced to the necessity of either leaving our distant possessions undefended or seeing France and Spain in the Channel with a superior fleet?[220]

At the time North was suffering from a nervous breakdown, and Suffolk was, on 19 December, too ill to attend to Sandwich's papers or to attend meetings of cabinet.[221] There is no record of a cabinet decision to implement Sandwich's recommendations, and the Admiralty Board minutes for this period are not preserved. Between 27 and 31 December, however, the Admiralty sent orders to the Navy Board to prepare for sea a total of ten additional ships of the line. An eleventh followed on 5 January. On 28 December Palliser sent to Sandwich a list of ships he considered suitable for commissioning.[222]

Although Sandwich continued to worry about the lead the Bourbon fleets had obtained in preparation for war, Britain's naval mobilization was now on the way to diminishing that margin. Mobilization in the eighteenth century was such a ponderous business that there was little reason for alarm, save that war is an alarming business. On 4 January Suffolk was able to write approvingly to North that, "Be the event . . . what it may, we certainly have not neglected to put the Country into a state of Preparation."[223] King George also congratulated North with the thought that "however insidious the conduct of France appear it is pleasant to feel we are taking all the steps that would be necessary if it should end in a War."[224] Preserved in the Thynne family papers are two précis of naval intelligence, mostly concerning developments at Toulon, which had come in through Suffolk's and Weymouth's offices. These show that, at least from 3 and 18 January when the précis were begun, the Secretaries of State were closely following the mobilization of the Toulon squadron.[225] However, they do not seem to have shared Sandwich's alarm. With the King, the Secretaries of State appear to have been able to face the prospect of war with France with considerable complacency. What they were concerned about was the need to make peace with the colonies before the storm broke in Europe. The hope was illusory; but it was nevertheless strongly held.

On the Duke of Richmond's motion, an enquiry on the state of the navy was opened in the Lords on 4 February. The debate did not have much support, but it did drag on intermittently for a month. On 13 February the Commons debated the Navy Estimates, and on 11 March a motion was made that "the Present State of the Royal Navy for the defence of Great Britain and Ireland, is inadequate to the dangerous crisis of public affairs."[226] Meanwhile in the Lords, a motion was made on 25 February for the attendance of the Surveyor of the Navy. Sandwich had to protest that "the noble duke who made the motion, knew that in every country there were ships upon paper which were not fit for service. That it was politic always to put the best face upon the state of the navy, and it never had been deemed wise to pry too minutely into particulars."[227] He insisted publicly that the navy was "in a most flourishing condition." In private he continued to plead with North for more forces, but when pressure in parliament forced him on 2 March to reveal the state of mobilization, it became evident that the British fleet was reasonably fit for war.[228] There were then fifty-one ships in commission, one of which was rotten, thirty-five of which were fully manned, and of which forty-two could, Sandwich claimed, be manned for sea in an emergency.

A few days before he received his recall from Paris in March, Stormont reported that Maurepas had boasted to him: "the great disadvantage the French have hitherto had in every naval war, arose from the beginning it with too small a force—The loss of one or two squadrons undid us, said he—but that will not be the case now."[229] The activity in French dockyards, and the relatively slow rate of Britain's response, appeared to have created a brief window of opportunity for France.[230] That was a fateful delusion. The British decision against preventive war had been rewarded by the temporary detachment of Spain from France, and without the Spanish fleet France did not have the numbers of ships needed to defeat Britain. The Comte d'Orvilliers was not able to bring annihilating numbers against Admiral Keppel in the July battle off Ushant.

More significant than matériel problems were those of political disunity. In the 2 March parliamentary debate on the state of the navy the Honourable Augustus Hervey, now the Earl of Bristol, declared, in an ominous foreshadowing of the future, that he would not serve in the fleet as it then was. Citing the fate of Admiral Byng, he said: "My Lords, I will be no scape-goat for any administration; let me go out with proper ships, properly manned, and I will defy all ministers whatever, and will be answerable for the rest."[231] It was political disunity within the fleet which prevented Admiral Keppel defeating the French at Ushant. The chance to end the war before Spain was persuaded to throw in her lot with France was thus lost, but the fault was not one of numerical weakness. Spain's entry into the war in 1779 certainly strained the capacity of the British navy, but the effect was temporary. French intervention in the war did suffice to ensure the victory for the revolutionaries, but wartime British strategic errors, and political disunity, were more significant than were matériel shortages.

It is as a departure from the established system of deterrence that the slow rate of mobilization is important. Maurepas' rejoicing appears rather sad in retrospect. Britain's foreign policy in the twelve years before Bunker Hill, based on the coercive use of naval forces, had had its limitations. Perhaps, however, the greatest of them was the difficulty experienced in abandoning the coercive approach when it was no longer wanted. The failure of Britain's exercise of minimal deterrence after Bunker Hill, a failure which obscured the country's real strength, had profoundly damaging effects on both states.

War had become inevitable because deterrence had failed and because London was no longer prepared to accept serious injury in order to avoid war. It was known in late 1777 that orders had been sent to Brest to hold in readiness three ships and a frigate, victualled for four months. It was believed they would be used to convoy gun-runners out of European waters. On 31 December, North advised King George that Sandwich intended to bring up in cabinet the next day the question of the orders under which Commodore Hood was watching the Biscay ports of France.[232] Two days later, secret orders were issued instructing Hood to intercept any convoy bound for North America and to seize ships found with warlike stores "notwithstanding any remonstrance from the convoy to the contrary." He was to instruct his captains to treat the French with "civility," but "For the more effectual performing this Service, you are not to allow your Ships to be less than two in Company." Similar orders were also sent to Captains Hughes, Brookes, and Digby, who were to proceed with a total of eleven ships of the line to cruise off Cape Finisterre.[233] As Camden remarked in the Lords on 2 February, "the ports of L'Orient and Nantz are blocked up by a British naval force. Three frigates are now cruizing off those ports, to intercept succours going to America, and to put a stop to that very commerce which the French King, in his public edicts, pretends to prohibit."[234] Had such orders been issued when Versailles first turned a blind eye on the American gun-runners and privateers, it is not improbable that the drift of the French ministry into war could have been arrested. Now, however, it was too late.

Camden was wrong only about the strength of the forces Sandwich had deployed to watch the French dockyards. It has become increasingly evident that considerable force could be required. Stormont was clear that the French were not going to risk a small detachment. On 19 January he reported that three ships and four frigates had sailed under the command of La Motte Picquet with sealed instructions, and that they were to be joined by five more ships and six frigates. These were to be replaced by others brought forward from ordinary. Two days later he reported that twenty-one ships were to be brought forward, and that all the sea officers had been ordered to hold themselves in readiness. On 25 January he added the report that all the ships of the line at Toulon were ordered to sail to Brest.[235] After an unsatisfactory interview with Maurepas, he concluded that the French were aiming at preparing and training as large a fleet as possible. Even before it was in fact concluded on 6 February he was convinced that France had signed a treaty with the rebels. "The general language of France," he wrote on that day, "at this moment is immediate War."[236] La Motte Picquet's squadron, now off Belle Isle, was reportedly ordered to convoy the American supply ships about 250 leagues off-shore. In a "Most Confidential" addition Stormont drew the obvious conclusion: "I have no Doubt that he has orders to protect the Ships under his Convoy at every Hazard and as I am persuaded our Rivals do us the Justice to believe that if these ships fall in our way we shall not let them pass, it is very natural they should expect immediate war."

It was Stormont's view, as he expressed it later to Weymouth, that "the Duration of the War will, in My poor Judgment depend much upon the Manner in w[hi]ch we begin it, if we are happy enough to stun France with a Great Blow this war may be as short as that which was begun and ended by Lord Torringtons Victory at Messina."[237] In the week following the conclusion of the alliance there was an invasion scare in France, which may have been intended, as Stormont suspected, to provide justification for the feverish military activity that was taking place.[238] Equally it could have been a move in Vergennes' game to draw Spain into the war. The simplest explanation is that the spectre of invasion came easily to the guilty consciences of those in France who knew the plot.[239] Weymouth, however, was far from planning the sort of stunning blow which Stormont thought so necessary. When the latter suggested he be authorized to demand an explanation for French preparations, Weymouth thought it unwise. Perhaps he was right; eighteenth-century naval technique rarely made possible spirited action. It was too late once the Franco-American treaties had been signed for any display of strength to intimidate the French.

The imminence of a French declaration in favour of the rebels did not bring the British to regard the American war as lost. London continued to seek delay in the inevitable hostilities with France, and did not make the radical strategic decision to concentrate on fighting France which hindsight suggests ought to have been done. The political problem had became one of finding some means of getting parliamentary sanction for concessions to the Americans which might persuade them to remain attached to the British Crown.[240] The military problem was to put pressure on the Americans to accept them, employing the major part of Howe's army which had not participated in the defeat, while guarding against French adventures. The strategic imperative continued to be time; war must be held off while political negotiations were conducted with the rebels. On 6 February, Weymouth went so far as to reassure the Lords that "nothing could be more pacific than the professions of that court [Versailles] at this time," although he hastily added that he would not "hold himself answerable or liable to be called upon, should a war break out shortly."[241] On 6 March he wrote to Stormont instructing him not to make any protest at La Motte Picquet's force: "Such a Measure cannot have been determined upon without fully weighing the consequences, and it is not to be supposed that the Orders, if given, will be withdrawn from any Arguments that can be stated."[242]

The policy of preparing for war but avoiding a confrontation, however, had failed. Four days earlier North had languidly agreed with Sandwich "that we should go forward in our military preparations with great diligence." He felt sure, however, that war would not come until the Spanish galleons were home. In any case he would not authorize anything without a cabinet meeting.[243] Sandwich replied:

> By the accounts this day received from France, it appears that the Duc de Chartres is actually at Brest taking upon him the command of the fleet, which consists of 21 ships of the line and 35 frigates; and that there are at Toulon 12 of the line and 13 frigates, making in all 33 of the line and 48 frigates in commission and ready for service. Spain has also, I believe, 32 of the line and 8 frigates, so that the House of Bourbon have in Europe an actual force of 65 of the line.
>
> You will find enclosed a note seemingly unintelligible, about brandy

N.º 10.

Turin the 21ᵗ February 1778.

Sir,

O)

The Levy of Sailors
3145. 2415. 56. 867. 2441.
continues with great activity on the Coast of
140. 771. 490. 552. 202. 2442. 1393. 195.
Languedoc, and they are immediately sent
893. 1110. 2657. 162. 2275. 1497. 1902. 1026.
under a proper guard to Toulon. The Press
717. 2936. 691. 1627. 2361. 3254. 966. 1037
for some time past has been so strong that the
1775. 390. 2292. 1981. 1391. 2073. 2470. 96.
trading Vessels are every where left without
1292. 1225. 1539. 2797. 2306. 1737. 169. 1710.
hands; and even the Masters of Ships which are
358. 640. 613. 1689. 96. 488. 656. 2259.
out of employ are forced into the Service to do
679. 1239. 1028. 1955. 1785. 491. 3515. 1456.
the duty of common Men : they inlist some of
3481. 3325. 401. 257. 1919. 1393. 72. 1868.

A. Chamier Esq.º   sixty 754.

Cipher letter from Dean Poyntz, Consul at Turin, to Anthony Chamier, 25 February 1778.
Courtesy of the Public Record Office, ref. no. sp 92/82

merchants: that note was brought to me yesterday from my friend at Morlaix, and is his mode of conveying to me that every exertion in point of preparing the fleet at Brest is now going on. Surely there is no longer any fear of our alarming France by our preparations; on the contrary, it seems to me that their preparations ought to be considered as very alarming to this country, and that not a moment should be lost in using every exertion on our part to make ourselves at least equal to our enemies; and this is the more necessary as there is every reason to expect that Captain Digby will fall in with Monsieur de La Motte-Picquet, which must occasion an immediate war. But even if that does not happen, I own I see a French war inevitable at a very little distance.[244]

Sandwich may not yet have received the warning from Poyntz at Turin which arrived in Weymouth's office 5 March that a general press had been ordered at Toulon.[245] On the 7th came Stormont's report that d'Estaing was leaving Paris to take command at Toulon.[246] Sandwich asked North: "As the French have commissioned their capital ships, can there be grounds for a moment's hesitation about putting the Victory into commission? And when the Duc de Chartres is at Brest, why should not Admiral Keppel be at Portsmouth?" Sandwich demanded permission to commission "every ship that is any forwardness" so that their officers could begin to look for men, and he asked whether ten or twelve frigates should not be recalled from America.

Sandwich was right that the time had passed when mobilization should be deferred out of concern for French sensitivities. It was the French who were setting the pace. When word of the French treaties leaked to the public through the Dutch *Gazette* there was no official British reaction. That did not serve Vergennes' purpose, for he wished to be at war before the American Congress could consider Britain's peace proposals. On 13 March M. de Noailles formally advised Weymouth that France had recognized the independence of the United States and had signed treaties of friendship and commerce. The same day Stormont was instructed to depart from Paris without taking leave.[247]

Notes

CHAPTER ONE: INTRODUCTION

1 Quoted in Michael Roberts, "Splendid Isolation, 1763-1780," Stenton Lecture 1969, University of Reading.
2 See W. L. Dorn, "Frederick the Great and Lord Bute."
3 "A Short View of the Present Situation," unsigned, *c.* 1763-66, PRO 30/8/70/5 f. 61.
4 SP 94/268 f. 37v.
5 See J. F. Ramsey, "Anglo-French Relations, 1763-1770," *passim.*
6 20 July 1765, SP 94/253.
7 22 September, SP 94/175. See V. L. Brown, "Studies in the History of Spain in the Second Half of the Eighteenth Century," *passim.*
8 See P. Coquelle, "Le Comte de Guerchy, ambassadeur de France à Londres, 1763-1767," p. 467.
9 Quoted in Roberts, "Splendid Isolation," p. 27.

CHAPTER TWO: THE BRITISH NAVY AFTER THE SEVEN YEARS' WAR

1 Add. MS 38,366 ff. 359-66, undated but subsequent to the economies of 1767. It can therefore only refer to the 1768 estimates.
2 "Account of the Number & Tonnage . . ." October 1763, Sandwich MS, F 1 no. 32.
3 ADM 106/2196, pp. 197-98.
4 "A Plan for the Disposition of His Majesty's Ships to be employed in time of Peace," 5 January 1763, ADM 2/371 p. 406, and SP 42/43 p. 27. See also "List of His Majesty's Ships Proposed to be employed," *c.* 1763, Sandwich MS F 1 no. 24-25.
5 ADM 8/41, Admiralty List Book for September 1765. See also Add. MS 38,340 ff. 187-88, a comparison of Grenville's plan of 1763 for the naval establishment, and the actual state in 1767.
6 See Neil R. Stout, *The Royal Navy in North America, passim.*
7 The sample consists of those ships the abstracts of whose journals appear between pages 200 and 209 of the Admiralty compilation ADM 7/574.
8 "An account of the Annual Charge of each of the Guardships in the last Peace at a Medium of Three Years," ADM 49/162 (bound volume).
9 Abstracted from ADM 7/651, Guardships 1764-70. See ADM 1/4126, 14 December 1765, and ADM 2/236 p. 157, 7 April 1765.
10 "An Abstract of His Majesty's Fleet . . ." 30 September 1764, ADM 7/186.

11 "An Account . . ." 1 September 1764, George March & Tho Hicks, Sandwich MS F 1 no. 34.

12 See J. E. D. Binney, *British Public Finance and Administration 1774-92*, pp. 134-49; and Daniel Baugh, *British Naval Administration in the Age of Walpole*, pp. 470-80.

13 See my article, "British Assessments of French and Spanish Naval Reconstruction between the Peace of Paris of 1763 and the Recommencement of Hostilities with France."

14 Goodricke to Sandwich, 20 September 1964, SP 95/105 f. 86. See Michael Roberts, *British Diplomacy and Swedish Politics 1758-1773*, pp. 79, 91-92, 124-25.

15 See Kenneth Ellis, *The Post Office in the Eighteenth Century*, pp. 60-77, 152-53.

16 ADM 1/3949-61 for the period of this book. See F. P. Renaut, *Le Secret Service de l'amirauté britannique au temps de la Guerre d'Amérique 1776-1783*.

17 Madrid Bill 1767, and Walters, 30 December 1769, SP 84/515 and 526.

18 Wolters to Stephens, 28 February 1769, ADM 1/3972.

19 Harcourt to Weymouth, 29 November 1769, SP 78/281 f. 180.

20 R. Mackay, *Admiral Hawke*, p. 323.

21 M. Wolters to Suffolk, 8 June 1773, ADM 1/4352; and see A. Cobban, *Ambassadors and Secret Agents: The Diplomacy of the First Earl of Malmesbury at The Hague*, p. 113. Cobban considers Wolters' service overrated in the period 1785-86, but quotes FO 97/246, Fraser to Harris, 4 January 1785, ordering the ending of the service because it was no longer as informative as it had been previously.

22 SP 81/142, in Cressener to Secretary of State, 24 January. See James Pritchard's study of the failure of the French naval finances during the Seven Years' War; *Louis XV's Navy, passim*.

23 Paris, 3 January 1763, and Geneva, 23 February 1763, SP 84/503.

24 See A. T. Patterson, *The Other Armada*, p. 30; and H.M. Scott, "The Importance of Bourbon Naval Reconstruction to the Strategy of Choiseul after the Seven Years' War."

25 E.F. Choiseul, Duc de, *Mémoires*, p. 406.

26 "Etat de la Marine de France," 1 November, SP 84/503. An undated copy is at Add. MS 35,898 f. 282.

27 ADM 1/4352.

28 SP 84/513.

29 Versailles, 12 April, and Paris, 5 July: in Cressener to Conway, nos 23 and 39, 20 April and 14 July 1767, SP 81/147.

30 PRO 30/885 f. 351; and Add. MS 38,339 f. 254.

31 SP 84/520. A copy of this list is in ADM 1/3972, and in the Hardwick Papers Add. MS 35,878.

32 Choiseul evidently overstated not only his success in rebuilding the French fleet, but also the size of the British fleet, which he numbered at 150 effective ships of the line. See Scott, "The Importance of Bourbon Naval Reconstruction."

33 SP 78/277 f. 147. See Lynch, April 1769, SP 92/74 no. 3, reporting that there were no ships building at Toulon.

34 SP 78/279 f. 192.

35 SP 84/536.

36 ADM 1/4352, and 26 May, SP 84/503. See Wolters to Halifax, 25 March, and

Sandwich to Wolters, 18 October 1763.

37 SP 84/506.
38 ADM 1/4352.
39 "A List of the Spanish Ships of War," in Rochford to Conway, SP 94/172.
40 PRO 30/8/93 f. 240.
41 Add. MS 38,339 f. 254.
42 "Liste de la Marine d'Espagne," SP 84/517.
43 "Répartition des vaisseaux de la Marine d'Espagne," SP 84/520.
44 ADM 1/3972.
45 Madrid Intelligence, SP 84/524.
46 ADM 1/524.
47 "A list of His Catholic Majesty's Ships of War," SP 42/103.
48 "Liste de la Marine d'Espagne," SP 84/526.
49 Madrid, 14 December 1766, SP 84/516.
50 In this view they apparently were in agreement with Choiseul himself. See Scott, "The Importance of Bourbon Naval Reconstruction."
51 See Binney, *British Public Finance and Administration 1774-92*, p. 249.
52 Sandwich to Grenville, September 1774, Grenville Papers, II, pp. 171, 290, 293, 441.
53 Admiralty to Navy Board, 7 April, ADM 2/234 p. 69; and Admiralty Board Minutes, ADM 3/71, for 7, 16, 30 April 1764, ADM 3/72, for 21 May (f. 251, 18 August (f. 72), and 8 September (f. 85) 1764.
54 Admiralty to Navy Board, 18 June, and Navy Board to Admiralty, 20 July 1764, ADM 49/162 (bound volume). See also ADM 106/2579, 20 July 1764.
55 ADM 2/234, p. 215. Also in ADM 49/162 (bound volume), 21 June.
56 ADM 106/2196, pp. 405-8, 431-34.
57 See "Reasons for the increase of the navy debt," 30 January 1764, ADM 106/2195, pp. 448, 452-53.
58 Mason to Stephens, 11 March 1765, ADM 7/703.
59 16 March 1765, ADM 106/2580.
60 Admiralty to Navy Board, "secret and private," 25 April, and Navy Board to Admiralty 10 May 1765, ADM 7/703.
61 30 May 1765, ADM 7/703.
62 July, T 29/37, p. 46; and ADM 106/2197, pp. 73, 140-44.
63 Order to Council, 6 September, ADM 49/162; and Navy Board to Admiralty 21 October 1765, ADM 49/162 and ADM 2/235, p. 447.
64 ADM 7/567 ff. 97-99.
65 ADM 3/73 f. 188.
66 T. Keppel, *The Life of Augustus Viscount Keppel* (1842), p. 382. Thomas Keppel acknowledges his source as the Rockingham Papers, but the original is not among those deposited in the Sheffield City Libraries.
67 Admiralty Office, 15 December 1767, Add. MS 38,340 f. 102.
68 ADM 106/2197, pp. 250-53.
69 R. Mackay, *Admiral Hawke*, p. 308.
70 A similar account is printed in J. G. Bullock, ed., *The Tomlinson Papers* (1935) p. 61.
71 See Saunders to Hood, 25 August 1766, MKH/C/1B; and Mackay, *Admiral Hawke*, pp. 295-332.
72 ADM 106/2198, pp. 90-91. See also Add. MS 38,340 f. 22.
73 ADM 3/75 f. 27.

74 ADM 106/2198, pp. 128-37.

75 This passage is crossed with an X and may not have been delivered.

76 ADM 3/75 f. 56. An additional copy in Add. MS 38,340 f. 56.

77 ADM 106/2198, pp. 150-56, 221-25. See also 21 April and 12 November 1767, ADM 2/237, pp. 93. 331.

78 "Heads of Defence of the Extra Estimate of the Navy": ADM 106/2198, pp. 348-49.

79 Egerton MS 220 f. 2, 2 February 1770.

80 Admiralty Board Minutes, 21 November 1769, ADM 3/77 f. 49.

81 PRO 30/8/79 f. 279. "The Utmost Efforts being exerted during the last War to raise Men / The first three Months 13,418 Men / The 2d three Months 7,301 / The 3d Do 4,241 / The 4th Do 864. Total Men rais'd for the Sea Service in the 1st Year of the last War 25,824.

Thus only 39 Ships of the Line & 474 Men over, can be fitted out within the whole first year in addition to the Peace Establishment. It also appears that the highest Number after 7 years War to which the navy attain'd or may ever be expected to attain are 87,019 borne 84,770 muster'd." See Sir J. Fortescue, *The Correspondence of King George the Third*, no. 3 (incorrectly dated 1763?).

82 22 August 1756, PRO 30/8/78 f. 76.

83 See Stephen Gradish, *The Manning of the British Navy during the Seven Years War*, pp. 29-53.

84 SP 78/277 f. 6.

85 1 January 1768, SP 84/520.

86 SP 84/517.

87 Accounts of the Spanish Navy, Bedfordshire County Records Office L29/353-72 (duodecimo).

88 Brian Lavery, *The Ship of the Line*, vol. 1, ch. 10.

89 Admiralty to Navy Board, 23 June, ADM 2/237; and Navy Board to Stephens, 5 and 17 June 1767, ADM 106/2198, pp. 221, 235-42.

90 Admiralty to Navy Board, 23 June 1767, ADM 3/75 f. 118, and ADM 2/237 p. 156 (words vary).

91 Hansard, ed., *Parliamentary History* xvi col. 607, 10 April 1769. For a general analysis of the dockyards at this time see R.J.B. Knight. "The Royal Dockyards in England at the time of the American War of Independence," London PH D, 1972. See also Daniel A. Baugh, *British Naval Administration in the Age of Walpole, s.v.* "The Dockyards," and Roger Morriss, *The Royal Dockyards during the Revolutionary and Napoleonic Wars, passim.*

92 Bradshaw to Grafton, 24 July 1770, West Suffolk Record Office 423/615.

93 A. H. Fitzroy, 3rd Duke of Grafton, *Autobiography of the Duke of Grafton,* Sir W.R. Anson, ed., p. 257; and West Suffolk Record Office 423/311 pt. 2.

94 Quoted in George Martelli, *Jemmy Twitcher*, p. 81.

95 25 October 1771, SP 78/283 f. 183.

96 Letter 42, 30 January 1771, *The Letters of Junius*, vol. 2, p. 51.

97 2 December 1772, *The Speeches of the Rt. Hon. Edmund Burke*, vol. 1, p. 138.

98 ADM 7/659 f. 111.

99 R 17-8. The 81 ships consisted of three of 100 guns, nine of 90 guns, 33 of 74 guns, six of 70, 19 of 64, and eight of 60. See R 17-5, List of Royal Navy, 29 December 1766, and 22 November 1768. The totals given are 135 and 139 capital ships, but it is noted: "Notwithstanding the total of 1768 you must suppose at least 50 of the line unfit for service & many of the smaller ships—& tho you was to reckon an increase by 8 [illegible word, ships by?] 1770. *I w[oul]d still not*

expect to be above 90 sail of y line.'' (Quotation with the permission of Earl Fitzwilliam and his Trustees.)

100 Sandwich MS F 3 no. 3.
101 29 January 1772, Egerton MS 232 f. 69.
102 ADM 7/660 ff. 16, 39, 61, 68, 75, 88.
103 ADM 7/661 ff. 13, 20, 37, 55, 60, 71.
104 See N. A. M. Roger, *The Admiralty*, pp. 71-80.
105 ADM 7/662 visitation of the dockyards. See J.M. Haas, ''The Introduction of Task Work in tne Royal Naval Dockyards, 1775.''
106 Sandwich MS F 4 no. 18. The style of writing is Sandwich's.
107 Sandwich MS F 12 no. 115, Navy Office, 27 February 1778.
108 G. R. Barns and J. H. Owen, eds., *The Private Papers of John, Earl of Sandwich, First Lord of Admiralty, 1771-1782*, vol. 2, pp. 258-65.
109 See R.J.B. Knight, ''The Royal Dockyards in England at the Time of the American War of Independence.''
110 Fortescue, *George III*, nos 986 (22 October 1771?) and 990 (15 November).
111 ADM 2/372, p. 293, and SP 42/48.
112 ADM 8/39-51.
113 The King to North, January 1771, Fortescue, *George III*, no. 901.
114 Sandwich MS F 4 no. 6.
115 ADM 7/659 f. 11, and ADM 2/241, p. 517.
116 See Barns and Owen, *Sandwich Papers*, vol. 1, p. 36, George III to [Sandwich?], 18 October 1773.
117 Egerton MS 232 f. 3 *et seq.*
118 Sandwich to a lord of the Admiralty, 13 June 1771, Sandwich MS F 2 no. 24.
119 ADM 7/659 f. 10, and ADM 8/48. For accounts of two training cruises see Spry to Stephens, 5 August 1774, ADM 1/805.
120 Captain Hervey was a member of the Board of Admiralty. Egerton MS 232 f. 3 *et seq.*
121 ADM 8/39-51.
122 Navy Debt, ADM 7/567. Other statements of the navy debt are to be found in the Sandwich MSS F 2 no. 10; F 3 no. 6; F 4 no. 6.
123 Admiralty Office, 11 March, 20 and 21 August 1772, Sandwich MS F 3 nos 15, 33, 34.
124 ''Ships built'' 1771, SP 84/532.
125 SP 84/536.
126 Sandwich MS F 3 no. 21.
127 J. R. Dull, ''The French Navy and American Independence'' (thesis), p. 6.
128 Sandwich MS F 4 no. 18. See Durnford to Rochford, 14 December 1772 (F 3 no. 45) giving 74 French ships of the line.
129 J. R. Dull, ''The French Navy and American Independence'' (thesis), p. 4.
130 ADM 1/3972.
131 17 and 24 May 1773, L 29/353-72.
132 Sandwich MS F 3 no. 22; and L 29/353-72.
133 SP 84/544.

CHAPTER THREE: THE UTILIZATION OF NAVAL SUPREMACY, 1763-68

1 For more detail concerning these events see my article, ''The Gunboat

Diplomacy of the Government of George Grenville, 1764-5, the Honduras, Turks Island, the Gambian Incidents.''

2 See R. Pares, *War and Trade in the West Indies, 1739-1763*; J. McLachlan, ''The Seven Years' Peace and the West Indian Policy of Carvajal and Wall''; Z. E. Rashed, *The Peace of Paris, 1763*, and V.L. Brown, ''Anglo-Spanish Relations in America, 1763-74.''

3 Lyttleton to Halifax, 3 April 1764, SP 94/167; and Burnaby to Stephens, 6 May 1764 (enclosing Yucatan to Maud, 29 December 1763), ADM 1/238.

4 Halifax to Rochford, 15 June and 3 July, and Masserano to Halifax, 18 June, SP 94/167; Admiralty to Halifax 28 June, ADM 2/371.

5 See Mrs. Grenville's diary; W. J. Smith, ed., *The Grenville Papers*, vol. 2, pp. 379, 511. J. R. G. Tomlinson, ed. of *The Additional Grenville Papers, 1763-1765*, considers that Mrs. Grenville must have been the author (pp. 4-11).

6 See Bedford to Sandwich, 22 July 1764, Sandwich MS v 14 no. 5.

7 Rochford to Halifax, 8 and 30 July, SP 94/167; and Sandwich to Bedford, 29 July, in Lord John Russell, ed., *Correspondence of John, Fourth Duke of Bedford*, vol. 3, p. 263.

8 ADM 1/238.

9 Stephens to Sedgwick (for Halifax), SP 42/43.

10 Shirley to Halifax (enclosing letter to d'Etaigne [sic], 19 July), CO 23/16 f. 23.

11 Sandwich MS v 14 no. 50, printed in F. Spence, ed., *The Fourth Earl of Sandwich, Diplomatic Correspondence, 1763-1765*, p. 192.

12 See Halifax to Grenville 8 August and Grenville to Halifax 9 August, Smith, *The Grenville Papers*, vol. 2, pp. 418, 422; *Journal of the Commissioners for Trade and Plantations, 1764-1775*, LXXI, pp. 426-28, 13 and 15 August; Spence, *Sandwich, Diplomatic Correspondence*, p. 197. There was a cabinet meeting on the 14th and Turks Island appears to have been discussed, although it was not recorded in Grenville's minutes (Tomlinson, *The Additional Grenville Papers*, p. 324).

13 J. M. Haas, ''The Pursuit of Political Success in 18th Century England: Sandwich, 1740-71.''

14 Tomlinson, *The Additional Grenville Papers*, p. 197 (Sandwich MS v 14 no. 6).

15 Bedford to Sandwich, 20 August, and Grenville to Sandwich, 24 August, Sandwich MS v 14 nos 7, 51. Bedford to Gower, 7, 9 September, Sandwich MS v 14 nos 8, 10 (printed in Spence, *Sandwich, Diplomatic Correspondence*, pp. 210, 217).

16 8 August, Smith, *The Grenville Papers*, vol. 2, p. 417.

17 See Burnaby to Stephens, 6 May 1764, ADM 1/238; Tomlinson, *The Additional Grenville Papers*, p. 325; Halifax to Admiralty, ADM 1/4126 no. 69 and SP 44/231; and ADM 2/92, p. 122.

18 18 August, Spence, *Sandwich, Diplomatic Correspondence*, p. 200.

19 SP 78/263 f. 48.

20 Rochford to Halifax, 6 and 13 August, SP 94/168.

21 ADM 1/4126 no. 17, and SP 44/231, p. 231.

22 SP 94/168.

23 Grenville to Sandwich, 31 August, Smith, *The Grenville Papers*, vol. 2, p. 435.

24 ADM 2/92, pp. 152, 159.

25 ''Rough Heads of a Resolution proposed to be submitted to the consideration of His Majesty's Šervants, in relation, to what has happened at Turk's Island,'' Sandwich MS v 14 no. 9. See also Hertford to Halifax, 28 August, SP 78/263 f. 83.

26 Cabinet Minute, 5 September, Spence, *Sandwich, Diplomatic Correspondence*, p. 208; ADM 1/4126 no. 75, SP 44/231, and SP 42/65; Admiralty to Burnaby, ADM 2/1332, p. 109.

27 P. Cunningham, ed., *The Letters of Horace Walpole*, vol. 4, p. 265. See also Horace Walpole, *Memoirs of the Reign of George III*, vol. 2, p. 12.

28 (Gower?) to Sandwich (Draft), 8 September, PRO 30/29/1/16 no. 5 f. 934.

29 Grenville to Bedford, 5 September, SP 78/263 f. 89; Halifax to Grenville, 9 September, and Grenville to Bedford, 12 September, Smith, *The Grenville Papers*, vol. 2, pp. 436, 438; ADM 2/1332, p. 109 and Admiralty Minutes, 25 September, ADM 3/72 f. 94.

30 Cabinet Minutes, Tomlinson, *The Additional Grenville Papers*, p. 328; and Burnaby to Admiralty, 15 July, ADM 1/238 (see Admiralty Minutes, 22 September, ADM 3/72 f. 92).

31 Halifax to Admiralty, 23 September, ADM 1/4126 no. 78, SP 44/231 p. 240, and SP 42/65; Halifax to Lyttleton 23 September, CO 123/3; and Halifax to Hertford, 25 September, SP 78/263 f. 132.

32 Secret orders to Burnaby, 25 September, ADM 2/1332, p. 119; and ADM 2/92 pp. 168-69 (see the captain's log of *Africa*, ADM 51/3755).

33 SP 94/168. See Orders to the Governor of Yucatan, 16 September, SP 44/168; ADM 1/4126 no. 79; Stephens to Sedgwick, 28 September, SP 42/65; Burnaby to Admiralty, 15 July and 4 September (enclosing Burnaby to d'Estaing, 16 July), ADM 1/238; and Shirley to Halifax, 20 July (enclosing Shirley to d'Etaigne [*sic*], 19 July) and 23 September, CO 23/16 ff. 23, 40; Captain's log of *Venus*, ADM 51/1033; Burnaby to Stephens, 11, 20 September, ADM 1/238; and Shirley to Halifax, 2 October, CO 23/16 f. 63; Burnaby to Stephens, 5 February and 21 September 1765, ADM 1/238; Admiralty to Halifax, 14 June 1765, SP 42/65; Burnaby's log, ADM 50/1; and Sir John Burdon, *Archives of British Honduras*, Admiralty to Halifax, 13 March 1765, ADM 2/371 p. 515, and SP 42/65; Halifax to Admiralty, 23 March, ADM 1/4126 and SP 42/65; and Halifax to Admiralty, 17 June, ADM 1/4126 and SP 44/231, p. 306.

34 Secret orders to Burnaby, 29 September, ADM 2/1332 p. 124; and ADM 2/92, p. 173. See Stephens to Sedgwick, 6 October, *Calendar of Home Office Papers 1760-1765*, no. 1474. On the 27th the Admiralty had ordered *Thunderer* to proceed to Jamaica, but the next day an express was sent to stop her (ADM 3/72 ff. 95-96).

35 SP 94/168.

36 Tomlinson, *The Additional Grenville Papers*, p. 331. See J.M. Gray, *History of the Gambia*, pp. 213-28; *Journal of the Commissioners for Trade and Plantations*, vol. 71 ff. 154, 247-48, 308, 399-400 (13 April, 31 May, 1 and 2 June, 18 and 20 July 1764); Petition of the Committee of the Company of Merchants Trading to Africa, to Pitt, 19 May 1761, CO 267/6; and Hillsborough to the King, 21 July 1764 (enclosing the Committee of the Company of Merchants' statement of British rights), CO 267/13.

37 ADM 2/92, pp. 166, 186.

38 Halifax to Admiralty, 16 October, SP 44/231, p. 246; ADM 1/4126, no. 80, and SP 44/231, p. 249; and Admiralty to Collier 22 October, ADM 2/92 p. 194. See Admiralty Minutes, 20 October, ADM 3/72 f. 110.

39 30 October, SP 78/263 f. 182.

40 *Journal of the Commissioners for Trade and Plantations*, vol. 71 f. 442, 19, 29 November; and Tomlinson, *The Additional Grenville Papers*, pp. 331-32.

41 ADM 2/92, pp. 222, 229; Admiralty Minutes, 1 December 1764 (and see 9 July 1765, 26 April, and 26 June 1766), ADM 3/72 f. 153 and ADM 3/73-74; and Stephens to Graves, 15 November, ADM 1/1836, no. 2. Graves was favoured by Egmont.

42 ADM 2/92, pp. 238-39.

43 11 December, ADM 1/1836, no. 2.

44 Admiralty to Halifax, 15 December, SP 42/65 (see ADM 3/72 f. 169); Secret Orders to Graves, ADM 2/1332 f. 126; Pye to Stephens, 1, 4, 6, 22 January 1765, ADM 1/804; and Graves to Stephens, 1, 6 January 1765, ADM 1/1836, no. 2.

45 20 January 1765, SP 78/265 f. 76.

46 21 January, Tomlinson, *The Additional Grenville Papers*, pp. 333-34; see Halifax to de Guerchy, 23 January, SP 78/265 f. 76.

47 23 January, ADM 1/804.

48 ADM 1/804. See the Admiralty Minutes, ADM 3/72 f. 207.

49 16 January, SP 78/265 f. 57.

50 31 January, SP 78/265 f. 72.

51 Pye to Stephens, 7 PM, 1 February, ADM 1/804. See the Admiralty Minutes for 31 January, ADM 3/72 f. 208.

52 31 January, SP 78/265 f. 72. See also Halifax to Admiralty, 11 February, ADM 1/4126 no. 93 and SP 44/231, p. 273.

53 ADM 2/1332 f. 131. See Admiralty Minutes, ADM 3/72 f. 220.

54 12 February, SP 78/265 f. 142.

55 Hertford to Halifax, 13 February, SP 78/265 f. 180.

56 SP 78/265 ff. 202, 206. Halifax had written the same thing to de Guerchy on the 11th.

57 ADM 1/4126 no. 98; ADM 2/1332 f. 133; and Admiralty to Halifax, 25 March, ADM 2/371, p. 517.

58 Admiralty to Conway, 25 July 1765, ADM 2/372, p. 1.

59 22 March 1765, ADM 1/1836 no. 2.

60 Admiralty to Halifax, 11 May 1765, ADM 2/371, p. 520 and SP 42/65. Graves to Stephens, 24 April *et seq.*, ADM 1/1836 no. 2; CO 267/1; and Admiralty to Conway, 29 July 1765, ADM 2/372, p. 2 and SP 42/65.

61 Admiralty to Edgcumbe, 7 August, ADM 2/93, p. 4; and Edgcumbe to Stephens, 11 August, ADM 1/804.

62 1 September 1764, CO 194/16 f. 1.

63 Palliser to Board of Trade, 9 October 1764, CO 194/16.

64 See Palliser to Stephens, 21 October 1764, SP 42/65; Hillsborough to the King, 11 December 1764 and 10 April 1765, CO 195/9, pp. 360, 369; 11 December 1764, *Journal of the Commissioners for Trade and Plantations, 1764-1775; Acts of the Privy Council of England, Colonial Series,* IV, p. 584; Admiralty to Halifax, 13 March 1765, ADM 2/371, p. 513; and Horace Walpole, *Memoirs*, vol. 2, p. 64.

65 See Conway-Hume correspondence, 14, 28 August 1764, SP 78/267; Palliser to Stephens, 16 July 1765, CO 194/27 f. 52; and Halifax to Admiralty, 8 May 1765, ADM 1/4126.

66 Palliser to d'Angeau 25 June 1765, CO 194/27 f. 58; and see CO 194/27 ff. 66, 70, 255.

67 SP 78/277 f. 6.

68 *Memoirs*, vol. 2, p. 64; and see Hertford to Halifax, 5 September 1764, SP 78/263 f. 89.

69 SP 78/267 f. 177.

70 See M. S. Anderson, "Great Britain and the Barbary States in the Eighteenth Century," and H.I. Lee, "Supervision of Barbary Consuls during the years 1756-1836."

71 11 December 1765, CO 91/14.

72 Conway-Irwin correspondence, 25 February and 31 March 1766, CO 91/14; CO 91/15 *passim*; and see Conway to Admiralty, 15 March 1766, SP 42/43; and Admiralty to Denis, 19 January 1774, ADM 2/1332.

73 8 June, CO 91/15.

74 SP 42/102 f. 184.

75 Egremont to Neville, 12 August 1763, SP 78/257.

76 Neville to Halifax, 31 August 1763, SP 78/257; and Memorandum on Dunkirk by Col. Desmaretz, 26 September 1763, SP 78/258 f. 55.

77 Neville to Halifax, 24 October 1763, SP 78/258 f. 211 (see also 11 and 23 November and 21 December, SP 78/258 f. 273, and SP 78/259 ff. 44, 184); Cabinet Minute, 23 February 1764, Tomlinson, *Additional Grenville Papers 1763-1765*, p. 320 (see also SP 44/231, p. 184 and SP 78/260 f. 284); and Halifax to Hertford, 11 May 1764, SP 78/261 f. 173.

78 Hertford-Halifax correspondence, 24 May, 5 June, and 20 August 1764, SP 78/261 ff. 224, 260, SP 78/263 f. 43.

79 Sandwich MS v 14 no. 8 (printed in Spence, *Sandwich, Diplomatic Correspondence*, p. 210).

80 8 September 1764, Spence, *Sandwich, Diplomatic Correspondence*, p. 212.

81 8 September 1764, PRO 30/29/1/16 no. 5 f. 934.

82 See SP 78/267 ff. 107, 183, and SP 78/268 f. 178.

83 See my article "The Capture of Manila, 1762," and my ms "Manila Ransomed."

84 Walpole, *Memoirs of the Reign of King George the Third*, vol. 2, p. 227.

85 Rochford to Conway, 6 September 1765 and 16 January 1766, SP 94/171 and 173.

86 To Junius, 17 February 1769, *The Letters of Junius*, no. 4.

87 To Shelburne?, 18 February 1767, SP 78/272 f. 101.

88 7 July 1766, H. Wallis, ed., *Carteret's Voyage Round the World, 1766-1769*, vol. 2, no. 12.

89 Devisme to Shelburne, 15 and 22 September 1766, SP 94/175; and Rochford to Shelburne, 4 February 1767, SP 78/272 f. 77.

90 Shelburne to Rochford, 17 November 1766, Add. MS 9242 f. 1.

91 Printed in B. G. Corney, ed., *The Quest and Occupation of Tahiti*, vol. 1, p. 108 (see "Minute," Grimaldi to Arriaga, 25 March 1768); see also my ms "Manila Ransomed," and J. Goebel, *The Struggle for the Falkland Islands*, p. 271.

92 6 July 1764, SP 95/104 f. 132.

93 22 May 1764, SP 95/104 f. 66. See Michael F. Metcalf, "Russia, England, and Swedish Party Politics 1762-1766."

94 Grafton to Goodricke, 24 January 1766, SP 95/109 f. 9.

95 Goodricke to Yorke, 5 February 1766, Add. MS 35,444 f. 41.

96 To Buckinghamshire, 20 January, SP 91/73 f. 32. See Roberts, *British Diplomacy and Swedish Politics, 1758-1773*, pp. 111-23, 179-212, 236-46.

97 George III to Chatham, 14 September 1766, W.S. Taylor and J.H. Pringle, eds., *Correspondence of William Pitt, Earl of Chatham*, vol. 3, p. 66.

98 7 October 1767, SP 91/78 f. 146.

99 See my article, "The Government of the Duke of Grafton, and the French Invasion of Corsica in 1768."

100 Hollford to Shelburne, 5 September 1767, SP 79/24; see 21 March 1767. Memorandum, misdated (May-June 1767), Shelburne MS v 40:7 pt. II; and Hollford to Shelburne, December 1767, 6, 25 February, and 9 April 1768, SP 79/24. See also Rochford to Shelburne, 21 April 1768, SP 78/274 f. 206.
101 Mann to Shelburne, 23 April 1768, SP 98/73 f. 89.
102 Shelburne to Rochford, 29 April 1768, SP 78/274 f. 210.
103 Shelburne to Rochford, 12 May 1768, SP 78/275 f. 11; and Rochford to Shelburne, 25, 26 May 1768, *ibid.*, ff. 39, 43.
104 Shelburne to Rochford, 27 May 1768, SP 78/275 f. 32.
105 Walpole, *Memoirs of the Reign of King George the Third*, vol. 3, p. 217, May 1768.
106 See Grafton, *Grafton Autobiography*, pp. 203 *ff.*; Lord Fitzmaurice, *Life of William, Earl of Shelburne*, vol. 1, p. 364; "Copy of John Stewart's account of a visit to Paoli," unsigned, Shelburne MS v 40:24, pt. II, p. 224; and John Stewart or Stuart to Lord Weymouth, December 1768, *ibid.*, 2, pt. II.
107 Spry to Shelburne, 18, 21, 28 June 1768, SP 42/102 ff. 171, 173, 180.
108 Copy of John Stewart's account of a visit to Paoli, pp. 221-22.
109 Debate on Seymour's motion, Egerton MS 215, pp. 161-95.
110 Fitzroy, *Grafton Autobiography*, p. 203.
111 Grafton to Shelburne, 15 September 1768, Fitzmaurice, *Life of Shelburne*, vol. 1, p. 385.
112 Rochford to Shelburne, 26 May 1768, SP 78/275 f. 43.
113 John Stewart's account of a visit to Paoli, p. 224. See also Fitzmaurice, *Life of Shelburne*, pp. 363, 365, 374; Rochford to Shelburne, 2 June 1768, SP 78/275 f. 59; Shelburne MS v 161 p. 18; and Fitzroy, *Grafton Autobiography*, p. 204.
114 Shelburne to Grey, 18 June 1768, SP 94/179; and Grey to Shelburne, 21 July 1768, SP 94/180.
115 See copy of order forbidding clandestine aid to Paoli, 29 December 1762, Bath MS; Fitzroy, *Grafton Autobiography*, p. 208; Weymouth to [Camden?] 17 August 1768, PRO 30/29/1/14 no. 64 f. 614; Fortescue, *George III*, no. 1075; and M. Roberts, "Great Britain and the Swedish Revolution, 1772-73"; and Mann to Shelburne, 1 November 1768, SP 98/73 f. 270.
116 Grafton MS no. 423; George III to [Grafton?], 12 August 1768, *ibid.*, no. 518.
117 Fortescue, *George III*, no. 653; see also nos 643, 644, 652.
118 See Minutes, 23 September 1768, Shelburne MS v 161, p. 18a; and Shelburne to Mann, 27 September 1768 (quoted), SP 98/73.
119 Rochford to Cathcart, 27 January 1769, Add. MS 9242 f. 48. See Rochford to Mitchell, 18 November 1768, Add. MS 6822 f. 34.
120 Lynch to Weymouth, 24 June 1769, SP 92/74. See Rochford to Mitchell, 1 September 1769, Add. MS 6822 f. 58; and Rochford to Mann, 22 March 1771, SP 98/76 f. 37; see also SP 98/75 ff. 163, 215.
121 Rochford to Gunning, 17 March and reply 29 April 1769, SP 75/122 ff. 10, 112.

CHAPTER FOUR: THE FALKLAND ISLANDS CRISIS

1 See Michael Roberts, *British Diplomacy and Swedish Politics*, pp. 276, 289-96.
2 Harcourt to Rochford, 29 January 1772, SP 78/284 f. 57.
3 See my article on "The Falkland Islands Crisis of 1770: Use of Naval Force."

4 See Goebel, *Falkland Islands*, p. 259 (Guerchy to Masserano 20 January); and M. C. Morison, "The Duc de Choiseul and the Invasion of England 1768-1770."

5 P. Coquelle, "Le Comte de Guerchy, ambassadeur de France à Londres, 1763-1767." Quoted above page 4.

6 22 June 1767, Add. MS 32, 300 f. 78; see ff. 60-80 *passim*.

7 Mitchell to Weymouth, 12 November 1768, HMS 99, p. 189.

8 Chamier to East India Co., 23 and 27 March in East India Co. to Weymouth, 29 March 1769, HMS 100, p. 79. See also HMS 99, pp. 213, 215, 221, 271, 28 November, 15 December, Intelligence, 15 and 20 December 1768.

9 President and Select Committee Fort William to Court of Directors, 13 September 1768, HMS 100, p. 209.

10 12 and 15 June, ADM 1/4127 nos 161 and 166; see Admiralty to Lee, 15 June, to Deane and Lloyd, 26 July 1769, ADM 2/95, p. 145.

11 Weymouth to Admiralty, 21 July 1769, ADM 1/4127 no. 167. Admiralty to Lindsay, ADM 2/95, p. 200; and Admiralty to Weymouth, 31 August 1769, ADM 2/372, p. 152. Draft of Sir John Lindsay's Full Powers, 7 September, and Weymouth to Lindsay, Secret, 13 September 1769, HMS 101, pp. 53, 101.

12 Harcourt to Weymouth, 13 December 1769, SP 78/279 f. 202.

13 Weymouth to Harcourt, 19 December 1769, SP 78/279 f. 206.

14 Harcourt to Weymouth, 26 December 1769, 18 February, 7 March, 28 April 1770, SP 78/279 f. 221 and SP 78/280 f. 60, 111, 210; Weymouth to Lindsey, 3 January 1770, HMS 103, p. 1; and Admiralty to Weymouth, 4 January 1770, SP 42/46.

15 See Michael Roberts, "Great Britain, Denmark, and Russia, 1763-1770," in Ragnhild Hatton and M.S. Anderson, eds., *Studies in Diplomatic History*; and Roberts, *British Diplomacy and Swedish Politics*, pp. 270-81.

16 Orville T. Murphy, *Charles Gravier, Comte de Vergennes*, pp. 136-64.

17 Weymouth to Murray, 1 November 1768, SP 97/44 f. 83 (see also Rochford to Yorke, 29 November 1768, SP 84/518); and Murray to Weymouth, 3 January 1769, SP 97/45 f. 1.

18 Weymouth to Sir John Dick, 15 September 1769, SP 98/74 f. 173.

19 Rochford to Admiralty, 11 August 1769, SP 44/232 f. 31.

20 Fenwick to Stephens, 23 September 1769, ADM 1/3837; Admiralty to Commissioners for Victualling, 4 October 1769, and to Proby 18 October, ADM 2/95, pp. 355, 243.

21 Fenwick to Stephens, 12 December 1769, ADM 1/3837; Admiralty Board Minutes, 15, 28 November, 20 December 1769 and 30 January 1770, ADM 3/77 ff. 48, 55, 67, 85; Admiralty to Rochford, 20 November, and 20 December 1769, ADM 2/371, pp. 163-64, 172; and Admiralty to Navy Board, 20 December 1769, ADM 2/239, p. 122.

22 Rochford to Cathcart, 29 September 1769, SP 91/82 f. 86.

23 Murray to Weymouth, 17 March 1770, SP 97/46 f. 53.

24 Rochford to Admiralty, 12 April, and to Cathcart, 17 April 1770, SP 91/84 f. 31.

25 Rochford to Cathcart, 24 October 1769, SP 91/82 f. 160.

26 Rochford to Stormont, 24 August 1770, Add. MS 35,500 f. 67.

27 Walpole to Weymouth, SP 78/278 f. 138. See Admiralty to Weymouth, 8 and 21 November 1769, and Weymouth to Harcourt, 21 November, *ibid.*, ff. 164, 166, 170.

28 23 November, ADM 2/95, pp. 285-86. See ADM 1/943 *passim*.

29 Harcourt to Weymouth, 22 November 1769, SP 78/279 f. 174. See also *ibid.*, ff. 178, 190, 192.

30 Grafton MS no. 423 pt. 326.

31 Lynch to Weymouth, 5 and 26 May and 9 June, SP 92/75; and SP 78/280 ff. 249, 251.

32 Admiralty to Weymouth, 6 June 1770, SP 42/47 (see ADM 2/372, p. 199); and Shelburne to Rochford, 16 November 1766, Add. MS 9,242 f. 1. See J. Goebel, *Falkland Islands*; and my ms "Manila Ransomed."

33 SP 42/46.

34 ADM 2/238, p. 344.

35 20 June 1770, SP 78/280 f. 254.

36 Walpole to Weymouth, 27 June and 11 July 1770, SP 78/281 ff. 1, 37; and Weymouth to Walpole, 6 July, *ibid.*, f. 13.

37 Woods to [Stephens?] 13 July 1770, SP 42/46 (see Admiralty to Capt. Clements and Charles Proby, 17 August 1771, ADM 2/95, pp. 509-10); Weymouth to Admiralty, 18 July 1770, SP 42/47 (see Edgcume to Stephens, 22 July 1770, ADM 1/804); Egerton MS 222 f. 273, 22 November; L. Blart, *Les Rapports de la France*, p. 165; and see Smith, *The Grenville Papers*, vol. 4, p. 505, Coleman to [Grenville?], 4 March 1770 (received June) warning of the probability of attack.

38 Add. MS 32,300 f. 108.

39 Hansard, *Parliamentary History*, XVI, cols 1053 (North) and 1101 (Chatham), 13 November 1770.

40 John Wilkes had been deprived of his seat. *Ibid.*, cols 1038 (Meredith, 13 November 1770) and 1343 (Barré, 25 January 1771).

41 Weymouth to Admiralty, 16 August, SP 42/47; and Admiralty to Navy Board, 20 August, ADM 2/238. See Admiralty to Clements, St. John and Proby, 17 August 1770, MS 2/95, pp. 509-10.

42 Weymouth to Proby, 18 August 1770, SP 42/104 ff. 9-11.

43 Rochford to Cathcart, 25 August 1770, SP 91/85 f. 59. See also Weymouth to Murray, 18 August 1770, SP 97/46 f. 137.

44 Proby's log 24 and 29 September, ADM 51/683 (see Navy Board to Stephens, 26 November, ADM 106/2200, p. 186. An inquiry had been ordered into the defects found in Edgar); logs of *Dorsetshire* and *Montreal*, ADM 51/224 and /595; and Hollford to Stephens, 25 August, ADM 51/3837 (see Admiralty to Rochford, 2 October, SP 91/85 f. 170; and Proby and G. S. Goodall to Stephens, 27 August and 3 September, ADM 1/386). Proby to Weymouth, 21 September, SP 42/104 f. 56. See also M. S. Anderson, "Great Britain and the Russian Fleet"; W. Woodward, *The Russians at Sea*, p. 53; and D. Ozanam and M. Antoine, eds., *Correspondance secrète du Comte de Broglie avec Louis XV, 1756-1774*, p. 88.

45 SP 94/184.

46 Corney, *The Quest and Occupation of Tahiti*, vol. 1, p. 42.

47 Weymouth to Admiralty, 7 September, SP 42/47; ADM 2/96, p. 1; and Admiralty to Weymouth, 17 October, SP 42/46.

48 York to Weymouth, 21 September, SP 84/529.

49 P. 258.

50 R. Mackay, *Admiral Hawke*, p. 323.

51 Fortescue, *George III*, no. 813.

52 See *The Gentlemen's Magazine* (1770), p. 612. It was publicly reported that the Spanish commander, presumably Madariaga, told Farmer "That he had orders from his Court to drive them from . . . [Port Egmont] three years before, but

could not find the harbour out, till the two Spanish frigates discovered it.''
53 Weymouth to Harris, 12 September 1770, SP 94/185. See Harris to Weymouth, 23 August 1770, SP 94/184.
54 Walpole to Weymouth, 18 September, SP 78/281 ff. 133, 137, 140.
55 SP 42/47; also in ADM 1/4128 no. 40.
56 SP 78/281 f. 144.
57 Blart, *Les Rapports de la France*, p. 171.
58 Admiralty to Weymouth, 24 September 1770, SP 42/47 and ADM 2/372, p. 220.
59 ADM 1/4128 no. 48; see Admiralty to Cs-in-C Jamaica, Barbados and Halifax, 29 September, ADM 2/1332 f. 178.
60 Hansard, *Parliamentary History*, XVI, col. 1039, 13 November.
61 Walpole to Weymouth, 26 September, SP 78/281 f. 148.
62 Rochford to Walpole, 22 September, SP 78/281 f. 146; and Walpole to Weymouth, 26 September, *ibid.*, f. 151; Harris to Weymouth, 28 September, 11 and 18 October, SP 94/185; Intelligence from Paris, 28 September, 5 and 13 October and from Brest, 31 October, SP 84/527; and see Admiralty to Weymouth, 2 October, SP 42/46; Lynch to Weymouth, 6 October, SP 92/75; and J. Goebel, *Falkland Islands*, p. 286.
63 Admiralty to Weymouth, 17 and 23 October, SP 42/46 (the first also in ADM 2/372 p. 232); and Weymouth to Admiralty, 19 October, and Stephens to Wood, 30 October, *ibid.*
64 Philip Stephens to Robert Wood, 30 October 1770, SP 42/46. The Navy Board estimated the damage at Portsmouth, at £149,880. See *The Annual Register* (1771), p. 13.
65 ADM 2/96, 17 and 19 September 1770; and ADM 3/77 f. 213. See *The Annual Register* (1770), p. 249.
66 12 and 15 October, MS 3/77 f. 239 and 244. See also ADM 2/272, p. 232; and SP 42/46, 17, 19, 23 October; and ADM 3/77 f. 256.
67 ADM 2/96, pp. 120, 129, 130, 135. Some of these ships later recruited to full complement.
68 Harris to Weymouth, 28 September, SP 94/185.
69 Goebel, *Falkland Islands*, pp. 290, 295.
70 Walpole to Weymouth, 9 October, SP 78/281 f. 165.
71 Weymouth to Walpole, 17 October, SP 78/281 f. 173.
72 Weymouth to Harris, 17 October, SP 94/185.
73 Fortescue, *George III*, no. 822, 9 November.
74 North to George III, 10 November, Fortescue, *George III*, no. 825.
75 Walpole, *Memoirs of the Reign of King George the Third*, IV, p. 128.
76 Speech printed in *The Annual Register* (1770), p. 258.
77 *The Letters of Junius*, vol. 2, p. 47, letter no. 42.
78 13 November, Fortescue, *George III*, no. 825.
79 Hansard, *Parliamentary History*, XVI, col. 1053.
80 See Admiralty to Weymouth, 16 November, SP 42/47; Walpole, *Memoirs of the Reign of King George Third*, vol. 4, p. 191; ADM 2/372, pp. 220, 259; ADM 1/4128 no. 71; *The Annual Register* (1770), pp. 203, 205; and see C. Lloyd, *The British Seaman*, p. 170.
81 Admiralty to Weymouth, 21 November, ADM 2/372, p. 260, and in SP 42/47.
82 SP 78/281 f. 206.
83 [George III?] to Weymouth, 21 November, Thynne MS 38 f. 36.
84 The King to North, 23 November, Fortescue, *George III*, no. 838.

85 WO 1/680.
86 SP 94/185.
87 George III to North, 28 November, Fortescue, *George III*, no. 841; and see Goebel, *Falkland Islands*, pp. 308, 310.
88 Weymouth to Admiralty, 4 December, ADM 1/4128 no. 77.
89 J. Wright, ed., *Sir Henry Cavendish's Debates of the House of Commons*, II, pp. 172, 194, 28 November and 12 December. See also the Admiralty minutes, 26 November, ADM 3/78 f. 46.
90 Rochford-George III correspondence 6-11 December, Fortescue, *George III*, nos 843-45, 848, 852, 854. See Weymouth to the Chairman and Deputy Chairman of the East India Company, 7 December, HMS 102, p. 603. See I.R. Christie, *Myth and Reality*, p. 99 ff.
91 SP 42/47, Weymouth to Admiralty, 2 October (also in ADM 1/4128 no. 52) and 16 October, and Admiralty to Weymouth 6 and 8 October, 16 and 27 November, and 30 November and 3 December (both also in ADM 2/372, p. 272), and 5 December; Weymouth to Admiralty, 10 October, ADM 1/4128 no. 53; Admiralty to Cs-in-C, 12 November, and to Vice-Admiral Geary, 26 November, ADM 2/96, pp. 104, 246; Geary to Stephens 14, 21 October, 15, 27 November, and 2 December, ADM 1/945; and Navy Board to Stephens 26, 30 November and 3 December, ADM 106/2000, pp. 143-44.
92 Rochford-George III correspondence 6-9 December, Fortescue, *George III*, nos 843, 846, 851.
93 Egerton MS 223 f. 181. See Admiralty to Navy Board, 1 December, ADM 2/544 p. 461, and reply, 10 December, ADM/B/184.
94 Goebel, *Falkland Islands*, p. 317, Choiseul to Masserano, 3 December.
95 Admiralty to Geary, Edgcombe, and Denis, 18 December, ADM 2/96, p. 313; Admiralty minutes, ADM 3/78 ff. 66, 82; and Rochford to George III, 9 December, Fortescue, *George III*, no. 850.
96 Minutes of Council, *Calendar of Home Office Papers 1760-1775*, no. 383.
97 Rochford to Harris, SP 94/185, and to Proby, SP 42/104 f. 94.
98 Weymouth-Mann, 16 October and 20 November, SP 98/75 f. 163.
99 Thynne MS "Foreign Affairs c. 1770-79," and Fortescue, *George III*, no. 875.
100 Admiralty to Weymouth, 25 September, 9, 11, 23 October, 8, 13, 21 November, and Weymouth to Admiralty, 28 September and 17 December, SP 42/46; Admiralty minutes, ADM 3/77 f. 213; Admiralty to Richards, and Fielding, 25 September and 17 November, and to Elliot, 5 January, ADM 2/96, pp. 59, 224, 353; Geary to Stephens, 22 November and 25 December, ADM 1/945; Weymouth to (Admiralty?) 15 December, ADM 1/4128 no. 80; and *The Annual Register* (1770), p. 166.
101 Weymouth to Boyde, 29 October, and to Board of Ordnance, 23 October, CO 91/17.
102 Johnson to Weymouth, 20 October, and reply, 14 December, CO 174/6 ff. 88, 110.
103 Cornwallis to Shelburne, 18 September 1768, CO 91/16.
104 Weymouth to Proby, 16 October, SP 42/104, f. 64; Weymouth to Admiralty 9, 19, 29 October, SP 42/47 (19 October also in ADM 1/4128 no. 58); Admiralty to Weymouth, 24 October, SP 42/47 and ADM 2/96, p. 133; Wood to (Stephens?) 26 October, and Rochford to Admiralty, 28 December, SP 42/47; Rochford to Admiralty, 8 January 1771, ADM 1/4128 no. 97; Hansard, *Parliamentary History*, vol. 16, col. 1331; Egerton MS 223 f. 194, Hawke 12 December (see

Mackay, *Admiral Hawke*, p. 103; and Proby's Log, 31 June 1770, ADM 51/683).

105 Egerton MS 223 f. 186.

106 Proby to Stephens, 10 December, ADM 1/386, and to Weymouth, 29 December, SP 42/104 f. 112; Admiralty to Rochford, 31 December, ADM 2/372, p. 276; Admiralty to Locker, 5 January 1771, ADM 2/96, p. 351; and Rochford to Proby, 14 January, SP 42/47 f. 102.

107 Admiralty to Rochford, 25 December, and Rochford to Admiralty, 21 and 26 December, SP 42/47; Rochford to Secretary at War, 26 December, WO 1/680; and "State of the Guardships etc. 31 December," in Stephens to Sutton, 4 January 1771, SP 42/48. See also "State of Guardships, 7 January 1771," Sandwich MS F 2 no. 2.

108 ADM 36 series. See also Sandwich's royal patent, ADM 3/78 f. 93 (see R. Mackay, *Admiral Hawke*, p. 330 and Fortescue, *George III*, nos 878 and 880); Visitation of the Dockyards, ADM 7/659 f. 111; ADM 8/46-47; Sandwich MS F 2 nos 9-10 and F 3 no. 5.

109 SP 83/526, List of the French Fleet, January 1770; /527, Brest 7 November, Toulon 8 November; and /532 Toulon 5 January 1771, "Ships built . . . " 1771, Toulon 23 January. And "Intelligence received at different times, Leghorn," 17 December, ADM 1/386.

110 SP 84/532 (see Harris to Weymouth, 7 November, SP 94/185).

111 J. Flammermont, *Le Chancelier Maupou et les Parlements*, p. 190, 21 December. See also p. 165 and Goebel, *Falkland Islands*, p. 319, 10 December.

112 Blart, *Les Rapports de la France*, p. 193.

113 Goebel, *Falkland Islands*, p. 341, 2 January 1771.

114 Harcourt to Rochford 17 January 1771, SP 78/282 f. 31, and Harris, 14 February 1771, SP 78/282 f. 31.

115 Rochford to George III, 3 and 17 January, and George III to North, Fortescue, *George III*, nos 876, 895, 896; Rochford to Harcourt, 7 January, SP 78/282 f. 5; Goebel, *Falkland Islands*, p. 351; and see *The Annual Register* (1771), p. 45.

116 Rochford to Harris, 18 January, SP 94/186; and *The Annual Register* (1771), p. 238.

117 Admiralty to Admiral Bockle, 23 January, ADM 2/96, p. 394. Rochford to Secretary at War, 24 and 26 January and 22 February, and to Barrington, 31 January, WO 1/680, pp. 97, 101, 105, 113.

118 ADM 3/78 f. 107.

119 Rochford to Harris, SP 94/186. See Rochford-Harris correspondence, 7 and 23 April 1771.

120 Admiralty to Rochford, 11 December 1771, SP 94/188. See ADM 2/1332 ff. 187, 19 March; ADM 1/4129 no. 13, 15 October; ADM 2/97, p. 256, 16 October 1771; and ADM 2/324, 15 February 1771.

121 Admiralty-Rochford correspondence, 24, 29 February, SP 94/189; Admiralty to Rochford, 26 February 1772, ADM 2/372, p. 327.

122 Rochford to Grantham, 6 March 1772, SP 94/189.

123 Admiralty to Lt. Gordon, 1 September, to Commissioners for Victualling, 7 October, to Captain Barr, 13 November, and to Lt. Gordon, 13 November, ADM 2/98, pp. 60, 100, 143, 144.

124 Rochford to Blanquière, 27 December 1771, SP 78/283 f. 301; Blanquière to Rochford, 1 January 1772, SP 78/284 f. 5; Rochford-St. Paul correspondence 10, 19 November and 1 December 1773, SP 78/290 ff. 78, 86, 121; and Rochford to Stormont, 25 February 1774, SP 78/291 f. 107.

125 Published 1771.
126 W.S. Lewis, gen. ed., *Horace Walpole's Correspondence with Sir Horace Mann*, VII, p. 239.
127 P. 40. See J.P. Hardy, ed., *The Political Writings of Dr. Johnson*, p. 76n.

CHAPTER FIVE: BUSINESS AS USUAL: INDIA AND SWEDEN

1 See my article "Parry of a Threat to India, 1768-1774."
2 Admiralty to Rochford, 1 March 1771, ADM 2/372, p. 293 and SP 42/48. See also Chairman and Deputy to (Rochford) 3 January, reply 26 January 1771, HMS 103, pp. 1, 25. The Admiralty dispatched *Northumberland, Orford, Buckingham*, and *Warwick* 50. Admiralty to Harland, 2 and 18 March, ADM 2/96, p. 446; Stephens to Porten, 16 March, SP 42/48. Harland was instructed to take his orders from the Secretary of State. [Rochford?] to Admiralty, 18 March 1771, ADM 1/4128. Rochford stopped Harland at St.Helens on the 24th but let him proceed the next day. Harland to Stephens, 24, 25 March 1771, ADM 1/163 ff. 81-82.
3 Rochford to Harris, 8 March 1771, SP 94/186.
4 Harcourt to Rochford, 13 August, SP 78/283 f. 65; Chairman to Rochford, 3 and 10 August, reply 22 August, and Bombay to Company, 4 February 1771, HMS 105, pp. 337, 353 , 367, 381. This last report touched off the first British survey of the Indian Ocean Islands; see W. A. Spray, "British Surveys in the Changos Archipelago and Attempts to Form a Settlement at Diego Garcia in the Late Eighteenth Century."
5 Intelligence, Fortescue, *George III*, no. 1181.
6 Intelligence from the East Indies, from Mr. Purling, July 1771, from a Danish captain, received 14 January 1772, HMS 106, pp. 1, 5.
7 Rochford to Harcourt, 24 January 1772, SP 78/284 f. 27.
8 Egerton MS 232 ff. 1-86, 29 January 1772 (Saunders f. 15; Palmerston f. 21; North f. 54).
9 Harcourt to Rochford (Most Secret and Private), 4 March, and see *ibid.*, 18 March 1772, SP 78/284 f. 148.
10 "An Account of French Ships and Forces in the East Indies" 1772, Sandwich MS F 34 no. 4.
11 Rochford to Harcourt (Most Secret and Private), 13 March 1772, SP 78/284 f. 160.
12 ADM 2/372, p. 331.
13 Rochford to Harcourt (Secret), 3 April 1772, SP 78/284 f. 282.
14 Rochford to Admiralty, SP 44/232 f. 48 and ADM 1/4129 no. 33; and Admiralty to Clerke (Prudent), 7 April 1772, ADM 2/97, p. 409. HMS 109, 7 April 1772, and see Sir H.W. Richmond, *The Navy in India*, p. 63.
15 Rochford to Harcourt, 10 April 1772, SP 78/284 f. 305.
16 Hillsborough to Rochford, 21 April 1772, SP 78/284 f. 321.
17 Rochford to Admiralty, 30 April 1772, ADM 1/4129 no. 41. See W.H. Wilkins, *A Queen of Tears*, chap. 11 in particular.
18 Rochford to Admiralty, 8 and 18 April, ADM 1/4129 nos 35 and 39; ADM 2/97, p. 417, Orders, 16 April 1772.
19 A year later d'Aiguillon gave the impression, possibly disingenuously, that the Danish crisis had not affected the situation. Stormont to Rochford, 10 April 1773, SP 78/287 f. 203.

20 Harcourt to Rochford, 21 April, and see 22 April 1772, SP 78/284 ff. 331-33.
21 Harcourt to Rochford, SP 78/285 f. 29.
22 Harcourt to Rochford, 20 May 1772, SP 78/285 ff. 203-5.
23 Admiralty to Harland, 27 August 1772, ADM 2/98, p. 56.
24 5 September 1772, and Sandwich to North, 10 September, J.R. Barns and J.H. Owen, eds., *The Private Papers of John, Earl of Sandwich, First Lord of Admiralty, 1771-1782*, vol. 1, p. 19 and 23.
25 Chairman to Rochford, 5 August, enclosing Russel to Court of Directors [March?] 1772, HMS 106, p. 187.
26 Harland to Stephens, 22 February 1772, ADM 1/663 f. 106.
27 Cabinet minute, 7 October 1772, PRO 30/29/1/14 no. 91 f. 669; Rochford to Admiralty, 14 October 1772, ADM 1/4129 no. 69; and see HMS 110, p. 475; Admiralty to Harland, 12 November, ADM 2/98, p. 135; Rochford to Harland (Secret) 16 November 1772, HMS 110, p. 475; Harland to Stephens, 20 September 1773, ADM 1/163 f. 239; and see Sandwich to [Rochford?] 30 October 1772, SP 42/48.
28 12 April 1771, SP 97/47 f. 66.
29 25 October 1771, SP 91/88 f. 150.
30 24 July 1772, SP 91/90 f. 101.
31 Admiralty to Denis, 4 July 1772, ADM 2/1332 f. 204. See Rochford to Harcourt, 13 March, SP 78/284 f. 161; and Rochford to the Admiralty, 3 July, SP 78/285 ff. 263, 271.
32 Roberts, *British Diplomacy and Swedish Politics*, pp. 339-41 and ff.; and Murphy, *Comte to Vergennes*, pp. 172-201.
33 SP 91/91 f. 105, p. 319.
34 [Suffolk?] to Gunning, 8 September 1772, SP 91/90 f. 186.
35 To Goodricke, SP 95/118 f. 778; see similar to Cathcart, SP 91/87 f. 90.
36 10 October 1772, PRO 30/29/1/14 no. 91 ff. 667, 669.
37 SP 91/91 f. 124.
38 29 January 1772, Egerton MS 232 ff. 3-84 (Saunders, North Hawke ff. 68, 82).
39 5 and 10 September 1772, Barns and Owen, *Sandwich Papers*, vol. 1, pp. 19, 23.
40 Fortescue, *George III*, no. 1151.
41 To Sandwich [12?] November 1772, Sandwich MS F 3 no. 40, and printed in Barns and Owen, *Sandwich Papers*, vol. 1, p. 30.
42 To Rochford, 15 November 1772, Sandwich MS F 3 no. 41, and printed in Barns and Owen, *Sandwich Papers*, vol. 1, p. 29.
43 See "Memoradum on the Partition of Poland" [end of 1772?], Fortescue, *George III*, no. 1180; Rochford to St. Paul, 11 December 1772, Add. MS 9242 f. 89; Gunning to Suffolk, 11 December 1772, SP 91/91 f. 213; Goodricke to Suffolk, 26 January and 19 March 1773, SP 95/123 ff. 24 and 76; Gunning to Suffolk, 30 March/10 April 1773, SP 91/93 f. 10; Murray to Rochford, 3 April 1773, SP 97/49 f. 43; and see D. de Fraquier, "Le Duc d'Aiguillon et L'Angleterre (Juin 1771-Avril 1773)"; and Roberts, "Great Britain and the Swedish Revolution 1772-3."
44 12 February 1773, SP 78/287 f. 46.
45 See Roberts, "Great Britain and the Swedish Revolution"; also Rochford to St. Paul, 16 March 1773, Add. MS 9242 f. 146.
46 Admiralty to Rochford, 22 December 1772, ADM 2/372 p. 367. See also Grantham to Rochford, 23 November, SP 94/191.
47 7 April 1773, SP 78/287 f. 197.

48 SP 78/287 f. 170.

49 SP 94/192.

50 Stormont to Rochford, 10 April 1773, SP 78/287 f. 203.

51 Suffolk to Stormont, 14 April 1773, SP 78/287 f. 220.

52 25 April 1773, Taylor and Pringle, *Pitt Correspondence*, vol. 4, p. 261n.

53 Gunning to Suffolk, 30 March/10 April 1773, SP 91/93.

54 Add. MS 9242 f. 154.

55 Fortescue, *George III*, no. 1225.

56 To Stormont, 16 April, SP 78/287 f. 288.

57 20 April 1773, Fortescue, *George III*, no. 1228.

58 Rochford to Admiralty, 21 April 1773, SP 78/288 f. 27, and ADM 1/4129 no. 96.
The Admiralty ordered fitted for sea: Chatham—*Marlborough*; Sheerness—
Resolution; Portsmouth—*Barfleur, Egmont, Lenox, Royal Oak, Terrible, St.
Albans, Worcester*; Plymouth—*Albion, Dublin, Kent, Torbay, Boyne, Sommerset*
(see Admiralty to Navy Board, 21 April, ADM 2/242, p. 17; Admiralty to several
captains 21 April, ADM 2/98, p. 249; Admiralty to Pye and Spry, 22 April, ADM
2/98, p. 254; and Pye to Stephens, 25 April, ADM 1/949.) The Admiralty
selected the ships from a short-list provided on request by the Navy Board.
Stephens to Navy Board, 21 April, ADM 2/547, p. 454; Navy Board to Stephens,
22 April, ADM 106/2202, p. 75; and Admiralty to Navy Board, 23 April, ADM
2/242, p. 24.

59 Admiralty to Navy Board, 23 April and 28 May, ADM 2/242, pp. 24, 82. See also
Admiralty to Privy Council, 21 April, ADM 7/341.

60 Stormont to Rochford, 21 April, SP 78/288 f. 43.

61 Rochford to Stormont, 23 April, SP 78/288 f. 29.

62 Stormont to Rochford, 27 April, SP 78/288 f. 77.

63 Grantham to Rochford, 27 and 29 April, SP 94/192.

64 Fortescue, *George III*, no. 1231. See also Admiralty to Navy Board, 27 April,
ADM 2/242, p. 31, suspending the work ordered on 23 April.

65 Fortescue, *George III*, no. 1235. See also Rochford to Stormont, 27 April, Add.
MS 9242 f. 153.

66 3 May, Fortescue, *George III*, no. 1236.

67 Rochford to the King, 4 May, Fortescue, *George III*, no. 1238.

68 Toulon 12 April, SP 84/540. The ships were: Toulon—*Languedoc* 80, *Tonnant*
80, *Zélé* 74, *Bourgogne* 74, *César* 74, *Hardy* 64, *Vaillant* 64, *Fantasque* 64,
Sagittaire 50, *Atalante* 32, *Sultane* 32. Brest—*Protecteur* 74, *Lion* 64, *Triton* 64.
Frigates concentrating on Toulon—*Chimère, Mignonne, Pleyade, Clue, Sar-
daigne, Engageante, Eclair*.

69 Johnson to Secretary of State, 12/14 April, CO 174/8 f. 19.

70 Toulon 26 April, SP 84/540.

71 Cook to Rochford, 1 May, SP 92/77.

72 Consul Davidson (Nice) to Denis, 27 May, ADM 1/386. "Annext is a list of the
ships they were busy arming with all the expedition which the state they were in
would admit of. When orders came for suspending the Armament, they had
most of their Provisions and water on board, and would have been ready for sea
in a few days." The list was the same as that noted above with the addition of
Souveraine 74, excluding *César* 74 and *Vaillant* 64, and including the frigates
Engageante and *Pléiade* as preparing in port.

73 Pye to Sandwich 28 April, Sandwich MS F 4 no. 25 (printed in Barns and Owen,
Sandwich Papers, vol. 1, p. 35).

74 SP 94/192.
75 Rochford to Admiralty, 6 May, SP 78/288 f. 119, and ADM 1/4129 no. 98. See also Admiralty to Pye, 7 May, and to Suckling, 6 May, ADM 2/98, pp. 293-94; and Pye to Stephens, 9 May, ADM 1/949.
76 See ADM 1/949 *passim*. On 25 April the seven guardships ordered fitted for sea at Portsmouth were 1,958 men short of complement. On the 30th they were ready for sea save for men, on 13 May 173 supernumeraries in *Barfleur* were reported discharged, and on the 28th a further 700 were reported as having slops charged against their bounty. In the middle of May the fourteen guardships mobilized which returned muster-books, however, bore only 5,513 seamen and supernumeraries on their books, against a complement of 8,640 needed (see ADM 36 series). Rochford may have been bluffing, or ill informed, but probably the necessary men were still in the receiving ships, and therefore not on the ships' muster-books.
77 Toulon, 9 and 16 May, SP 84/540; Cook to Rochford, 12 May, SP 92/77; Davison to Denis, 27 May, ADM 1/386.
78 Rochford to Stormont, 12 May, Add. MS 9242 f. 174; see office letter in SP 78/288 f. 139.
79 Stephens to Pye, ADM 2/549. See also Admiralty Board minutes, 12 May, ADM 3/80 f. 44. While the order of the 12th originated with the Admiralty Board it was not executed with orders from the Lords to Stephens. The impression that this order (for reasons of secrecy) was not processed through the normal channels is heightened by the complete lack of formal authorization for Stephens' order of the 26th.
80 Pye to Stephens, 13 May 1773, ADM 1/949.
81 SP 78/288 f. 165.
82 Fortescue, *George III*, no. 1236.
83 SAN/T/6 pt. 1. See also Stephens to Pye, 26 May, ADM 2/547, p. 520, and Pye to Stephens, 28 May, ADM 1/949.
84 Rochford to Grantham, 28 May, SP 94/192. See also Rochford to the King, 3 May, Fortescue, *George III*, no. 1236.
85 Grantham to Rochford, 24 April, SP 94/192.
86 Byrne to Denis, 16 June, ADM 1/386.
87 Suffolk to Yorke, 11 June, SP 84/536. See also Suffolk to Gunning, 11 June, Egerton MS 2702 f. 28.
88 See Pye to Stephens, 22 June, ADM 1/949, "Ceremonys at Spithead during His Majesty's Visitation of the Fleet."
89 27 April, P. Toynbee, ed., *The Letters of Horace Walpole*, vol. 8, p. 266. See also Walpole, *The Last Journals*, vol. 1, p. 196.
90 See Anderson, "Great Britain and the Russo-Turkish War."
91 Murray to Rochford, 17 June, SP 97/49 f. 105; (Rochford?) to Murray, 29 June, SP 97/49 f. 88.
92 Intelligence from Cape, 8 July 1772, and from St. Helena, 1 February 1773, HMS 107, pp. 37, 63. In April 1773 further information was received from Harland of the withdrawal of troops from Mauritius. Lt. Colpoys had visited Port Louis in June 1772 and had seen only 1,420 soldiers of the French Crown, although it was thought that there might be 2,000. Harland to Stephens, 2 October 1772, ADM 1/163 f. 239.
93 Rochford to Admiralty, 16 August 1773, ADM 1/4129 no. 106. Rochford to Admiralty, 2 November, ADM 1/4129 no. 116 and SP 44/232; Admiralty to

Collingwood, Hughes, Harland, Walters, Farmer, 2 November 1773, ADM 2/98, pp. 389-96. See Sir Edward Hughes Papers, including a letter from Rochford, telling of plans of the French at Pondicherry to act aggressively, and apparently forbidden by Paris, ADM 7/746.

94 J. Debrett (printer), *Proceedings of Both Houses of Parliament*, VII, p. 21, 21 January 1774.

CHAPTER SIX: MINIMAL DETERRENCE

1 The King to North, 3 April 1774, reply 3 April, and Rochford to the King, 4 April, Fortescue, *George III*, nos 1436-38. See also Suffolk to Gunning, 12 October, and to Sandwich, 17 December, SP 91/94 ff. 52, 163; Sandwich to [Suffolk?], 18 December, SP 91/94 ff. 52, 163, 165; Rochford (17 December) and Suffolk (17, 19, and 27 December) to the King, Fortescue, *George III*, nos 1350, 1352-53; Spry to Stephens, 17 December, ADM 1/805; Rochford to Grantham, 21 January and 25 March 1774, SP 94/195; Stormont to Rochford, 31 March 1774, SP 78/291 f. 208; Suffolk to Eden, 17 August 1774, add. MS 34412 f. 290; and see Grantham's naval file L 29/353-72.

2 The most recent study of the naval reforms and preparations of Gabriel de Sartine is J.R. Dull's *The French Navy and American Independence: A Study of Arms and Diplomacy, 1774-1787*.

3 Rochford to [Sandwich], 1 and 4 August 1774; see also Stormont to Rochford, 27 July, and Minute of Cabinet, 7 August, transcribed in SAN/T/6, p. 1 (original of first two in Sandwich MS F 5 nos 14, 16).

4 See Hansard, *Parliamentary History*, vol. 18, col. 305; Lord John Cavendish, Almon, *Parliamentary Register*, vol. 1 p. 13; and ADM 7.567 f. 95.

5 Almon, *Parliamentary Register*, vol. 1 p. 51.

6 27 January and 1 February 1775, SP 78/295 ff. 41, 73.

7 SP 42/49 ff. 17, 21, and 43.

8 10 March 1775, SP 78/295 f. 171.

9 Rochford to Stormont, 3 March 1775, SP 78/295 ff. 86, 160; see ff. 88, 94, 98, 114, 154.

10 Rochford to St. Paul, 14 April 1775, SP 78/295 ff. 204, 223, 237.

11 See SP 78/295 ff. 173, 232, 270.

12 St. Paul to Suffolk, 20 April, SP 78/295 ff. 221, 241, 250 and 256. Grantham to Suffolk, 27 March, SP 94/197. Lynch to Suffolk, 1 April, SP 92/79. Eden to Gower, PRO 30/29/1/15 ff. 706, 708. Dull, *The French Navy and American Independence*, p. 20. See also: H. Doniol, *Histoire de la participation de la France . . .* , pp. 42, 43, 48, and 51.

13 PRO 30/29/1/15 no. 3.

14 Rochford to the King and reply 21 April, Fortescue, *George III*, nos. 1645-46; 21 and 26 April, SP 78/295 ff. 262-68.

15 Rochford to [Sandwich], 1 and 4 August 1774, Stormont to Rochford, 27 July, and Minute of Cabinet, 3 August, transcribed in SAN/T/6 pt. 1 (originals of first two at Sandwich MS F 5 nos 14 and 16). See also Grantham's naval file, including letters from Hardy, and Rochford (21 September), and to Rochford (5 October 1774), L 29/357.

16 See Hardy (10, 13, and 27 February 1774), Banks (15 February and 3 March), and Grantham to Rochford (received 20 March), SP 94/197; Stormont to

Rochford, 3 March, SP 78/295 f. 160; Walpole to Rochford, 4 March, SP 89/79 f. 6; and Rochford to Lynch, 28 February, SP 92/79.

17 Hardy to Rochford, 4 April 1775, SP 94/197, and 18 April, 2 and 5 May 1775, SP 94/198; Mann to Rochford, ADM 1/386.

18 5 May 1775, SP 94/197.

19 Almon, *Parliamentary Register*, vol. 2, p. 141.

20 Grantham-Rochford correspondence, 25 May and 14 July 1775, SP 94/198.

21 Grantham to Rochford, 17 July 1775, SP 94/198.

22 Almon, *Parliamentary Register*, vol. 5, p. 1.

23 PC 2/119, pp. 9, 124, 166, 193.

24 Vote requested from Commons 1 November. See Almon, *Parliamentary Register*, vol. 3, p. 83 and Hansard, *Parliamentary History*, vol. 18, col. 841.

25 20 and 27 August 1775, Doniol, *Histoire de la participation de la France . . . ,* pp. 171-72; and Piers Mackesy, *The War for America*, p. 28.

26 To (Weymouth), 28 November 1775, Thynne MS, "Official Correspondence."

27 28 June 1775, SP 78/296 f. 118.

28 SP 78/296 f. 137. See also Rochford to St. Paul and to Frazer, 5 May 1775, SP 78/296 ff. 5, 7, 12 May 1775, SP 78/296 f. 20.

29 SP 78/296 f. 141.

30 SP 42/49 f. 71.

31 10 June 1775, SP 92/79 no. 25.

32 1 July (received 14th) 1775, SP 92/79 no. 28.

33 SP 78/296 f. 188.

34 SP 78/296 ff. 200, 210, 212, 214, 216, 221, 223, 235.

35 SP 92/79 nos 30, 8, 1; and SP 78/296 f. 291.

36 SP 78/296 f. 297.

37 22 and 29 September 1775, SP 78/297 ff. 301, 308.

38 SP 78/297 f. 29.

39 21 and 29 September, SP 94/199.

40 1 November 1775, SP 78/295. See Murphy, *Charles Gravier, Comte de Vergennes*, pp. 222-23; Grimaldi was also interested in preventive war, but Vergennes rejected any land campaigns as alarming to central European states.

41 3 November 1775, SP 78/297 f. 45.

42 7 October 1775, SP 89/80 no. 47.

43 7 November 1775, SP 89/90 no. 23. See Grantham and Hardy's letters, 27 and 31 October and 9 November, SP 94/199.

44 7 to 10 November 1775, Fortescue, *George III*, nos 1744-55.

45 SP 89/90 no. 28.

46 SP 78/297 f. 244.

47 19 November 1775, SP 89/90 no. 51.

48 14 February 1776, SP 78/298 f. 117.

49 SP 92/80 nos 1 (out) and 1, 3, 5, 6, 8 (in); and see Johnson to Porten, 13 February 1776, SP 42/49 f. 197.

50 7 February 1776, SP 78/298 f. 99.

51 Hardy to Weymouth, 1 March 1776, SP 94/200 no. 3; see also Sandwich to Weymouth 23 and 29 March, and 9 April, SP 42/49 ff. 205, 209, 213; Stormont to Weymouth, SP 78/298 f. 422; and in-Letter from Commodore Mann, 5 April 1776 (received 8 April), ADM 1/386.

52 SP 92/80 no. 11. See also nos 1 (out) and 1, 3, 5, 6, 8, 10 (in).

53 21 February and 13 March 1776, SP 78/298 ff. 136, 245.

54 SP 78/289 f. 66.

55 St. Paul to Weymouth, 8 May 1776, SP 78/299 f. 94.

56 Dull, *The French Navy and American Independence*, pp. 30-48, 52. See Clark and Morgan, *Naval Documents of the American Revolution*, vol. 4, pp. 966-70, 974-76, 1084.

57 Almon, *Parliamentary Register*, vol. 4, p. 131.

58 See SP 78/299 ff. 161, 171; Weymouth to Grantham, 28 May 1776, SP 94/200; and Weymouth to Walpole, 29 May 1776, SP 89/82 no. 10.

59 Walpole, *The Last Journals* . . . , vol. 2, p. 43.

60 SP 78/299 f. 193.

61 SP 42/49 ff. 225, 229, and Barns and Owen, *Sandwich Papers*, vol. 1, p. 212.

62 Dull, *The French Navy and American Independence*, p. 54.

63 18 April 1776, SP 94/200.

64 19 and 30 April 1776, SP 94/200.

65 SP 94/201.

66 20 May 1776, SP 94/201.

67 21 May 1776, SP 94/201.

68 See "From Lord Sandwich 1776," "Remarks on the State of His Maj.s Fleet 20 June 1776," "Precis of Advices & Intelligence 20 June 1776," and cabinet minutes 20 June 1776, in Thynne MS "Admiralty Affairs"; and cabinet minutes 20 June 1776, Barns and Owen, *Sandwich Papers*, vol. 1, p. 212; Fortescue, *George III*, nos 1894-96; and Clark and Morgan, *Naval Documents of the American Revolution*, vol. 5, pp. 427-28.

69 19 June 1776, SP 78/299.

70 Dull, *The French Navy and American Independence*, p. 54.

71 21 June 1776, SP 78/299; see St. Paul, 19 June, *ibid.*

72 21 June 1776, SP 78/299 f. 212.

73 SP 92/80 no. 16.

74 ADM 1/3963, pp. 361-8.

75 See Dull, *The French Navy and American Independence*, Appendix C.

76 To Weymouth, 26 June, SP 78/299 f. 218.

77 5 June, SP 78/299 f. 226.

78 8 June, SP 89/82 no. 28.

79 To Weymouth, 13 June 1776, SP 94/201 no. 22.

80 9 July 1776, SP 94/201.

81 SP 42/49 f. 237.

82 29 June 1776, SP 92/80 no. 19.

83 SP 78/299 f. 253.

84 Stormont-Weymouth correspondence 10, 19, 17 July 1776, SP 78/299 ff. 263, 280, 296.

85 See Stormont to Weymouth, 7 August 1776, SP 78/299 f. 353.

86 Grantham to Weymouth, 27 June 1776, SP 94/201.

87 To Weymouth from Hardy 5 and 9 July, Katenkamp 22 June and 14 July, and Marsh 19 July, SP 94/201.

88 Sandwich MS V 13, pp. 1-2 (printed in Barns and Owen, *Sandwich Papers*, vol. 1, p. 213).

89 21 July 1776, Sandwich MS F 9 no. 19 (printed in Barns and Owen, *Sandwich Papers*, vol. 1, p. 214).

90 Barns and Owen, *Sandwich Papers*, vol. 1, p. 215).

91 SP 42/49 f. 241.

92 ADM 1/244, pp. 352-68.
93 Hardy to Weymouth, 16 July 1776, SP 94/201.
94 Grantham to Weymouth, 1 August 1776, SP 94/201.
95 Grantham to Weymouth, 5 August 1776, SP 94/201.
96 SP 89/82 no. 15, and SP 89/83 no. 17.
97 17 August 1776, SP 89/83 no. 39.
98 10 September 1776, SP 89/83 no. 18. See also Walpole to Stormont, 23 August, SP 78/299 f. 390.
99 27 September 1776, SP 78/299.
100 See SP 89/83 nos 40 (in) and 20 (out); and Weymouth to Stormont, 4 October 1776, SP 78/300 f. 1.
101 26 September 1776, SP 78/299 f. 545.
102 SP 42/49 ff. 269, 273; and SP 92/80 nos 26, 27 (in).
103 SP 78/300 f. 36.
104 11 October 1776, SP 42/49 f. 277.
105 Murphy, *Charles Gravier, Comte de Vergennes*, pp. 232-41.
106 Dull, "The French Navy and American Independence" (thesis), p. 103.
107 *Ibid.*, p. 110.
108 SP 78/300 f. 42.
109 10 and 16 October 1776, SP 78/300 ff. 62, 90.
110 9 October 1776, SP 92/80 no. 2.
111 22 October, SP 89/83 no. 23.
112 Fortescue, *George III*, no. 1918; reprinted in Clark and Morgan, *Naval Documents of the American Revolution*, vol. 7, p. 709.
113 PC 2/120, p. 160.
114 SP 78/300 f. 108.
115 23 October 1776, SP 78/300 f. 114.
116 Secret Orders, ADM 1/1332 f. 154.
117 PC 2/120, p. 170, and ADM 1/5168.
118 ADM 2/244, pp. 512, 518; noted in Navy Board Minutes, 30 October, ADM 106/2594.
119 Dull, *The French Navy and American Independence*, p. 62.
120 Hansard, *Parliamentary History*, vol. 18, col. 1384; and Almon, *Parliamentary Register*, VIII, pp. 1-31.
121 Weymouth to Grantham and Walpole, 29 October 1776, SP 94/202 no. 22, and SP 89/83 no. 24.
122 26 November 1776, SP 94/202.
123 Grantham to Weymouth, 20 November 1776, SP 94/202.
124 Dull, "The French Navy and American Independence" (thesis), p. 114.
125 Grantham to Weymouth, 20 November 1776, and Hardy to Weymouth 12, 15, and 29 November 1776, SP 94/202.
126 23 October and 2 November, SP 92/80 nos 4, 5, 7.
127 SP 42/49 f. 281.
128 6 November 1776, SP 78/300 f. 208.
129 PC 2/120, p. 194; Hansard, *Parliamentary History*, vol. 18, col. 1449; and Sandwich MS V 13, pp. 28-29.
130 SP 78/300 f. 214; see also SP 78/300 *passim*.
131 Stormont to Weymouth, 13, 20, and 27 November 1776, SP 78/300 ff. 227, 245, 253 (the last printed in Clark and Morgan, *Navy Documents of the American Revolution*, vol. 7, pp. 765-69).

132 Admiralty to Howe, Gayton, and Young, ADM 2/1334.
133 Weymouth to (Sandwich), 19 December 1776, Sandwich MS F 9 no. 130.
134 See his letters of 13, 20, and 23 November 1776, SP 92/80.
135 SP 78/300 f. 376.
136 25 December 1776, SP 78/300 f. 471. As recently as 19 December, Weymouth
     had been unable to reassure Sandwich on that point, see SAN/T/6, p. 2.
137 13 December 1776, SP 78/300 f. 362. See also Stormont and Sandwich to
     Weymouth 8 and 10 January 1777, SP 78/301 ff. 22, 49.
138 To Stormont, 21 February 1777, SP 78/301 f. 262.
139 ADM 2/244, pp. 512, 518, 531, 532, 535, 536, 539, 543, 571.
140 Ordered 30 October and amended 4 November to allow *Foudroyant* 650 men,
     ADM 2/255, pp. 523, 538.
141 ADM 7/422.
142 ADM 8/53.
143 ADM 8/53-54 and ADM 2/102, Admiralty Orders.
144 18 August 1777, Sandwich MS F 10 no. 144.
145 Dull, *The French Navy and American Independence*, p. 71. See orders printed
     in Clark and Morgan, *Naval Documents of the American Revolution*, vol. 7, p.
     807 and vol. 8, pp. 503, 558, 601, 637, 811-12.
146 SP 92/80 no. 17 (in), and SP 92/81 nos 1, 3, 5, 11 (in); and SP 78/300 f. 390. See
     Edward S. Corwin, *French Policy and the American Alliance of 1778*, p. 95.
147 Stormont to Weymouth, 11 and 16 February 1777, and Sandwich to Weymouth
     9 February, SP 78/301 ff. 208, 214, 239.
148 Dull, "The French Navy and American Independence" (thesis), pp. 139-40. See
     Sartine to Chaffault, 4 May 1777, extract printed in Clark and Morgan, *Naval
     Documents of the American Revolution*, vol. 8, pp. 816-17.
149 Stormont to Weymouth, 18 and 25 December 1776, SP 78/300 ff. 427, 471.
150 To Weymouth, 29 January 1777, SP 78/301 f. 132.
151 10 February 1777, SP 94/203. See extract of Grantham to Weymouth, 10
     February 1777, printed in Clark and Morgan, *Naval Documents of the
     American Revolution*, vol. 8, p. 577.
152 Grantham to Weymouth, 17 February, SP 94/203.
153 SP 94/203.
154 Dull, "The French Navy and American Independence" (thesis), pp. 126-28.
155 7 and 11 November (in) and 26 November (out), SP 94/202; and 26 November
     (out); SP 89/83 no. 26.
156 SP 94/203.
157 See Poyntz to Weymouth, 12 and 22 February 1777, SP 92/81 nos 8, 9;
     Admiralty to Weymouth, 26 February, and Stormont to Weymouth, 26, 29 (two
     letters) February and 5 March, SP 78/301 ff. 276, 288, 296, 316.
158 12 March, SP 78/301 ff. 344, 355.
159 14 March 1777, Sandwich MS F 10 no. 57 (and SAN/T/6 pt. 2).
160 Robinson to George III, 14 March 1777, Add. MS 37,833.
161 14 and 20 March 1777, Fortescue, *George III* nos 1974-75.
162 15 March 1777, Add. MS 37,833, p. 170.
163 21 March 1777, SP 78/301 f. 400.
164 In Sandwich to Weymouth, 21 and 23 March 1777, SP 78/301 ff. 402, 406.
165 Poyntz to Chamier, 5, 15, and 22 March 1777, SP 92/81 nos 11-13.
166 To Weymouth, 26 March 1777, SP 78/301 f. 426.
167 Stormont to Weymouth, 9 April 1777, SP 78/302 f. 37.

168 10 April, SP 78/302 f. 49.
169 Sandwich to Weymouth, 15 April 1777, SP 78/302 f. 69; and Poyntz to Chamier, 2 April 1777, SP 92/81 no. 15.
170 Hardy to Weymouth, 18 March 1777, SP 94/202.
171 SP 78/302 f. 71.
172 SP 94/203 no. 8.
173 16 April 1777, SP 78/302 f. 81.
174 Stormont to Weymouth, 19, 21, and 23 April 1777, SP 78/302 ff. 97, 101, 111.
175 SP 78/302 f. 163.
176 27 April 1777, SP 94/203.
177 Hardy to Weymouth, 11 April 1777, SP 94/203 no. 12; and Weymouth to Stormont, 9 May 1777, SP 78/302 f. 191.
178 SP 78/302 ff. 191-261 *passim.*
179 SP 78/302 f. 77.
180 Poyntz to Chamier, 16 and 23 April 1777, SP 92/81 nos 17, 18.
181 24 May 1777, SP 92/81 no. 22.
182 George III to North, 4 June 1777, (misaddressed in) Fortescue, *George III*, no. 2009.
183 See Weymouth to Walpole, 31 December 1776, SP 89/83 no. 30; Walpole to Weymouth, 19 and 29 March and 12 April 1777, SP 89/84 nos 14-17, 19; and Grantham to Weymouth, 8 May 1777, SP 94/203. See also Weymouth to Stormont and Grantham, 30 May, SP 78/302 and SP 94/203.
184 Grantham to Weymouth, 29 May and 11 June 1777, SP 94/203. See also SP 89/84 nos 12 (out) and 27 (in); and Stormont to Weymouth, 11 June 1777, SP 78/302 f. 338.
185 See Stormont to Weymouth, 4 and 25 June 1777, SP 78/302 f. 403; and Suffolk to Sandwich 29 June, Barns and Owen, *Sandwich Papers*, vol. 1, p. 226.
186 Suffolk to Stormont, 4 and 9 July 1777, and Stormont to Weymouth (Separate and Secret), 9 July 1777, SP 78/303 ff. 93, 136, 142. See also intelligence reports, SP 94/203 and SP 78/302 ff. 375, 403, 410 (Stormont 20 and 25 June); and see Dull, "The French Navy and American Independence" (thesis), p. 139.
187 2 July, SP 78/303 f. 136.
188 Weymouth to Stormont, and to Grantham, 25 June, SP 78/303 f. 243, and SP 94/204. See also Stormont to Weymouth, 15 July 1777, and Weymouth to Stormont, 18 July, SP 78/303 ff. 174, 211; Stephens to Porten, 14 July, and Jackson to Porten, 20 July, SP 42/51 ff. 26, 40; and the King to North, Fortescue, *George III*, no. 2030.
189 1 August 1777, SP 78/303 f. 291; see also SP 94/204, 1 August.
190 Stormont to Weymouth, 6 August 1777, SP 78/303 f. 322.
191 Logs of *Mars* and *Monarch*, ADM 51/566 and ADM 51/609. See Palliser to Sandwich, Sandwich MS F 10 no. 130 (printed in Barns and Owen, *Sandwich Papers*, vol. 1, p. 232). See account of ships and frigates in home waters sent by "A Cockney" to the *London Chronicle*, 15-17 July 1777, reprinted in Clark and Morgan, *Naval Documents of the American Revolution*, vol. 9, pp. 508-10.
192 Sandwich to [North], 3 August 1777, Barns and Owen, *Sandwich Papers*, vol. 1, p. 235.
193 Dull, "The French Navy and American Independence" (thesis), p. 146, n97; refers to Weymouth-Stormont correspondence, 8 and 20 August, SP 78/303 ff. 334, 390.
194 See Stormont to Weymouth, 6 and 9 August, SP 78/303 f. 297, 356.

195 SP 78/303 ff. 366, 372. Sandwich had also been warned of the French embargo on outboard fishermen by J. Thornton who had word from one of Sartine's secretaries, Sandwich MS F 10 no. 142, 15 August 1777. See also Stormont to Weymouth, 20 and 23 August 1777, SP 78/303 ff. 390, 402, 418; and Dull, "The French Navy and American Independence" (thesis), p. 146, n98.

196 Dull, "The French Navy and American Independence" (thesis), p. 79.

197 North to Sandwich, 21 August 1777, Sandwich MS F 10 no. 147 (printed in Barns and Owen, *Sandwich Papers*, vol. 1, p. 241). See also North to the King, 22 August 1777, Fortescue, *George III*, no. 2049.

198 Barns and Owen, *Sandwich Papers*, vol. 1, p. 242.

199 *Ibid.*, p. 245.

200 22 August 1777, Fortescue, *George III*, no. 2050; and Weymouth to Stormont 29 August, SP 78/303 ff. 452-60.

201 Stormont to Weymouth, 4 September 1777, SP 78/304 f. 27.

202 See Stormont to Weymouth, 3 and 4 September 1777, SP 78/304 ff. 9, 27 (extract of the latter printed in Clark and Morgan, *Naval Documents of the American Revolution*, vol. 9, pp. 626-27); and see Dull, *The French Navy and American Independence*, p. 80.

203 SP 42/51 ff. 156-58.

204 SP 78/304 f. 70.

205 17 September 1777, SP 78/304 f. 68.

206 To North, 27 September 1777, Fortescue, *George III*, no. 2064. See also intelligence in Admiralty to Weymouth, 26 September, SP 42/51 ff. 184-217.

207 Stormont to Weymouth, 19 and 24 September 1777, SP 78/304.

208 8 October 1777, SP 78/304 f. 176. See also separate letter by same messenger, f. 182.

209 Dull, "The French Navy and American Independence" (thesis), p. 150.

210 SP 78/304 f. 258.

211 SP 42/51 no. 253.

212 12 November 1777, SP 92/81 no. 46.

213 Almon, *Parliamentary Register*, X, p. 1. See also North to William Eden, 8 November, Add. MS 34,414 f. 335; and Stormont to Weymouth, 14 November 1777, SP 78/305 ff. 43, 113.

214 Almon, *Parliamentary Register*, X, p. 52.

215 *Ibid.*, pp. 64-68. See also "An account of Papers called for by the House of Lords," 27 November 1777, Sandwich MS F 11 no. 116.

216 Fortescue, *George III*, nos 2179, 2182.

217 Stormont to Weymouth 14, 17, 18, 25, and 28 December 1777, SP 78/305 ff. 200, 208, 234, 256, 264; and Suffolk to North, 4 January 1778, Fortescue, *George III*, no. 2147.

218 To North, Fortescue, *George III* no. 2195.

219 E.S. Corwin, *French Policy and the American Alliance of 1778*, p. 398, and Doniol, *Histoire de la participation de la France . . .* , vol. 2, pp. 144, 733 ff.

220 Barns and Owen, *Sandwich Papers*, vol. 1, pp. 333-34.

221 Suffolk to Sandwich, 19 December 1777, SAN/T/6.

222 ADM 2/246, pp. 353-73, and "General Conditions of Service," SAN/T/16.

223 Fortescue, *George III*, no. 2147.

224 7 January 1778, Fortescue, *George III*, no. 2150.

225 Miscellaneous Confidential Reports, Thynne MS, "Foreign Affairs."

226 Hansard, *Parliamentary History*, vol. 19, cols. 726, 874.

227 *Ibid.*, vol. 19, col. 817.
228 27 February, Sandwich MS F 12 no. 112 (Barns and Owen, *Sandwich Papers*, vol. 1, p. 342).
229 SP 78/306 f. 351.
230 Dull, *The French Navy and American Independence*, pp. 97-98.
231 Almon, *Parliamentary Register*, X, p. 269.
232 Fortescue, *George III*, no. 1945; see Stormont to Weymouth, 6 January 1778, SP 78/306 f. 34.
233 2 January 1778, ADM 2/1334.
234 Almon, *Parliamentary Register*, X, p. 174.
235 Stormont to Weymouth 19, 21, and 25 January, SP 78/306 ff. 70, 111, 124.
236 28 January and 6 February 1778, SP 78/306 ff. 128, 166.
237 18 and 19 February (in)? February (out) 1778, SP 78/306 ff. 218-29, 290.
238 9 February 1778, SP 78/306 f. 189.
239 Dull, *The French Navy and American Independence*, p. 102.
240 The King to North, 31 January, Fortescue, *George III*, no. 2182.
241 Almon, *Parliamentary Register*, X, p. 223.
242 SP 78/306 f. 307.
243 North to Sandwich (2 March 1778), Barns and Owen, *Sandwich Papers*, vol. 1, p. 347.
244 Barns and Owen, *Sandwich Papers*, vol. 1, p. 349.
245 SP 92/82 no. 10.
246 SP 78/306 f. 293.
247 SP 78/306 f. 341.

Bibliography

MANUSCRIPTS

Bedfordshire County Record Office

Lucas Manuscripts (Thomas Robinson, 2nd Lord Grantham):
L 29/353-72 Lord Grantham's naval file
L 29/547 Grantham's correspondence with Rochford concerning Portugal

British Library

Additional Manuscripts

6822   Original dispatches from secretaries of state to Sir Andrew Mitchell, 1768-71
9242   Archdeacon Coxe Papers, correspondence of Rochford with Shelburne and others
32258   Deciphers of dispatches passing between foreign governments and their ministers in England & France
32300   "   —Spain
32970 and 32977 Newcastle Papers concerning Cornish
34412, 34414-15 Aukland Papers, correspondence of Suffolk with William Eden
35438   Hardwick Papers
35444   Hardwick Papers Yorke-Goodricke correspondence
35500-3   "   diplomatic correspondence
35547   "   "
35898   Hardwick Papers, Naval Papers
36215   "   Prize-appeal cases
37833, 37836 John Robinson Papers
38205, 38335-40, 38373 Liverpool Papers
38428   "   —Navy estimates
47053   Egmont Papers, Nova Scotia estates
47106   "   Log of *Dolphin*, 1766-68
Egerton manuscripts
215-63 and 3711 Cavendish's Records of Parliamentary Debates, May 1768-13 June 1774
King's manuscripts
44

Bodleian Library

MS Lyell Empt. 37 Diary of Henry Zuylestein, 4th Earl of Rochford

India Office Records

B 86 Court Book, 11 April 1770-10 April 1771
E 1/53-54 Miscellaneous letters received, 1770
HMS 99, 101-10 Home Miscellaneous Series

Longleat House

Thynne Papers (3rd Viscount Weymouth)
    Admiralty affairs 1770-78
    Foreign affairs—miscellaneous confidential reports
    Official correspondence

Mapperton House

Sandwich Papers (John Montagu, 4th Earl)
    F 1-5, 8-13, 33a-b, and 34. Loose papers filed chronologically
    V 6, 9, 10, 10a, and 11. Journals of dockyard visitations
    V 12-14. Bound volumes of correspondence

National Maritime Museum

ADM/B/184 Navy Board Letters to Admiralty, 1770
MKH/C/1B Howe's letters
SAN/T/1-8 Transcripts of Sandwich Papers

Public Record Office

Admiralty Papers

    Secretary's Department—in-letters:
    ADM 1/94 Channel Fleet
    ADM 1/163-4 East Indies
    ADM 1/238, 240 Jamaica
    ADM 1/308, 310 Leeward Islands
    ADM 1/385-6 Mediterranean
    ADM 1/804-6 Plymouth
    ADM 1/945-6, 949-52 Portsmouth
    ADM 1/1836 no. 2 Thomas Graves
    ADM 1/2300 Hugh Palliser
    ADM 1/3837 British Consuls
    ADM 1/3949-65 intelligence "First Series" (duplicates of secret service letters

of naval interest from Rotterdam; see SP 84)
ADM 1/3972 intelligence "Second Series"
ADM 1/4126-35 Secretaries of State
ADM 1/4350, 4352 secret letters
ADM 1/5117, 5168 miscellaneous
Secretary's Department—out-letters:
ADM 2/90-102 orders and instructions
ADM 2/232-47 Lords' letters
ADM 2/371-72 To Secretaries of State
ADM 2/536-54 Secretary's letters
ADM 2/1332-34 secret orders and letters
ADM 3/71/82 Admiralty Board Minutes
Secretary's Department—miscellanea:
ADM 7/171 estimates, abstracts of impressment
ADM 7/179 ordinary estimates of the navy
ADM 7/186 return of sums necessary for completing new ships, 1764
ADM 7/421 muster-books (abstracts of ships' condition in sea pay) May 1772-73 April
ADM 7/422 abstract of state and condition of ships in sea pay at home
ADM 7/553 partial survey of fleet, 1763
ADM 7/567 view of progress of navy, fleet strengths, and navy debt, 1754-1806
ADM 7/568 list of ships sold or taken to pieces, 1762-64
ADM 7/574 abstracts of ship's journals, 1761-76
ADM 7/651 weekly returns of manning of guardships, 1764-70
ADM 7/659-662 minutes of visitations to dockyards by Sandwich
ADM 7/703 correspondence about estimates for 1765
ADM 7/704 description of Falkland's Island, 1774
ADM 7/745-6 Hughes correspondence, 1764-1860
ADM 8/39-54 list-books
Accountant-Generals' Department
ADM 49/162 miscellaneous papers, 1764-1860
Admirals' Journals
ADM 50/1 Sir William Burnaby
ADM 50/14 Sir J. Lindsay

Captains' logs

ADM 51/1	*Achilles*	ADM 51/17	*Ajax*
ADM 51/64	*Arrogant*	ADM 51/98	*Belleisle*
ADM 51/172	*Centaur*	ADM 51/224	*Dorsetshire*
ADM 51/235	*Defence*	ADM 51/301	*Edgar*
ADM 51/310	*Emerald*	ADM 51/347	*Favorite*
ADM 51/566	*Mars*	ADM 51/595	*Montreal*
ADM 51/603	*Merlin*	ADM 51/609	*Monarch*
ADM 51/683	*Proby*'s journal (misnumbered)		
ADM 51/765	*Ramillies*	ADM 51/788	*Rippon*
ADM 51/1033	*Venus*	ADM 51/1090	*Yarmouth*

ADM 51/3755 *Africa*
Controller of the Navy
ADM 95/84 ships built, repaired, etc., 1771-83
Navy Board
ADM 106/2195-2205 out-letters to Admiralty, cover only, see ADM/B series, National Maritime Museum, Greenwich
ADM 106/2577-91, minutes

Colonial Office Papers

CO 23/16 Bahamas
CO 91/14-20 Gibraltar
CO 123/1, 3 British Honduras
CO 174/3-8 Minorca
CO 194/15-18 Newfoundland
CO 194/26-28   "
CO 195/9 (entry books of instructions)
CO 267/6 Sierra Leone
CO 267/13 African forts
CO 268/1 (entry books of commissions, instructions, charters, etc.)
Gifts and deposits
PRO 30/8/70 Chatham Papers, notebooks, and letter-book
PRO 30/8/78-9 Chatham Papers, Admiralty Papers, 1759-67
PRO 30/8/85 Chatham Papers, France
PRO 30/8/93-4   "   "   Spain
PRO 30/29/1/14-16 Granville Papers, Earl Gower
PRO 30/29/3/1, 3   "   "   "   "

State Papers

Domestic, naval
SP 42/43-52 Lords of the Admiralty, 1762-78
SP 42/64-5   "   supplementary, 1760-75
SP 42/101-4 naval commanders: Cleveland, Spry, Harrison, Proby, and Denis
SP 42/136 miscellaneous, sick and wounded
SP 44/231-32, naval entry books, 1760-84
Foreign
SP 75/122 Denmark
SP 78/256-306 France
SP 79/23-25 Genoa
SP 81/142-53 German states, intelligence reports from Versailles through Cologne
SP 84/501-45 Holland, 22 vols contain intelligence from Wolters in Rotterdam
SP 89/79-84 Portugal
SP 91/71-97 Russia
SP 91/108 letters from British mission in Russia to that at the Porte

SP 92/70-82 Savoy and Sardinia
SP 93/20-29 Sicily and Naples
SP 94/165-205 Spain
SP 94/253-54 Spain, supplementary, miscellaneous
SP 95/104-124 Sweden
SP 97/42-50 Turkey
SP 98/69-79 Tuscany
Treasury
   T 29/37 Treasury Board Minutes, 1765-66
   T 38/649 Treasury Accounts, Naval, 1772
War Office
   WO 1/680 in-letters, Secretary of State, Miscellaneous, 1770-75

Sheffield Central Libraries, Department of Local History

Wentworth-Woodhouse Muniments
   Earl Fitzwilliam Collection: Rockingham Letters and Papers—Correspondence
   of Charles, 2nd Marquis of Rockingham
   R 17-5 lists of the Royal Navy, 27 December 1766 and 22 November 1768
   R 17-8 Case for Investigating Conduct of Navy Department, 1781

West Suffolk Record Office

423 Grafton Papers

West Sussex Record Office

Goodwood 192 The Political Journal of 3rd Duke of Richmond, 17 June-17 July 1766

William L. Clements Library, Ann Arbor, Michigan

Shelburne Papers, vol. 40: 2, 7, 24 (part II)

PRINTED CONTEMPORARY SOURCES

Acts of the Privy Council of England, Colonial Series. HMSO, vols 3-4. 1911-12
Almon, J. (Printer). *The Parliamentary Register.* vols 1-10. London 1775
Annual Register, The. London periodical
Barns, G. R. and J. H. Owen, editors. *The Private Papers of John, Earl of Sandwich, First Lord of Admiralty, 1771-1782.* 4 vols. London 1932-38
Baugh, Daniel A., editor. *Naval Administration 1715-1750.* London 1977
Bullocke, J. G., editor. *The Tomlinson Papers.* London 1935
Burdon, Sir J., editor. *Archives of British Honduras.* London 1931-35
Burke, E. *The Speeches of the Rt. Hon. Edmund Burke.* London 1816

Burrell, Sir W., editor. *Reports of Cases Determined by the High Court of Admiralty, 1758-1774*, R. G. Marsden edition. London 1885

Calendar of Home Office Papers, 1760-1775. 4 vols. London 1878-99

Choiseul, E-F. Duc de. *Mémoires*. Paris 1904

Clark, William Bell, and William James Morgan, editors. *Naval Documents of the American Revolution*. Washington 1964-86

Cobbett, W. and J. Wright, editors. *Parliamentary History of England*. Vols 16-17. London 1806

Corney, B. G., editor. *The Quest and Occupation of Tahiti by Emissaries of Spain During the Years 1772-1776*. 3 vols. London 1913-19

Cornish, S. *A Plain Narrative of the Reduction of Manila and the Philippine Islands*. London 1764

Cunningham, P., editor. *The Letters of Horace Walpole*. 9 vols. London 1891

Debrett, J., printer. *The History, Debates, and Proceedings of Both Houses of Parliament of Great Britain from the year 1743 to the year 1774*. 7 vols. London 1792

Draper, W. *Colonel Draper's Answer to the Spanish Arguments, Claiming the Galeon, and Refusing Payment of the Ransom Bills, For Preserving Manila from Pillage and Destruction in a letter addressed to the Earl of Halifax*. London 1764

Erskin, D., editor. *Augustus Hervey's Journal*. London 1953

Fitzroy, A. H., 3rd Duke of Grafton. *Autobiography of the Duke of Grafton*, Sir W. R. Anson, editor. London 1898

Fortescue, the Hon. Sir J., editor. *The Correspondence of King George the Third*. 6 vols. London 1927

Gallager, R. E., editor. *Byron's Journal of His Circumnavigation, 1764-1766*. London 1964

Hansard, Luke, editor. *Parliamentary History*. London 1763-78

Johnson, S. *Thoughts on the Late Transactions Respecting Falkland's Island*. London 1771

Journal of the Commissioners for Trade and Plantations, 1764-1775. London 1936-37

Journals of the House of Commons. London 1763-78

Jucker, N. S., editor. *The Jenkinson Papers, 1760-1766*. London 1949

Junius (pseud.) *The Letters of Junius*. 2 vols. London 1810

Keppel, G. T., Earl of Albemarle, editor. *Memoirs of the Marquis of Rockingham*. London 1852

Malmesbury, 3rd Earl of, editor. *Diaries and Correspondence of James Harris, First Earl of Malmesbury*. London 1844

Nautical Almanac for 1770. Published by order of the Commission of Longitude

Ozanam, D., and M. Antoine, editors. *Correspondance secrète du Comte de Broglie avec Louis XV, 1756-1774*. Paris 1956

Russell, Lord J., editor. *Correspondence of John, Fourth Duke of Bedford*. 3 vols. London 1846

Schomberg, I. *Naval Chronology*. 4 vols. London 1802

Smith, W. J., editor. *The Grenville Papers*. 4 vols. London 1852

Spence, F., editor, *The Fourth Earl of Sandwich, Diplomatic Correspondence, 1763-1765*. Manchester 1961

Taylor, W. S., and J. H. Pringle, editors. *Correspondence of William Pitt, Earl of Chatham*. 4 vols. London 1838

Tomlinson, J. R. G., editor. *Additional Grenville Papers, 1763-1765*. Manchester 1961

Toynbee, P., editor. *The Letters of Horace Walpole*. 19 vols. London 1903-25

Wallis, H., editor. *Carteret's Voyage Round the World, 1766-1769*. 2 vols. London 1965

Walpole, H., *The Last Journals of Horace Walpole During the Reign of George III from 1771-1783*. 4 vols. London 1845; and 2 vols. 1859

Williams, G., editor. *Documents Relating to Anson's Voyage Round the World*. London 1967

Wright, J., editor. *Sir Henry Cavendish's Debates of the House of Commons*. 2 vols. London 1841

MODERN WORKS

Unpublished theses

Down, W. C. "The Occupation of the Falkland Islands." Cambridge 1927

Dull, J. R. "The French Navy and American Independence: Naval Factors in French Diplomacy and War Strategy, 1774-1780." University of California at Berkeley 1972

Knight, R. J. B. "The Royal Dockyards in England at the Time of the American War of Independence." London 1972

Rothney, G. O. "The History of Newfoundland and Labrador, 1754-1783." London 1934

Williams, M. J., "The Naval Administration of the Fourth Earl of Sandwich, 1771-1782." Oxford 1962

Printed books

Acomb, F., *Anglophobia in France 1763-1789*. Paris 1950

Albion, R. G. *Forests and Sea Power*. Cambridge, MA 1926

Ambrosi, C. *La Corse insurgée et la seconde intervention française au XVIIIème siècle 1743-1753*. Grenoble 1950

Asher, E. L. *Resistance to Maritime Classes*. University of California Publications in History vol. 66. Berkeley 1960

Bamford, P. W. *Forests and French Sea Power 1660-1789*. Toronto 1956

Basye, A. H. *The Lords Commissioners of Trade and Plantations*. New Haven 1925

Baugh, Daniel A. *British Naval Administration in the Age of Walpole*. Princeton 1965

Bemis, S. F., *The Diplomacy of the American Revolution*. Indiana 1967

Binney, J. E. D. *British Public Finance and Administration, 1774-92*. Oxford 1958

Blart, L. *Les Rapports de la France et de l'Espagne après la Pacte de Famille jusqu'à la fin du ministère du Duc de Choiseul.* Paris 1915
Brooke, J. *The Chatham Administration 1766-1768.* London 1956
Butterfield, H. *George III and the Historians.* London 1957
Christie, I. R. *Myth and Reality.* London 1970
Cobban, A., *Ambassadors and Secret Agents: The Diplomacy of the First Earl of Malmesbury at The Hague.* London 1954
Collinge, J. M. *Navy Board Officials, 1660-1832.* London 1978
Conn, S. *Gibraltar in British Diplomacy in the Eighteenth Century.* New Haven 1942
Corbett, J. S. *England in the Mediterranean.* London 1904
—*Some Principles of Maritime Strategy.* London 1911
Corwin, E. S. *French Policy and the American Alliance of 1778.* Princeton 1916
Davis, K. G. *The Royal Africa Company.* London 1957
Deacon, R. *The Silent War.* London 1978
Doniol, H. *Histoire de la participation de la France à l'Etablissement des Etats-Unis d'Amérique.* 5 vols. Paris 1886-92
Dull, J. R. *The French Navy and American Independence: A Study of Arms and Diplomacy, 1774-1787.* Princeton 1975
Dunmore, J. *French Explorers in the Pacific.* 2 vols. Oxford 1965
Fernandez Doro, C. *Armada Espanola.* 9 vols. Madrid 1895-1903
Ellis, Kenneth. *The Post Office in the Eighteenth Century.* London 1969
Fisher, Sir G. *Barbary Legend.* Oxford 1957
Fitzmaurice, Lord. *Life of William, Earl of Shelburne.* London 1912
Flammermont, J. *Le Chancelier Maupeau et les Parlements.* Paris 1884
Foster, G. J. *Doctors' Commons: Its Courts and Registers.* London 1871
Goebel, J. *The Struggle for the Falkland Islands.* London 1927
Gooch, G. P. *Frederick the Great.* London 1947
Gradish, Stephen F. *The Manning of the British Navy During the Seven Years' War.* London 1980
Graham, G. S. *Empire of the North Atlantic.* Toronto 1958
—*Politics of Naval Supremacy.* Cambridge 1965
Gray, I. *Catherine the Great.* London 1961
Gray, J. M. *A History of Gambia.* Cambridge 1940
de Guignard, F. E. *Count de Saint-Priest: Mémoires sur l'ambassade de France en Turquie.* Paris 1877
Hampson, N. *La Marine de l'An II.* Paris 1959
Haring, C. H. *The Spanish Empire in America.* New York 1947
Harlow, V. T. *The Founding of the Second British Empire 1763-1793.* 2 vols. London 1952-64
Horne, D. B. *Great Britain and Europe in the Eighteenth Century.* Oxford 1967
—*British Public Opinion and the First Partition of Poland.* London 1945
Humphreys, R. A. *The Diplomatic History of British Honduras 1638-1901.* London 1961
Innis, H. A. *The Cod Fisheries.* New Haven 1940
Kaplan, H. H. *The First Partition of Poland.* London 1962
Klaus, E. K. *British Colonial Theories 1570-1850.* Toronto 1963

Lacour-Gayet, G. *La Marine militaire de la France sous le règne de Louis XV*. Paris 1902

—*La Marine militaire de la France sous le règne de Louis XVI*. Paris 1905

Larradbee, H. A. *Decision at the Chesapeake*. London 1965

Lavery, Brian *The Ship of the Line*. 2 vols. London 1983

Lloyd, C. *The British Seaman 1200-1860*. London 1968

Lynch, J. *Spanish Colonial Administration 1782-1810*. London 1958

Mackay, R. *Admiral Hawke*. Oxford 1965

Mackesy, P. *The War for America 1775-83*. London 1964

Mahan, A. T. *The Influence of Sea Power upon History*. London 1889

Marshall, D. *Eighteenth Century England*. London 1962

Martelli, G. *Jemmy Twitcher*. London 1962

Martin, E. C. *The British West African Settlements 1750-1821*. London 1927

Martin-Allanic, J. E. *Bougainville, navigateur, et les découvertes de son temps*. Paris 1964

Metcalf, Michael F. *Russia, England, and Swedish Party Politics, 1762-1766*. London 1977

Monk, W. E. *Britain in the Western Mediterranean*. London 1953

Morandière, C. de la. *Histoire de la pêche française de la morue dans l'Amérique septentrionale des origines à 1789*. Paris 1962

Morriss, Roger *The Royal Dockyards During the Revolutionary and Napoleonic Wars*. Leicester 1983

Murphy, Orville T. *Charles Gravier, Comte de Vergennes*. Albany, NY 1982

Namier, L. B. *England in the Age of the American Revolution*. London 1930

Neatby, H. *Quebec: The Revolutionary Age, 1760-1791*. Toronto 1966

Olson, A. B. *The Radical Duke*. Oxford 1961

Pares, R. *Limited Monarchy in Great Britain in the Eighteenth Century*. London 1957

—*Yankees and Creoles*. London 1956

—*War and Trade in the West Indies 1739-1763*. London 1963

—*King George III and the Politicians*. London 1967

Patterson, A. T. *The Other Armada*. Manchester 1960

Pool, Bernard. *Navy Board Contracts 1660-1632*. London 1966

Pottle, F. A. *James Boswell: The Earlier Years, 1740-1769*. London 1966

Priestley, H. I. *Jose de Galvez, Visitor-General of New Spain 1765-1771*. University of California Publications in History vol. 5. Berkeley 1916

Pritchard, James *Louis XV's Navy 1748-1762: A Study of Organization and Administration*. Kingston and Montreal 1987

Ramsey, J. F. *Anglo-French Relations 1763-1770*, University of California Publications in History vol. 17 no. 3. Berkeley 1939

Rashed, Z. E. *The Peace of Paris 1763*. Liverpool 1951

Renaut, F. P. *Le Secret Service de l'Amirauté britannique au temps de la Guerre d'Amérique 1776-1783*. Paris 1936

Richmond, Sir H. *The Navy in India*. London 1931

—*Sea Power in the Modern World*. London 1934

—*The Navy as an Instrument of Policy, 1558-1727*. Cambridge 1953

Roberts, Michael. *British Diplomacy and Swedish Politics, 1758-1773.* Minneapolis 1980
Roger, N. A. M. *The Admiralty.* Lavenham, Suffolk 1979
Sainty, J. C. *Admiralty Officials, 1660-1870.* London 1975
Sherrard,O. A. *Lord Chatham and America.* London 1958
Spinney, D. *Rodney.* London 1969
Stout, Neil R. *Royal Navy in America 1760-1775.* Annapolis, MD 1973
Toussaint, A. *History of the Indian Ocean,* translator, J. Guicharnaud. London 1966
Ward, W. R. *The English Land Tax in the Eighteenth Century.* London 1953
Wilkins, W. H. *A Queen of Tears, Caroline Matilda.* London 1904
Williams, A. F. B. *The Life of William Pitt, Earl of Chatham.* 2 vols. London 1913
Winstanley, D. A. *Personal and Party Government.* Cambridge 1910
—*Lord Chatham and the Whig Opposition.* Cambridge 1912
Woodward, D. *The Russians at Sea.* London 1965

Articles

Abbreviations of periodicals frequently cited:

BIHR   *Bulletin of the Institute of Historical Research*
CHR   *Canadian Historical Review*
EHR   *English Historical Review*
HAHR   *Hispanic-American Historical Review*
HJ   *The Historical Journal*
JMH   *Journal of Modern History*
MM   *Mariners' Mirror*
RHD   *Revue d'Histoire Diplomatique*

Anderson, M. S. "Great Britain and the Russian Fleet, 1769-1770," *The Slavonic and East European Review,* 31 (1952-53):148-63
—"Great Britain and the Russo-Turkish War of 1768-1774," *EHR* 69 (1954):39-58
—"Great Britain and the Barbary States in the Eighteenth Century," *BIHR* 29 (1956):87-107
Anderson, Olive. "The Establishment of British Supremacy at Sea and the Exchange of Naval Prisoners of War, 1689-1783," *EHR* 75 (1960):77-89
Breen, K. "The Foundering of H.M.S. *Ramillies,*" *MM* 56:2 (1970):187-97
Broomfield, J. H. "Lord Sandwich at the Admiralty Board: Politics and the British Navy, 1771-1778," *MM* 51:1 (1965):7-17
Brown, V. L. "Studies in the History of Spain in the Second half of the Eighteenth Century," *Smith College Studies in History,* 15 (Oct. 1929-Jan. 1930)
—"Anglo-Spanish Relations in America, 1763-1774," *HAHR* (August 1922)
Butterfield, H. "Review Article: British Foreign Policy, 1762-1765," *HJ* 6 (1963): 131-39
Carrillo, E. A. "The Corsican Kingdom of George III," *JMH* 34 (1962):254-74
Chapman, W. C. "Prelude to Chesme," *MM* 52:1 (1966):61-76
Christelow, A. "French Interest in the Spanish Empire During the Ministry of the

Duc de Choiseul, 1759-1771," *HAHR* 21 (1941):515-37
Coquelle, P. "Le Comte de Guerchy, Ambassadeur de France à Londres, 1763-1767," *Review des Etudes Historiques*, 64 (1908):432-72
"Projets de descente en Angleterre," *RHD* 3, 4 (1901) 1 (1902)
Delumeau, J. "Les Terre-Neuviers Malovines à la fin du XVIIe siècle," *Annales*, year 16, no. 4 (July-Aug. 1961)
Desdevises du Dezert, G. "Les Institutions de l'Espagne," *Revue Hispanique*, 70 (1927)
Dorn, W. L. "Frederick the Great and Lord Bute," *JMH* 1 (1929):529
Fraquier, B. de. "Le Duc d'Aiguillon et l'Angleterre (juin 1771-avril 1773)," *RHD* 26 (1912):607
Fry, H. T. "Early British Interests in the Changos Archipelago and the Maldive Islands," *MM* 53:4 (1969):343-56
Graham, G. S. "Fisheries and Sea Power," in *Historical Essays on the Atlantic Provinces*, pp. 7-16, G. A. Rawlyk, editor, Toronto 1967
Grose, C. L. "England and Dunkirk," *American Historical Review*, 39 (1933-34):1-27
Haas, J. M. "The Royal Dockyards: The Earliest Visitations and Reforms 1749-1778," *HJ* 13 (1970):191-215
—"Introduction of Task Work into the Royal Dockyards, 1775," *Journal of British Studies*, 8:2 (1969):44-68
—"The Pursuit of Political Success in Eighteenth Century England: Sandwich, 1740-71," *BIHR* 43:107 (May 1970):56-77
Irvine, D. D. "Newfoundland Fishery: A French Objective in the War of American Independence," *CHR* 13 (1932):268-84
Jarrett, D. "The Regency Crisis of 1765," *EHR* 85:335 (1970):282-315
Lee, H. I. "The Supervision of Barbary Consuls During the Years 1756-1836," *BIHR* 23 (1950):191-99
McLachlan, J. "The Seven Years Peace and the West Indian Policy of Carvajal and Wall," *EHR*, 53 (1934):472
Morison, M. C. "The Duc de Choiseul and the Invasion of England 1768-1770," *Transactions of the Royal Historical Society*, series III 4 (1910):82-115
Morton, W. L. "A Note on Palliser's Act," *CHR* 34 (1953):33-38
Murphy, O. T. "The Comte de Vergennes, the Newfoundland Fisheries, and the Peace Negotiations of 1783: A Reconsideration," *CHR* 46 (1955):32-46
Reddaway, W. F. "Macartney in Russia, 1765-67," *Cambridge Historical Journal*, 3 (1931):260-94
Renaut, F. P. "Etudes sur le Pacte de Famille et la politique coloniale française," *Revue de l'histoire des colonies françaises*, 9-11 (1921-23)
Roberts, M. "Great Britain and the Swedish Revolution, 1772-3," *HJ* 8:1 (1964):1-46
—"Great Britain, Denmark and Russia, 1763-1770," in Ragnhild Hatton and M. S. Anderson, editors, *Studies in Diplomatic History*. London 1970
Scott, H. M. "The Importance of Bourbon Naval Reconstruction to the Strategy of Choiseul after the Seven Years' War," *The International History Review*, 1:1 (January 1979):17-35
Spray, W. A. "British Surveys in the Changos Archipelago and Attempts to Form a

Settlement at Diego Garcia in the Late Eighteenth Century," *MM* 56:1 (1970):59-76

Syrett, D. "Defeat at Sea: The Impact of American Naval Operations upon the British, 1775-1778," in *Maritime Dimensions of the American Revolution*, Naval History Division, Dept. of the Navy (77-14804). Washington 1977

Tracy, N. "The Capture of Manila, 1762," *MM* 55:3 (1969):331-23

—"Parry of a Threat to India, 1768-1774," *MM* 59:1 (1973):35-48

—"The Gunboat Diplomacy of the Government of George Grenville, 1764-5: The Honduras, Turks Island, and Gambian Incidents," *HJ* 17:4 (1974):711-31

—"The Government of the Duke of Grafton, and the French Invasion of Corsica in 1768," *Eighteenth-Century Studies* 8:2 (Winter 1974-5):169-82

—"The Falkland Islands Crisis of 1770: Use of Naval Force," *EHR* 90:354 (Jan. 1975):40-75

—"British Assessments of French and Spanish Naval Reconstruction between the Peace of Paris of 1763 and the Recommencement of Hostilities with France," *MM* 61:1 (Feb. 1975):73-85

Whiteley, W. H. "The Establishment of the Moravian Mission in Labrador and British Policy, 1763-83," *CHR* 45 (1964):29-50

—"Governor Hugh Palliser and the Newfoundland and Labrador Fishery, 1764-1768," *CHR* 1 (1969):141-63

Wilson, A. M. "The Logwood Trade in the Seventeenth and Eighteenth Centuries," in *Essays in the History of Modern Europe*, D. C. McKay, editor. London 1936

Woods, J. A. "The City of London and Impressment, 1776-1777," *Leeds Philosophical and Literary Society Proceedings,*, 8:2 (1956):111

Index